communication,
family, and
marriage

D0701226

SCIENCE AND BEHAVIOR BOOKS
OF RELATED INTEREST

Communication, Family, and Marriage, edited by

Don D. Jackson

An Anthology of Human Communication, two-hour tape

and companion text by Paul Watzlawick

Conjoint Family Therapy, by Virginia Satir

Family Therapy and Disturbed Families, edited by

Gerald H. Zuk & Ivan Boszormenyi-Nagy

Family Dynamics and Female Sexual Delinquency,

edited by Otto Pollak & Alfred S. Friedman

Research in Family Interaction, edited by William D.

Winter & Antonio J. Ferreira

communication, family, and marriage

Human Communication
Volume 1

Edited by Don D. Jackson

SCIENCE AND BEHAVIOR BOOKS, INC.

Palo Alto, California

COMMUNICATION, FAMILY, AND MARRIAGE

Human Communication, Volume 1

Library of Congress card catalog number: 68-21576
ISBN 0-8314-0015-3

FOREWORD TO THE MRI VOLUMES

On a bleak January day in 1954, I gave the Frieda Fromm-Reichmann lecture at the Palo Alto Veterans Administration Hospital. In the audience was Gregory Bateson, and he approached me after the lecture. My topic was the question of family homeostasis, and Bateson felt the subject matter related to interests that he shared on a project with Jay Haley, John Weakland, and William Fry.

From that moment on, I became more closely related to the social sciences than to medical psychiatry, I have never regretted this decision.

Once the research bug bit, I felt for the first time the pressing need in the San Francisco Bay Area of a behavioral science research foundation. In November, 1958, with the help of some influential friends, the Mental Research Institute was born. Our first grant started in March, 1959, and the staff then consisted of myself, Jules Riskin, M.D., Virginia Satir, A.C.S.W., and an inexperienced, frightened secretary. The Bateson project maintained its autonomy, but we had a close working relationship. The MRI operated under the umbrella of the Palo Alto Medical Research Foundation (thanks to Dr. Marcus Krupp) and continued to grow until it split off as an autonomous research foundation with its own administrative staff and board of Directors.

The Bateson project was never formally under the MRI label, even though Jay Haley and John Weakland subsequently became full-time principal investigators at the MRI. Gregory Bateson became a research associate and participated in teaching, as well as in generously acknowledging requests for his time from puzzled investigators.

Thus, in the first two volumes of the MRI papers, there is a mixture of pre-MRI papers, early MRI papers, papers from the Bateson project, and papers of Haley and Weakland after they were formally MRI research associates.

About the papers themselves, it is necessary to give a brief note about orientation context and selection. We did not select all the papers of all principal investigators, since some obviously had been hastily prepared for trivial occasions. In 1954 there was no conjoint family therapy or family research in the literature, and as far as we were concerned, the MRI investigators were pioneering because the then-extant family studies were of individual family members and dea. with quite different phenomena from those encountered when the family is seen together as a unit. Haley's brilliant laboratory research with intact families demonstrates how totally different the family as a unit is from the "family" created by amalgamating the results of studies of its individual members.

To the extent that the MRI has influenced psychiatry and the behavioral sciences, it has probably occurred because of our common conviction that group phenomena cannot be clearly depicted in the language of the individual's psyche. The grasp that psychoanalysis has had on the body politic in psychiatry and on the thinking of behavioral science academicians (many of whom are arriving on the scene ten years late) makes it difficult to transmit the simple message that individual and group at the present time are discontinuous phenomena. We haven't even the language to handle our insights, let alone a holistic theory.

It is my hope that the papers in these volumes will depict a course and a struggle. It is a further hope that papers even ten years old contain semblances of fresh information to some of the readers. It is also simple expediency to collect articles that stem from some well-known, some obscure sources and the finding of which presents the student with manifold logistical problems.

Finally, I must call attention to the fact that a research institute is not just a body of happy scholars and experimenters. Without the generous help of our Board of Directors, our administrative assistants, secretaries, research assistants, and receptionists, we would since have settled beneath the waters of obscurity.

These papers, then, representing my own early work, the efforts of the Bateson project and the MRI staff, are presented more as a challenge than a monument.

Don D. Jackson

November 1967

PREFACE TO VOLUME I

The papers included in this volume cover a considerable span of time, substantive focus, and levels of generality, yet there is a unity in their manifest diversity. To aid the reader unfamiliar with this body of work, we have attempted to indicate this unity by the arrangement of the papers, without adding undue commentaries to the presentation.

The arrangement of these papers derives from both logical and chronological considerations.

The first section contains some early theoretically-oriented papers based on observation of specific types of clinical phenomena.

The second section focuses on the double bind theory, presenting four papers ranging from the original double bind article to a review of the whole area that subsequently evolved.

The third section broadens the focus to embrace the complex and subtle relationships among topics of communication, human systems, and the pathologies of individuals and of the groups in which they function.

The fourth section comprises an introduction to a body of newly evolving family research approaches and methods. The papers in this section serve only to hint at the richness of this developing area; this foretaste will be followed by another volume in this series dealing specifically with family research.

CONTRIBUTORS

DON D. JACKSON, M.D., Director, Mental Research Institute, Palo Alto, California; Associate Clinical Professor of Psychiatry, Stanford University School of Medicine. *

GREGORY BATESON, currently working on a Research Career Grant under the auspices of the National Institute of Mental Health, at the Oceanic Foundation, Sea Life Park, Oahu, Hawaii.

WILLIAM F. FRY, M.D., Research Associate, Mental Research Institute; Clinical Staff Member, Psychiatry Department, Palo Alto—Stanford Medical Center.

JAY HALEY, Director, Philadelphia Child Guidance Clinic; Editor, Family Process; formerly Research Associate, Mental Research Institute.

ROBERT E. KANTOR, Ph.D., Research Associate, Mental Research Institute; Lecturer, Department of Art and Architecture, Stanford University.

JULES RISKIN, M.D., Associate Director and Research Associate, Mental Research Institute.

VIRGINIA SATIR, A.C.S.W., Secretary-Treasurer, Esalen Institute, Big Sur, California; Consultant, Mental Research Institute.

PAUL WATZLAWICK, Ph.D., Research Associate, Mental Research Institute.

JOHN H. WEAKLAND, Research Associate, Mental Research Institute; Research Associate, Studies in International Conflict and Integration, Institute of Political Studies, Stanford University.

---

*Publisher's Note: Dr. Jackson died suddenly on January 29, 1968, just as this book was going to press.

CONTENTS

IV. RESEARCH: APPROACHES AND METHODS

THE QUESTION OF FAMILY HOMEOSTASIS

Don D. Jackson

A growing tendency is evident in psychiatry to regard the emotionally ill individual as only an instance in a field of force that extends from intrapsychic processes to the broadest aspect of the culture in which he lives. There are those who would see man as a collection of unique individuals strictly limited by their biological propensities; such individuals scorn the "culturists," whose prestige, nevertheless, continues to rise. The contributions of Horney, Sullivan, Fromm and others in the psychiatric field as well as many contributors from psychology, sociology and anthropology require no adumbration.

More recently, Johnson and Szurek, and others have rendered an impressive service by demonstrating, by collaborative therapy, specific instances in which unconscious wishes of the parent influence the behavior of the child. The importance of interaction with others in determining behavioral patterns has resulted in technical changes in therapeutic method. Thus, one hears of child clinics that insist on seeing the mother and father, and of group therapy for the mothers of schizophrenics or the wives of alcoholics.

The purpose of this presentation is not to restate the already stated, but to consider certain technical and theoretical aspects of family interactional patterns: 1) the importance of changes in other family members as the result of change in the patient during psychiatric treatment; and 2) the relation of family interactional patterns (especially parental interaction) to psychiatric nosological categories.

The term family homeostasis is chosen from the concepts of Claude Bernard and Cannon because it implies the relative constancy of the internal environment, a constancy, however, which

Reprinted from THE PSYCHIATRIC QUARTERLY SUPPLEMENT, 31, Part 1:79–90 (1957). Copyright, New York State Department of Mental Hygiene, Utica, New York; reproduced by permission.

is maintained by a continuous interplay of dynamic forces. Another way of considering the topic of "family homeostasis" would be in terms of communication theory: that is, depicting family interaction as a closed information system in which variations in output or behavior are fed back in order to correct the system's response. For example, a boy won a popularity contest in his grammar school, and, in riding home with his mother afterward, was able to tell that she was not entirely pleased by his success. This was one event that helped set into motion various adaptive responses, including his not being so popular henceforth. One aspect of his reaction was his father's indifference toward his mother and the tacit bargain that the child was to supply <u>her</u> needs. It was apparent to the psychiatrist that an integral part of this boy's treatment would be making provisions for an upset in the mother.

The topic of family homeostasis in no way concerns itself with a sociological approach to the American family, but rather is aimed at a very practical problem nearly every psychiatrist must encounter: What effect will the appearance of a patient in his office have upon the patient's family? In particular, if long-term psychotherapy or psychoanalysis is undertaken, the psychiatrist must take into account the effect a change in the patient's interpersonal dealings will have on the most contiguous members of his family. It is true, that in most cases this problem can be dismissed quickly because there will be a fortunate outcome for both the patient and his family. In a minority of situations, however, adequate psychiatric planning will require an understanding of the total family situation. The term "family," as used in this paper, refers to the "significant others" in the patient's life, whether mother, father, sister, brother, wife or others. In addition, "family" refers to the group with which the psychiatrist becomes acquainted through his distillation and translation of the patient's recollections. The individuals include real people of today, the members of the family of the patient's childhood (who are similar to, but not necessarily identical with, those of the present-day family) and the family members who are distortions created out of the special biological conditions of childhood. Thus, to view the patient's family, the psychiatrist must have a four-dimensional concept, with time serving as the fourth dimension. The view of "how it must have been" is obscured by the fog of family fictions--the family, as members tell themselves they were, usually contrasts with how they actually were. The family first presented by the patient is usually the version offered for public consumption; and, only after several interviews does the real family emerge for the psychiatrist's scrutiny. If the therapist refuses to bother with understanding complicated family interrelations, with knowing who meant what to whom, he will be apt to see the patient in terms of extremes. The patient will be conceptualized either as a hostile individual busily throwing out projections like radar signals, or as a violet dying on the desert of other people's unfriendliness.

In our attempts to understand our patients we deal with matters as yet little understood, such as "psychic energy" and "instinctual forces." The fact is sometimes overlooked that <u>one reason why many of us continue to manifest our neurotic woes is that we manage to find people with whom to integrate on a neurotic level</u>. The tendency to live the present in terms of the past is as constant, consistent and impressive in the human as the heartbeat. With increasing awareness of interpersonal relations, it appears that the particular dramatis personae with whom each of us plays out his life are as rarely chosen by accident as the cast of a Broadway production. The lonely psychiatrist, working with one individual, may tend to see him as a bundle of intrapersonal forces much as the company commander's interest is centered about the disposition of forces within his particular sector. If one overworks the concept of projection, the significant others in the patient's life can so easily be seen as constructs of his mental machinations that they never achieve real form and substance within the therapist's office.

It is usual that the psychiatrist treating adults attempts to alter symptoms in his patient and thus is not apt to think of the family as a homeostatic unit. Child psychiatrists have, with few exceptions, come to treat the child and the "significant others" in so-called collaborative therapy. Even in child clinics, the tendency is to concentrate on the mother and not on the family as a whole-- thereby excluding potentially important people such as the father, grandmother and others. Some authorities have called attention to the potential fallacy in this practice. It may be that failure to take a total approach toward the family group creates certain obscurities in our understanding, for example, why severe maternal rejection seems to produce schizophrenia in certain cases and not in others. Before we rush in with the cry of "constitution" or "heredity," it should be important to notice what effect rejection of the child by the mother has in the father, or whether there is a third person somewhere on the periphery who manifests occasional tenderness toward the child, thereby possibly saving him from the psychosis.

It is a fairly recondite matter to attempt to place the patient in a setting and to imagine the interplay of emotional forces. Perhaps the greatest aid is our understanding of the phenomena of transference and countertransference, but even here we are dealing with limited concepts. For example, if the therapist feels the patient is in a "father transference," he may tend to think in terms of the patient's father alone, rather than to think "father as a Gestalt" composed of father as a different person under different conditions; or rather than to think of the parental interaction, the mother's relationship to the patient, the mother's, and other individuals' attitudes toward the father and so on. Is it possible that a child who notices a striking difference between father-in-the-home and father-at-his-club perceives this as father having hateful feelings toward mother--despite the even temperature of the home? The presence of relatives and others as continuing members of the household geometrically increases the possibility of the child's picking up cues about who feels what toward whom. Thus, implications mother makes about other members of father's family may be sensed by the child as mother's rejection of certain aspects of father and of the child himself. If the despised relative is one from whom the child has also received tenderness, a very conflictual situation arises. Occasionally the covert aspects of such a situation are ineradicably etched into the child's memory by such a relative moving out of the home, whereupon there ensue overt difficulties between father and mother and/or difficulties with that aspect of the child that the relative represented.

The paternal uncle of a woman patient had lived with her parents until she was 10 when he married. Her mother's hatred of him was partially overt; however, his presence seemed to deflect some of the mother's hostility toward her husband away from the husband, and the brother gave moral support to the father. Following this uncle's departure, four events occurred that seemed hardly coincidental: The parents began openly quarreling, the mother made a potentially serious suicide attempt, the father took a traveling job, and the patient quietly broke out in a rash of phobias.

The incredibly complex picture one obtains in studying family interrelations may be compared to the mathematics of the motion of bodies in relation to one another--the simultaneous consideration of more than three such instances is, at present, an insuperable task for the mind of man. Since man is the measure of all things, we accept our conceptual limitations and make the most of certain aids available. One of these aids is collaborative therapy, and it is a beautiful thing if done properly. The unfolding of the psychic drama as two or more therapists relate and correlate their findings embodies the dynamics of chess and the topological fasci-

nation of a jig saw puzzle. Unfortunately, collaborative psychotherapy is difficult because the therapists must deal with each other
in addition to their patients.

Another aid to conceptualizing is the adding of a temporal concept to our more or less spatial image of the family. Such a temporal concept may be achieved by constructing a picture of the
probable family interaction at a period the patient is discussing,
or at that period where such-and-such a symptom seems most
likely to have been engendered. We can make use of our information about the patients' siblings, about the age of one or other of
the parents when significant events occurred, about the differential
handling of the children by the parents, and so forth to help obtain
the proper setting for understanding what might have been momen-
tous to the patient at that period in his life.

Considering the difficulties in forming a concept of the emotional
interactions of a family group, the obvious rejoinder might be:
"What is the value of such brain-wracking exercise on the part of
the psychiatrist?" It is felt that two main benefits may ensue:
facility in understanding the patient and in helping those who will
undergo change as the result of the patient's change; and theoretical
and research implications brought to light by this kind of orientation.

There are two rather well-known situations in which one automatically takes into account the "significant others" of the patient.
The best-known instance is that already mentioned where the treatment of a child would be futile or even dangerous without mother
and/or father consenting to therapy as well. Another more spec-
tacular situation is that of folie a deux, or as Gralnick aptly labels
it, "psychosis of association." Actually, folie a deux is merely a
caricature of the underlying principals of any family interaction.
Acquaintance with this fact may mean that a psychiatrist will not
--in certain situations--undertake treatment of a patient, especially
long term psychotherapy, unless the other significant family member, or members, enter treatment, or unless provision is made
for therapy if the need in another family member becomes evident.
Most of us are acquainted with situations where one person has
started treatment, and soon the entire family has been parcelled
out among the circumambient psychiatric brotherhood. Such on-
the-spot instigation of treatment may work out well if money and
psychiatric facilities are available, but they are not always available; and in any event, it would seem helpful to have some data
with which to predict the potential need of other family members

for treatment. Furthermore, it seems likely that alert inquisitiveness into the entire family interrelationship will aid in understanding of the member who is in therapy. This applies as well to the family of the patient's childhood, where it is not only a question of what mother was like or what father was like but how they related to each other and what their relationship meant to the patient. The meanings of the patient's position in the family, of the patient's sex and of other matters constitute subtle but important dynamic factors in shaping emotional patterns. It is possible that our present largely descriptive classification of mental disorders might be made more meaningful by understanding diagnosis phenomenologically--in terms of parental interaction. For example, it may be possible to say that where there is a rejecting mother and a narcissistic father who can accept his daughter more fully than he can his wife, the daughter will tend to develop hysterical symptoms which include expressions of sexual difficulties and overevaluation of men, regardless of what other emotional difficulties she may manifest.

There seem to be few tools at present to measure or even delineate such a factor as parental interaction and its effect in shaping the child's emotional patterns. Epistemologically, we are not well acquainted with the variables here, and the quantitative aspects of these variables. The clinician has a ringside seat to study such forces, however, if he carefully notes changes in other family members as the patient in psychotherapy alters his reactions. The writer would like to give a few oversimplified examples of how one may conceptualize diagnostic categories in terms of family interactional patterns. These are offered only to illustrate a way of thinking; there is a good deal of research to be done before such patterns could be considered in etiological terms, and in every instance the patterns are to be considered as differing only in degree. Thus the hysterical situation blends into the schizophrenic one, and in fact, might become the schizophrenic one if unusual life stresses should occur, such as the death of one of the parents or severe physical illness in the child. When "child" is used in these examples it refers to the child, who, for a variety of reasons such as ordinal position, sex, appearance and so on, is the most important child in the particular interaction described.

1. The development of hysterical symptoms is favored by a situation in which a daughter serves as the main repository for unacceptable sexual and aggressive wishes on the part of both parents, especially if certain other factors are also present. These are: (a) An ambivalent mother who lends herself to being split

into "good" and "bad, " the splitting being further aided by the father's attraction to his daughter and the mother's tendency to push the girl in his direction. A third figure who serves as a "good" mother (such as a grandmother or older sibling) may minimize the tendency toward a psychotic situation but aid the development of the hysterical integration. (b) The mother must be able to manifest concern (especially in relation to illness) although she cannot manifest tenderness.

2. In a family where the parents' hostility toward each other is handled in part by covertly disagreeing over the child, but overtly appearing firm and united, special ways of integrating will be developed by the child. For example, if the mother is markedly fearful of any aggression, including her own; and the father, despite a stern front, allows her to exploit him with phobic symptoms (masking his hostility by assuming a protective role toward his wife and child), then the child caught in the middle of such a situation may manifest phobias, and particularly if a girl, may have a marked fear of "losing control"--a fear pertaining to sexual and aggressive expressions.

3. If the mother is a cold individual who veils rejection of the child by a martyr role and by maintaining that the father is "no good, " and if the father is dead, divorced or accepts a considerable maligning of himself there may be overwhelming pathogenic elements present for a boy. For example, if this boy is a marked disappointment because of his mother's wish for a daughter, there exists a nidus for various degrees of homosexual difficulties, and if the mother is markedly helpless and has the need to deny her own feelings--especially through the mechanism of saying one thing and meaning another--then the possibility exists of producing a pre-schizophrenic personality in the son.[1] Certain psycho-

---

[1] The present writer considers the designation "schizophrenogenic mother" a rather useless or possibly misleading one. He has never studied an instance of schizophrenic psychosis where the individual's environment, in general, had not let him down. In addition to "acts of God, " physical illness, unusual stress and so on, an important aspect of the schizophrenic situation is the inability or unwillingness of other family members to rescue the child from the unbelievably sadomasochistic tie to the mother. The father may be an apparently successful and aggressive individual, though more often a weak and passive character, but in either case, he cannot or will not intervene to give the child the so-

somatic disorders may occur in a somewhat similar situation, when, although the mother is strongly rejecting, the father is able to manifest spotty, but real tenderness: or these disorders may come at that point in intensive therapy when the therapist is invested with strong dependent and hostile feelings by the schizoid patient from the parental set-up just described.

4. Some severely obsessional individuals may arise out of a less pathogenic but similar family constellation to that just described (paragraph 3), with the addition that hypocrisy, intellectualization and religiosity may be an important aspect of the parents' techniques.

5. Where the family situation is unstable, and the child very early in life is confronted with multiple, shifting, nonaccepting figures, he may develop a psychopathic integration.

6. The manic-depressive integration may be associated with a somewhat special parental interaction in which the mother is an unhappy individual who emphasizes the child's obligation to make up to her for what the father and others have denied her. She is ambitious for her child, yet his striving, ambition, and success are threatening to her and may be handled by disparagement and pessimism. The father may be an apparently successful individual who also emphasizes his ambitions for his offspring but who is more aggressively and overtly threatened by his child than the mother is. Neither parent, however intelligent, is able to be of much aid in teaching the child about people. Somewhat in contrast to schizophrenogenic parents, these people stress performance and "appearances" in such a way that their superficial behavior may look like a relatively good adjustment.

It is hoped that these hypotheses will be seen as only a possible way of thinking about psychiatric nosology. All are sketchily presented. As has been previously indicated, the development of psychiatric thinking along such interactional lines might help in discovering, for example, situations where serious consequences will occur in a parent or spouse because the parent or spouse has been "buying" mental health from the illness of the person who is in treatment. Such a situation occurred in the following case.

---

necessary "other one." The child's tie to the mother prevents further growth, in part because other experiences have a diluted meaning, in the sense that every problem is the original problem.

A young male schizophrenic is brought to the psychiatrist's office by his fiancee and his older brother. He has been more or less abducted by these two from his parents, who feel he is incurably ill, and wish to devote themselves to taking care of him. The psychiatrist judges that intense hostility between the fiancee and the brother is veiled by their mutual concern over the patient; and he guesses that the same situation obtains between the parents of the patient. He advises intensive psychotherapy for the patient and recommends that the brother and fiancee do not rent a house and care for the patient as they had planned. He is especially interested in discouraging this arrangement, since he is puzzled about why the young woman should be so attached to this patient as to leave her home, her job, and friends in order to care for him, and as to why the brother has taken a leave of absence from an important position when he was away from home so much during the patient's growing-up period that it was hard to account for his strong affection for the patient.

Needless to say, the advice was disregarded by the two, and the psychiatrist felt forced to deal with the situation by strongly supporting the patient and bringing the conflict between the brother and the fiancee out into the open as soon as feasible. The young man made rapid progress in treatment; and a few months after its inception, the brother left in a rage, after a quarrel with the fiancee during which the patient sided with her. As an interesting aside, the brother did not return to his job, but became fanatically involved in psycho-religious matters that more or less pointed out that psychotherapy was crude, old-fashioned, and perhaps crooked. The patient meanwhile continued to improve so much that he took a job. His dissatisfaction with his fiancee became more obvious; and following what was more or less a declaration of independence by him, she immediately responded with a psychotic episode. Parenthetically, she had been seen in a psychiatric interview initially --that is while the patient was still very psychotic--and had not been judged to be more than mildly neurotic by the examining psychiatrist.

The emphasis on homeostatic mechanisms within the family group carries implications for therapy. It would be a boon to the practice of psychiatry if we could increase our ability to predict with reasonable probability what would be the outcome for patient and family if, say, a psychotic lives at home during his therapy --or if it could be predicted, if a woman is pregnant, whether childbirth could result in a postpartum psychosis, or in a schizophrenic episode in a husband. The following brief clinical examples depict some situations involving homeostatic mechanisms:

1. A young woman undergoing psychotherapy for recurrent depressions began to manifest increased self-assurance. Her husband, who initially was eager that she become less of a burden to him, called the psychiatrist rather frequently and generally alluded to her "worsening" condition. The therapist had not made an appraisal of the husband; and when the extent of the husband's alarm became clear, he had become too antagonistic to enter therapy. He became more and more uneasy, finally calling the therapist one evening, fearful that his wife would commit suicide. The next morning he shot himself to death.

2. A husband urged his wife into psychotherapy because of her frigidity. After several months of therapy she felt less sexually inhibited, whereupon the husband became impotent.

3. A young woman with anorexia nervosa was persuaded to enter psychotherapy by her husband. Following a period of intense, rather dangerous, acting out, she began to relate more intimately to her husband. The husband's initial pleasure at her response was marred by his developing a duodenal ulcer.

4. A young woman requested psychotherapy for a variety of reasons, none of which included dissatisfaction with her marriage. Her mother had died when she was two years old, as had the mother of her husband. The couple married in their late teens and, after a stormy beginning, apparently had made a pleasant, if markedly symbiotic, adjustment. The wife was fearful of having a child, but both she and her husband wanted one, and hoped therapy would make it possible to have one. With a good deal more information than there is time to present, the psychiatrist felt that therapy for her alone would endanger the marriage, and that if she became pregnant, the husband, unsupported, might become seriously disturbed. The husband agreed to start psychotherapy with another psychiatrist; and a somewhat stormy, but eventually fruitful, time was had by all.

CONCLUSION

The writer would like to suggest that emphasis on family interaction is but a logical development in the natural history of psychiatry. As the steps are logical from the single symptom to the patient's character, from his instinctual forces to emphasis on his interpersonal dealings and environmental possibilities, so it is but a logical step from the savant isolated from the community and scarcely seen abroad, to the role of "family" psychiatrist. In America, it has been the physician more than the family solicitor or the minister who has played the counseling role. This long tradition is undergoing change, as the family doctor dies out and the psychiatrist gains importance.

But with the help of the sociologist, the social psychologist, and the anthropologist, psychiatrists are amassing a body of data on the family that has possibilities for use in devising therapeutic interventions. The importance of studying the complex interactions within a family group is stressed the more because of the value of data from such a study in treating patients psychotherapeutically, because of the possibility of being helpful to a family member other than the patient and of avoiding unpleasant counterreactions in such other members, because of the possible economy and expeditiousness of collaborative therapy, and, finally, because of possible research implications for understanding psychiatric nosology genetically. It becomes a matter of some practical importance for the psychiatrist to employ every conceivable aid for predicting behavior. The postulated outcome of the patient's responses to therapy, as well as the responses of those persons significantly interacting with the patient, become matters upon which the outcome of therapy may hinge. Aids to predicting behavior are not a firm aspect of our psychodynamic formulations or teaching.

A prediction that has been successful in the writer's own experience is one in regard to the mate of the overtly-dependent person who enters psychotherapy. If therapy is at all successful, the patient will feel more competent and the mate will become more upset for several reasons: (a) He cannot disguise his own fear of dependency by his complaints about his spouse; (b) his spouse's greater freedom and competency increase his own wish to be dependent; and (c) both of these circumstances weaken his "controls."

Psychiatrists should be increasingly able to predict such situations before, for example, the husband develops an ulcer. The psychiatrist who is oriented to "this-patient-in-my-office" may, in some cases, be misapplying his ability. Unless one sees the patient as a dynamic social force interacting with other people, the finger of psychiatric knowledge may truly muddy the waters of inquiry.

Author's Note: It is nearly four years since this paper was written. Although some of the ideas expressed here have been subsequently modified, the author feels it important to publish this paper without changes, so that future modifications will be obvious.

GUILT AND THE CONTROL OF PLEASURE
IN SCHIZOID PERSONALITIES

Don D. Jackson

It is the thesis of this brief presentation that guilt over masturbation, and mutatis mutandi other pleasurable activity, stems in part from the fact that the child dares to determine the nature of his relationships. His providing of pleasure for himself is autonomous, assertive behavior which particularly in schizoid personalities may be experienced as dangerous activity. Through the mechanism of guilt feelings the child attempts to reinstate the parental control in reality and within himself which in turn may continue the cycle by creating a further urge toward autonomy.

It is a necessary extension of this thesis that the mother of the schizoid fears the loss of control of her child; and for her, masturbatory activity may exemplify such loss of control. The mother's (or parents') reaction to suspecting or witnessing her child masturbating is anachronistic, because she cannot help but translate the activity into her own adult sexual phantasies. As a result, a complex communication is set up in which the child accepts blame for activity that he cannot comprehend because he has no notion yet of the framework for his mother's phantasies. The mother, in turn, may feel very possessive toward the child yet reject it because union connotes sexuality to her. Normal adult orgiastic pleasure consists of an explosive autonomy and, at the same time, a feeling of union with another. It is not satisfactory if it is rape, at one extreme, or a nursing situation at the other. The reconciliation of these two poles are impossible for some mothers, and the conflict is communicated to the child over the issue of masturbation. The healthy body–pleasure and ego mastery of the activity gets connected with an unclear notion of doing something wrong.

Reprinted from THE BRITISH JOURNAL OF MEDICAL PSYCHOLOGY, 31, Part 2:124–130 (1958). Copyright, British Psychological Society, London; reproduced by permission.

There is more involved, in my opinion, in the masturbation conflict between parent and child than the acknowledged deep-seated cultural prohibition against sexual activity. The additional factor involves control, that is, who determines the nature of the relationship. Whereas parents may want children to grow up and manage themselves, they may have difficulty in letting the child develop mastery or autonomy. In this situation, it is handy if the child develops guilt feelings, since he may then express himself autonomously and reinstate the parents' control of himself by feeling guilty. Guilt, in this sense, is an integrative phenomenon both in phantasy and in the communication that the adult perceives. Ethologists have described 'submissive' behavior in many animal species that communicates 'You have control of me'. This behavior in the animal can be life-saving--perhaps the analogy to guilt is not inappropriate. In short, both the parent and the child are reactions to more than the lust component of masturbatory activity.

In order to develop the 'control' framework, I will review some historical and etymological aspects of masturbation and compare this theoretical framework with some of Freud's and Fairbairn's concepts.

PLEASURE VERSUS CONTROL

It is trite to note that for the infant it is a life and death matter that his parents assume virtually complete charge of his existence. Those activities that the parents do not control, for example crying, defecation, etc., the parents may define as being 'normal' or usual for an infant so that the infant is permitted to be in control of these functions. Obviously, parents vary greatly in the extent to which they have to define who is in control--that is, how much autonomy they can allow the infant just as cultures vary enormously in what kind of activities are considered 'normal' for infants. The anxious young mother who is upset because her child cries 'too much' may be relieved if an expert defines the activity as normal. If an outsider defines the nature of the mother's relationship to the child for her, the conflict over wanting to be in control and fearing seeing herself as controlling may be avoided.

As the infant grows from an 'it' to a 'he' or 'she' the parents increasingly need their definition of the relationship to be observed and acted upon by the child. An interesting phenomena occurs in, for example, those mothers who can permit infants to play with their genitals but who are driven to distraction by the same activity occurring in an 18-month or 2-year-old child. Somewhere along in this period comes the imputation of badness to the child, and the mother's need to control this badness or even to stamp it out. My belief is that the difference in the mother's reaction is caused by her suspicion that said child is phantasizing and not merely producing a pleasurable physical sensation. (The mother who cannot permit even the infant to have pleasurable sensation is probably reacting, via identification, as if it were phantasizing.) Why should phantasy (or the suspicion of it) require the mother to strengthen her control? Perhaps because phantasy involves the independent creation of relationships by the child. Masturbatory activity may mean to the mother that the child is defining his relationship to her as one in which he can have pleasure separate from his mother. Even more disturbing, it may mean that he is defining their relationship as one in which he is able to control her as, for example, by obtaining sexual pleasure from her in phantasy. In any case, the mother's suspicion that the child is phantasizing makes his behavior meaningful, a communication rather than a mere wiggling of some fortunately flexible piece of anatomy.

I suspect that the mother of the schizophrenic, in particular, cannot permit the child to have separate relationships, nor permit him to emit those signals that indicate he is having separate relationships, even in phantasy. On the other hand, she cannot permit him to indicate that he is controlling her in reality or in phantasy (Bateson et al. 1956; Jackson, 1957). The mother's dilemma—namely, that she cannot tolerate the thought of being the sexual object of the child's phantasies and cannot tolerate the thought that she is not such an object—is avoided as long as she denies those signals from the child which indicate an attempt to define the nature of his relationship to her, and as long as additionally she can deny her wish to control or rationalize it via 'God', 'sin' and 'for your own good'.

Some of the secrecy, on a conscious level, surrounding masturbatory activity even in fairly healthy families may be an avoidance of how to handle such an independent act on the part of the child. As long as both parties pretend ignorance, the authority problem is not encountered. It is not uncommon to see this same issue occurring between husband and wife when they are not clear on who is defining the nature of the marital relationship. For example, a young woman came to her therapist quite upset because she had discovered her husband was homosexual. What she actually had discovered was evidence (presumably a communication from him) that he was masturbating and since it was 'the same thing as being in love with a man,' she assumed he was homosexual. This was a very controlling woman who constantly attempted in all areas, including sex, to define her husband's relationship to her. However, although he went along with her on most issues, she could not control an involuntary activity like his having an erection, and more than once he failed her in the clinches. What is especially pertinent is her denial that he might be having heterosexual phantasies. This fact, in addition to her general alarm about his mental state, provides a rather analogous situation to the parent who fears the child will go insane because he masturbates.

EVIL, INSANITY AND MASTURBATION

The word 'masturbation' appears to have arisen in the late eighteenth century. Its etymology may be from a combination of the Latin roots 'man', hand; 'sutpra', debauchery; and 'turbo' or 'tupra', motion. Thus we have the connotation of evil doing through manipulation. However, the term 'onanism' preceded 'masturbation' and was in rather good repute until relatively recently. Tuke, an eighteenth-century English psychiatrist, stated: 'Onanism is frequently seen in insanity and often is a cause of it.' The term 'self-pollution' was a popular synonym at the time and appears to have had a similar origin to 'onanism'; namely, the story in Genesis, ch. 38, of Onan, son of Judah and brother of Er. Er married Tamar and was dispatched by the Lord for reasons unknown. The next son, Onan, was ordered by Judah, his father, to 'go into your brother's widow, do your duty to her as a husband's brother and produce a child for your brother.' But as the Bible states further, since Onan knew that the child would not belong to him, he used to spill his seed on the ground whenever he went into his brother's widow to avoid producing a child for his brother. For this disobedience the Lord 'cut him off' and interestingly enough, Judah, the father, was then tricked into impregnating Tamar when she disguised herself as a whore and he came upon her outside the city gates. To me, it appears that Onan practiced coitus interruptus, not masturbation, and that the point of the story is not the fact that father cuts off the little boy's penis for playing with it, but that father feels like another son in a matriarchal situation. For example, despite his being head man of the group, Judah is tricked by Tamar into impregnating her and in addition has to pay a fee of some fine young goats for the privilege. Thus the woman has been indirectly responsible for determining the fate of Er, Onan, and the powerful Judah.

Some scholars feel that Onan and Er refer to deceased tribes of the Judahites, and if one dwells for a moment on the facts of that period the Biblical passage makes good sense. The Judahites were nomadic tribes and by reason of circumstances were matriarchal. The men roamed the countryside with their flocks while the women maintained a fireside of sorts, presumably an oasis, and raised the children. Evidently, the men returned to camp in a staggered fashion and would cohabit with any available female. The importance of the father was thus lessened since he was not wise enough to know his own child, and since the life or death of the tribe depended upon the woman's getting impregnated and rearing the children. It is obvious that masturbation, zoobestry, and homosexuality would be threats to such a way of life and it may have been to point up such a lesson that the story of Onan originated. Onan was killed for defiance--he refused to accept a communal woman for purposes of furthering the tribe.

There is another story that is perhaps pertinent in a consideration of masturbation myths, the Greek tale of Narcissus. Certainly the term 'self-love', 'self-abuse' and 'Narcissism' are linked in our psychiatric vocabulary, and Freud's choice of this legend for the coining of his term 'Narcissism' may have been over-determined. You will recall that this is also essentially a matriarchal story in that Echo, one of the Oreades, the mountain nymphs who were tall women and ardent hunters, falls in love with a youth called Narcissus and wastes away to an echo when he spurns her. Narcissus, in turn, is punished by Aphrodite for refusing the maid and is caused to fall in love with his own reflection, which he sees as a fountain goddess looking up at him from the water. Some accounts have him hearing Echo's voice as he steadfastly gazes at his own image. The fact that he is described as youthful and pale, that he wastes away, and that he changed into a flower which grows from seeds impregnated into the ground are all perhaps relevant to our topic. To overstate the case, when the man refuses to define his relationship to the woman in terms of her having control via the progeny, she becomes the embodiment of emptiness and nothingness--an echo--and he destroys himself in the process. Note that additionally by virtue of the nice touch of having Narcissus hear Echo's voice and seeing his image as a fountain goddess we have analogues to a psychotic state. Narcissus further reveals his schizoid nature by the fact that what really destroys him is his attachment to the woman in himself--the internalized maternal object which he projects as a reflection from the fountain.

Medicine has done its share to perpetuate myths about masturbation. In 1760 Andre D. Simon Tissot published <u>A</u> <u>Treatise</u> <u>on</u> <u>the</u> <u>Diseases</u> <u>Produced</u> <u>by</u> <u>Onanism</u> which many authorities regard as having caused a longlasting condemnation of masturbation. It was re-published as late as 1832. In 1932 Malamud and Palmer reviewed the literature and a series of their own patients in a very thorough study on the role played by masturbation and the causation of mental disturbances. They concluded that in one group of patients masturbation was responsible for the mental illness since it caused a conflict between the ability to stop the habit and the fear of its consequences. Among other disturbances they felt resulted from such conflict were neurasthenia, depression, hysterical manifestations, and paranoid episodes. They felt psychotherapy was definitely a benefit in such cases.

Freud appears as a somewhat equivocal figure in the masturbation-mental illness question. Although he made lasting original observations regarding masturbation, he does not seem to have taken a clear stand on sanctioning the activity. It is understandable that Freud would not have been free to do so when the culture he lived in is considered. However, Freud's theory itself provides additional reason why the practice might be regarded as harmful. In his paper 'On the Passing of the Oedipus Complex' (1924) Freud states that a conflict is established in the little boy over the desire for the love object (mother) and fear of losing the penis, and this conflict is solved by his renouncing the love object in favor of the penis. In the little girl, Freud feels, external intimidation leads to the renouncing of the Oedipal desires and the cessation of masturbatory activity during latency. Huschka (1938) has confirmed Freud's idea that the main intimidating threats in both sexes come from women. Dr. Huschka studied information regarding masturbation that was obtained from the parents of 320 problem children. One hundred and twenty-eight of the children's parents stated that the child masturbated and 85% of the children were severely threatened in order to stop the activity, 67% of these threats being physical in character. The majority of threats were made by the mother.

If Freud's theory is altered from regarding the organ (penis) as the crucial element to putting the emphasis on the feeling state (assertiveness, control) there need not be separate theories for male and female. Freud himself (1924) equates masturbation and enuresis. Unfortunately, he did not follow this lead to its natural conclusion, namely, the emphasis on assertion and defiance of the parental prescriptions and the consequent guilt feelings.

PSYCHOANALYTIC THEORY

According to Freud, we have to discriminate between two kinds of feelings of guilt. One makes itself known as social fear, fear of outer authority; the other is a fear of inner authority or pangs of conscience. The feeling of guilt originating from the fear of outer authority coincides with the fear of the loss of love. The fear of the inner authority coincides with the fear of the super ego. Freud's derivation of the feeling of guilt is well known. The incorporation of the aggression, that is, the turning of the destructive instincts against the ego, originates the feeling of guilt and makes its appearance in the ego as an unconscious need for punishment. For this reason he has equated the term 'feeling of guilt' with the concept of 'the need for punishment'.

According to Freud's theory, especially as developed in 'Totem and Taboo' (1912) the Oedipus complex is the source of man's sense of guilt and of his morality. Freud supposes that in the primal horde the father was murdered, dismembered and devoured by the sons. Having perpetrated this act they were seized for a longing for the father whom they had thus lost. This longing was converted into dread of the community which is another term for sense of guilt. As time went on and the longing for the father recurred, being the expression of unsatisfied libido fixated to the father, it became the principal source of the various religions in which the power of the father was re-established by the mechanism of projection. The father was exalted while the son was abased and the primal transgression was redressed. The father's image was revived and in a sublimated form the passive homosexual libido directed toward him attained its goal again. Freud's ideas on the role of the super ego and castration fear can of course apply to any aggressive attempt to achieve gratification --including masturbation.

It is useful to consider Fairbairn's reformulation of the classical psychoanalytic viewpoint (1949) because, to me, it serves as a bridge between the classical view and the concept of control presented here. Taking as his text Freud's statement: 'The super ego is, however, not merely a deposit left by the earliest object choices of the Id, it also represents an energetic reaction formation against these choices', Fairbairn points out that in describing the super ego as a reaction formation against object choices that Freud is describing it as the instigator of repression, and that if repression involves the reaction against object choices it must be directed against objects and not against guilty impulses. Guilt, or the sense of personal moral badness, thus becomes secondary to a sense of badness in the object. Fairbairn feels that guilt is thus a defense against relationships with bad objects. The guilt over masturbation thus might be regarded as arising from the relationship of this activity to forbidding internal objects rather than over the necessity of controlling libidinal impulses. Guilt, in this sense, is conjunctive and adaptational since it keeps the bad object preserved (and hence the 'good' object remains 'good') and the conscience pain is offered up as payment for the attempt to control the internalized objects. The sequence described above is perhaps most impressively seen in the repetitious sequence of masturbation, guilt, promise to abstain, and subsequent masturbation that can virtually destroy the rest of life on earth for the schizoid adolescent. The compulsive repetitiousness of such cycles is difficult for me to conceive of as sexual tension, discharge, and rebuilding of charge, but it can be understood in terms of the wish to control the object and the fear of abandonment that such control brings with it. Some wit once remarked about women that 'you can't get along with them, and you can't get along without them.' Unfortunately some schizoids are in the same position vis-a-vis the maternal object. That the body itself as an object is important in such masturbatory conflict can be noted clinically by the following observations:

1) Rising sexual tension could be handled via nocturnal emissions and then the hand would not be blamed. Obviously this route is not sufficient for such adolescents despite their intense guilt. Perhaps the desire for conscious control of phantasies is an important factor as well as the pleasurable relationship to the body.

2) Hypochondriacal fears are common in such adolescents and again can be understood, in part, as a struggle of the individual for uniqueness, a private totality, a complete managing of the internal objects and the expiation of such unwelcome ideas of independence. The inability to define the nature of his relationships with external objects results in a chaotic state vis-a-vis internal objects and a consequent confusion about who he is and what is his. In this, I am very much in accord with Szasz's ideas (1957).

3) There may be in such individuals a need to suffer self-inflected physical or ideational pain. Tics, blushing, excoriations and physical pain and shame are common and have not only an exhibitionistic and self-punitive aspect but may also be unconscious attempts of the individual to define who he is and where he is. In a certain sense, the ability to inflict pain upon oneself, bear it, and feel it subside is much like drawing a line around one's prop-

erty to declare what is his. That this kind of definition is unacceptable to the mother can be noted clinically in patients who pick their noses, scratch or break out in tics. Such activities may goad the mother to frenzy and she may accuse the child of trying to upset her.

4) The attempt to use one's own body as a substitute for a lost object is discussed below.

To summarize the application of Freudian, Fairbairnian and control theories to masturbation, we might say that they agree that: (a) It is the phantasies that are important and guilt about the act serves as a displacement and hence a safeguard for repression. (b) Problems regularly connected with over-frequent masturbation are conflicts centering about the lacking satisfaction and there is an expectation of punishment for this aggressiveness.

The differences in the theories are that the non-Freudian theories deal with objects--by Fairbairn as intrapsychic occurrences, by the control theory as intrapsychic occurrences directly related to real objects. The latter is thus but a logical extension of Fairbairn's work. For example, the dilemma posed by the child's attempt to define the nature of his relationship to his mother can be understood when one postulates that she is also an object within him. As one schizophrenic patient stated: 'In the end we hurt only ourselves.' Non-schizophrenics may experience the dilemma as a fear of going crazy because of masturbation. Such fear may develop when the individual is growing closer, socially and physiologically, to making his phantasies become reality of a sort. Going crazy may represent the wild gratification of every whim, and at the same time it forces 'them' to take care of him via the punishment of incarceration in an asylum.

MASTURBATION, AUDITORY HALLUCINATIONS AND ABANDONMENT

There are two clinical observations that have struck me as pertinent to my thesis, but neither has been carefully verified. The first is that although the auditory hallucinations of a schizophrenic may accuse him of all manner of possible and occasionally improbable anatomical combinations with others, they do not accuse him of being, in effect, 'a dirty masturbator.' If this observation is true, then the following speculation might be pertinent: the voices accuse the schizophrenic of activities in which there is an object other than himself. When his own body is the object, the activity, masturbation, provides a frame which states, 'my phantasies are not real' or 'this is only masturbation.' Though a forbidden activity, masturbation may be a necessary activity (apart from the sexual gratification) in order that the transactions that occur as masturbatory phantasies do not become thoughts which frighten one lest they take over and result in action. According to this explanation then, masturbation does not result merely from the sequence: tension--phantasy--sexual excitement --masturbation--relief of tension. But in schizoid people there is also the cycle: fear of abandonment--attempt to define the nature of the control of one's relationships--phantasy--increased fear of abandonment--the necessity to define the message as 'only masturbation' (solitary activity)--fear of the autonomy of self-pleasure--guilt and hence reinstatement of the significant other's control, and so on.

The second observation concerns the correspondence between the individual's feeling abandoned and masturbatory activity. In my experience, it is common for schizoid people when they find no one at home to experience a sudden masturbatory urge. Such urges are common also in stressful situations like final examinations and figuring out their income tax. In understanding such phenomena it is helpful to postulate internal and external objects and the dilemma that controlling them produces. For example, the schizophrenic individual who finds himself alone may experience the phenomena as if he had been abandoned. He immediately turns for gratification to the internal objects which were once external love objects and forces them to gratify him, via phantasy, as well as the taking over of a pleasure-giving function himself, in reality. Often he will experience a momentary return of euphoria only to run headlong into his past and thus to experience guilt and self-abnegation. Now you see, he has behaved in a fashion so that he deserves to be left and is again threatened with abandonment which he now attempts to handle by shame and guilt. The healthy adolescent may also react to abandonment with a masturbatory urge but he finds some comfort in his own body much as a child stroking his blanket while he chews on a corner of it. Stressful situations may produce a masturbatory urge for additional reasons than mere release of tension. The threat of failure or of success, the urge to defy the authorities by cheating or refusing to comply may light up the old problem about who determines the nature of the relationship. The conflict is acted out in miniature through the masturbatory act and the individual may be freer to take his examination or pay his full pound of flesh.

The concept presented is built around the theme that it becomes increasingly important to the individual from infancy onward to determine the nature of his relationships. The schizoid individual is handicapped in such efforts by his relationship to his mother who is controlling, but who must not be regarded as controlling. The child must therefore develop covert means of handling pleasurable or assertive activity and masturbation becomes an especially meaningful situation because:

1) Pleasure is obtained from one's own body but guilt feelings make restitution for the assertiveness or defiance involved.

2) The secretive, bad behaviour provides a frame for phantasies that labels them as only phantasies. Disgust cloaks any connections with real wishes and guilt washes over any notions of assertiveness or mastery.

3) Although masturbation can be an attempt at mastery, at ego growth via a differentiation of one's self from them, it leads to a fear of abandonment and a wish for outside control. Whether there is an appeal to God or one's better nature, a new cycle will be set in motion and a new attempt to determine the nature of one's relationships.

REFERENCES

1. Bateson, G., et al. Toward a theory of schizophrenia. Behavior. Sci., 1, 1956. (See p. 31, this vol.)
2. Fairbairn, W. R. D. Steps in the development of an object relations theory of personality. Brit. J. Med. Psychol., 22:26, 1949.
3. Freud, S. (1912) Totem and Taboo, Moffat, Yard and Co., New York, 1918.
4. Freud, S. (1924) The passing of the Oedipus Complex. In Collected Papers, Vol. II. Hogarth Press, London, 1948.
5. Huschka, M. The incidence and character of masturbation threats in a group of problem children. Psychoanal. Quart., 7:339, 1938.
6. Jackson, D. D. A note on the importance of trauma in the genesis of schizophrenia. Psychiatry, 20:181, 1957. (See p. 23, this vol.)
7. Malamud, W. and Palmer, G. The role of masturbation in mental disease. J. Nerv. Ment. Dis., 76:366, 1932.
8. Szasz, T. Pain and Pleasure, Basic Books, New York, 1957.
9. Tissot, S. A. D. (1760) A Treatise on the Diseases Produced by Onanism, Collins and Hannay, New York, 1832.

A NOTE ON THE IMPORTANCE OF TRAUMA
IN THE GENESIS OF SCHIZOPHRENIA

Don D. Jackson

Adelaide Johnson and her colleagues, in their "Studies in Schizophrenia at the Mayo Clinic,"[1] have made an important contribution to the understanding of the psychopathology of schizophrenia. Following the presentation of this paper at the American Psychoanalytic Association meeting in 1955, I heard a good deal of muttering as some of the audience filed into the lobby. One distinguished analyst remarked to a companion: "Good heavens, don't they realize there is such a thing as heredity? Many of my patients have had just the kind of experience she reported and they aren't schizophrenic." Since many psychiatrists and psychoanalysts have great difficulty in considering a theory of psychogenic causation for schizophrenia, this is an almost predictable response to the Mayo Clinic thesis, and one that is not entirely met by postulating a quantitative factor, such as the amount or frequency of the trauma. Thus it is especially important, when such a theory is presented, that it not lend itself to easy dismissal by the skeptical.

It seems to me that the thesis presented in this paper about the relation between "traumatic assaults" and schizophrenia is essentially correct, but that it suffers from the present conceptualization of trauma and punishment. Webster's New International Dic-

---

[1] Peter G. S. Beckett and others. Studies in schizophrenia at the Mayo Clinic: I. The significance of exogenous traumata in the genesis of schizophrenia. *Psychiatry*, 19:137–142, 1956.
Adelaide M. Johnson and others. Studies in schizophrenia at the Mayo Clinic: II. Observations on ego functions in schizophrenia. *Psychiatry*, 19:143–148, 1956.

Reprinted from PSYCHIATRY, 20, No. 2:181–184 (May 1957).
Copyright, The William Alanson White Psychiatric Foundation, Inc., Washington, D. C.; reproduced by permission.

tionary defines trauma as: "A mental shock, a disturbing experience to which a neurosis may be traced." This is the definition which permeates the paper of Johnson and her colleagues and which, in my opinion, does not render justice to the complexity and subtlety of the kinds of human interaction that predispose people to schizophrenia. The authors say, "Certain types of physical or psychological assault occur too frequently in our series to be fortuitous. Furthermore, in the earliest delusions of the schizophrenic episode, the type of assault is so often specifically reflected as to make a chance relationship seem most unlikely. The types of assault fall into two main groups--first, persistent obstruction to ego differentiation; and, second, discrete physical or psychological assault."[2]

Certainly the first type of "assault" mentioned--namely, "persistent obstruction to ego differentiation"--indicates recognition by the authors that a schizophrenic is not produced only by a series of unholy beatings and an occasional rape. Unfortunately, however, the main focus of the paper seems to be on the second category--"discrete physical or psychological assault"--and this, to me, has a flavor that renders schizophrenia perilously close to a kind of psychological subdural hematoma.

While I have puzzled over the etiology and pathogenesis of schizophrenia since 1943, when the late Jacob Kasanin interested me in the topic, only during the last two years have I felt any real understanding of either. Before that, concepts such as "overwhelming anxiety," "rejection," "flooding of the ego by the id," "breakdown of repression," and so on were conceptual aids, but they had limited meaning, even though I saw schizophrenic patients in collaborative therapy, group therapy, intensive individual therapy, and multiple therapy. But finally, by participating in the interaction of the families of schizophrenics, I have gotten a feel for what the patient has been up against.

The Mayo group has played a large part in the development of collaborative therapy and has documented its usefulness. They have made it clear that the process is only as good as the therapists' ability to communicate with each other. However, apart from the undisputed value of collaborative therapy as a therapeutic method, I am not sure that as a research tool, even under optimal conditions, it can precipitate and crystallize out the patterns of a schizophrenic

---

[2] Beckett et al., op. cit., p. 139.

family interaction in their appropriate subtlety, complexity, and intensity. Even when the parents are seen more often than once a week, their therapy is apt to be oriented toward event-reporting. This is partially appropriate to the situation because, after all, the patient is the patient. Yet although a therapist working in the collaborative setting can get a feel of the parents' personalities, he cannot really appreciate the Gestalt when the parent being seen by one therapist, the other parent being seen by a colleague, and the schizophrenic patient in treatment with still a third colleague are blended into a chiaroscuro of blame, hate, dependency, jealousy, and above all, the terrible, all-pervading Who am I? that underlies the family tragedy.

A group of colleagues and I have undertaken conjoint therapy with schizophrenic patients and their parents, taperecording the psychotherapeutic sessions and later checking with the patient regarding some of the events reported by the parents. [3] Our experience has indicated that often the traumatic assault, to use Johnson's terminology, is of such a nature that trauma is hardly an appropriate word. Rather, it has constituted a condition operating in the patient's environment, which has been nondiscrete and continuing.

A second point of variance with the Mayo group's conclusions concerns their comment that if the child is to survive within the family, the details of the traumatic assault must be dealt with first by denial and then by repression. In our investigations, we have often found that the reporting of the patient is more complicated than can be accounted for by repression or denial, as these terms are ordinarily used. There is truly a perceptual difficulty involved, which is partly a matter of what is paid attention to.

For example, the mother says to the patient, in effect, "Tell me anything, I can take it," whereas the father says explicitly, "Don't be ungrateful and criticize us." The patient turns on the father with angry righteous indignation, but the mother's remark turns out to be the more deadly. The patient, in reporting what went on, doubts that what he told his mother was really his own idea. That is, he feels he was saying something that she put him up to. One might say that there is a psychic trauma involved in

---

[3] This research has been supported in part by the Josiah Macy, Jr. Foundation, USPHS grant #M1673, and the Palo Alto Medical Research Foundation. My colleagues are Gregory Bateson, Jay Haley, John Weakland, and William Fry.

this sort of ploy on the mother's part, but it is nondiscrete and continuing. The sudden absence of oxygen is a physiological trauma for the human, but a chronically lowered partial pressure of oxygen is a condition that the human can adapt to. To push the analogy further, the person who has adapted to lowered oxygen tension may be unaware that he is 'different' until he is confronted with 'normal' atmospheric conditions. Then his adaptive measures may cause him difficulty. In a similar way, would there be schizophrenics if the entirety of the circumambient environment were identical to the home situation? Elsewhere, Bateson, Haley, Weakland, and I have tried to demonstrate how schizophrenia can be viewed as appropriate to the patient's particular ecologic niche. [4]

The idea that trauma floods the child's psyche with more affect or instinctual energy than can be mastered might be refined by noting that the effect of a trauma cannot be measured simply by the amount of trauma, or by the chronological age and maturational level of the child. Rather the vital factors are the contextual or operational setting in which it occurs and the relation of the event to the sequence.

The work of Hebb[5] and Lilly[6] might lend support to the idea that not only is the codifying of perceptions essential to the maintenance of 'who I am,' but vast alterations in classes of percepts and their sequential relationships can be devastating to the maintenance of an intact ego. While the implication by mother that Johnny may become a murderer is undoubtedly traumatic to his future social relations and to his notion of his own personal worth, he may grow up and become a murderer--even of his own mother-- without exhibiting notable schizophrenic phenomena. If the implication that he has enough badness, violence, and what not in him to become a murderer leads to a perception of himself that is in unresolvable opposition to the percepts that generally keep him in harmony with his family's interactional patterns, then there may be a

---

[4] Gregory Bateson, Don Jackson, Jay Haley, and John Weakland. Toward a theory of schizophrenia. Behavioral Sci., 1:251-264, 1956.

[5] Hebb, O. The Mammal and his environment. Amer. J. Psychiatry, 111:826-831, 1955.

[6] Lilly, J.C. Effects of Physical Restraint and of Ordinary Levels of Physical Stimuli on Intact, Healthy Persons. Presented at Group for Advancement of Psychiatry, Asbury Park, New Jersey, November 13, 1955.

dissolution of his ego to the extent that he would be called schizo-phrenic. For example, the implication that he is dangerous may upset the mother's other signals that she is in control of the defini-tion of their relationship. It may mean the revelation to the child that she sees him as more like his father, when previously he has been dealing with his lack of identification with his father by going along with the mother's control as if he were part of her. To the child who does not see himself as being allowed to blow his own nose because although his hand does it, it was really his mother's idea, being regarded as potentially evil may be a rather different trauma than it is to the child who has known he was nothing but trouble from the start.

Another problem that must be answered in presenting a theory of schizophrenia based on psychogenic trauma concerns those pa-tients who do not present such a history. Kant, for example, stu-died 56 consecutive cases of schizophrenia and found no precipita-ting factors involved.[7] The growing literature differentiating be-tween process and reactive schizophrenia would seem to support the belief that in some cases schizophrenia just happens. It may not be enough to say that the lack of a traumatic history is a re-flection of the incompleteness of the investigation of the patient, al-though I am sure that this is often, if not usually, the case. It may be that those patients who have a history and a recollection of trau-ma, and from whose parents these events can be elicited, are ac-tually the 'healthier' schizophrenics, and that those who can offer no clear-cut cause for their illness are in worse shape. This is another way of saying that the reporting of traumatic events may be but a caricature of more enduring events, and that patients who have been reared with subtle malignancy cannot even report trauma, nor can their parents in all honesty report any horrendous occurrences.

The idea of trauma introduces also, by implication, a corollary, 'constitution.' Obviously, if a patient falters or falls before a 'mild trauma,' then he is of a sensitive make-up. While this is possibly a correct notion, it has some pitfalls, for it requires of the psychiatrist value judgments about what constitutes a trauma and how much is much. An incredible amount of information is re-quired to be able to judge a trauma in reference to context, timing, and sequence--and these matters are crucial. Rats that will put up with electric shocks in order to obtain food, water, and sex will

---

[7]Kant, O. The problem of psychogenic precipitation in schizo-phrenia. Psychiatric Quart., 16:341-350, 1942.

completely forgo these basic requirements if the shock is properly timed. Thus if a young male rat just about to mount is shocked, he will renounce his sex life forever. [8]

A final point deals with the concept of "identification with the hostile aggressor." There is no question in my mind that the phenomenon as described by the Mayo group does occur and is important to label. However, it is not clear to me that a sufficiently satisfactory theoretical framework is available to explain why a preschizophrenic will assume responsibility for something he did not do. Identification with the hostile aggressor is a description, not an explanation. It might, for example, fit in with the concept of the importance of the definition of control in a relationship. [9] The schizophrenic might have to identify with the aggressor because of habitual experience in relationships in which there is no appropriate definition of who is in control of the control. If one conceives that there are two sets of signals involved, the first acknowledging control and the second, a metacommunicative comment on the first signal, acknowledging who is in control of the one in control, then it is possible to depict mental pathology stemming from confusion and lack of resolution of these signals. Ideally, the mother-child relationship would be one in which the mother increasingly operates with signals of the second sort so that the child has experience in being in control--experience of mastery--and in recognizing who is in control of the control. As the child grows older, the mother relinquishes control of the second kind in an expanding number of areas. Thus the child's playtime may literally be with himself in control, and ideally the mother can allow the child control expressed as "Feed me," "Read me a story," and so on. The mother of a schizophrenic may be seen as having difficulty in distinguishing between the two levels of signals. She can acknowledge neither that she is in control nor that she is not. This situation could theoretically encourage helplessness and withdrawal as ploys on the child's part to force the definition of control. However, such forcing leads to the paradox of power by giving up power, and identification with the aggressor is appropriate to such a context.

---

[8] Personal communication from David McK. Rioch.

[9] I am indebted to Jay Haley for the idea that the control of the definition of a relationship might be used as a descriptive tool for depicting family interaction.

These comments are offered in no final way, but only to indicate that various frames of reference can be usefully employed in attempting to expand one's thinking beyond the concept of "psychic trauma." I have attempted to raise some questions about the relationship of trauma to schizophrenia because I feel that the important contribution of the Mayo group can best be viewed as having limited implications.

Schizophrenia is a response to a perduring situation for which it is, in some sense, appropriate, and the discernible trauma are but labelable situations in an otherwise misty and blurred picture. It may even be that those schizophrenics who have such well-defined situations at their command are more capable of resolving their psychosis. This is not to underestimate the importance in therapy of seeking out and confronting the patient with traumatic events. Since schizophrenics are reputed to be rather unreliable folk who project all over the place, the clinician would do well to take Johnson and her colleagues seriously, and by doing so they will be taking the patient seriously.

I have raised the trauma question also because it has serious implications for research. Investigators of schizophrenia have for some time been in an anatomical and pathological phase, with emphasis on dissecting individual psychodynamics. Historically the place of psychogenic trauma in etiology appears to be shifting from Freud's original idea of a single traumatic event to the concept of repetitive trauma. The next step would be not who does what to whom, but how who does what. Perhaps the next phase will include a study of schizophrenia (or schizophrenias) as a family-borne disease involving a complicated host-vector-recipient cycle that includes much more than can be connoted by the term "schizophrenogenic mother."[10] One can even speculate whether schizophrenia, as it is known today, would exist if parthenogenesis were the usual mode of propagation of the human species, or if women were impersonally impregnated and gave birth to infants who were reared by state nurses in a communal setting.

[10] Don D. Jackson. Reprinted from THE PSYCHIATRIC QUARTERLY SUPPLEMENT, 31, Part 1:79-90 (1957).

TOWARD A THEORY OF SCHIZOPHRENIA

Gregory Bateson, Don D. Jackson
Jay Haley and John H. Weakland

Schizophrenia—its nature, etiology, and the kind of therapy to use for it—remains one of the most puzzling of the mental illnesses. The theory of schizophrenia presented here is based on communications analysis, and specifically on the Theory of Logical Types. From this theory and from observations of schizophrenic patients is derived a description, and the necessary conditions for, a situation called the "double bind"—a situation in which no matter what a person does, he "can't win." It is hypothesized that a person caught in the double bind may develop schizophrenic symptoms. How and why the double bind may arise in a family situation is discussed, together with illustrations from clinical and experimental data.

This is a report[1] on a research project which has been formulating and testing a broad, systematic view of the nature, etiology,

---

[1] This paper derives from hypotheses first developed in a research project financed by the Rockefeller Foundation from 1952-54, administered by the Department of Sociology and Anthropology at Stanford University and directed by Gregory Bateson. Since 1954 the project has continued, financed by the Josiah Macy Jr. Foundation. To Jay Haley is due credit for recognizing that the symptoms of schizophrenia are suggestive of an inability to discriminate the Logical Types, and this was amplified by Bateson who added the notion that the symptoms and etiology could be formally described in terms of a double bind hypothesis. The hypothesis was communicated to D. D. Jackson and found to fit closely with his ideas of family homeostasis. Since then Dr. Jackson has worked closely with the project. The study of the formal analogies between hypnosis and schizophrenia has been the work of John H. Weakland and Jay Haley.

Reprinted from BEHAVIORAL SCIENCE, 1, No. 4:251-264 (October 1956). Copyright, Mental Health Research Institute, Ann Arbor, Michigan; reproduced by permission.

and therapy of schizophrenia. Our research in this field has proceeded by discussion of a varied body of data and ideas, with all of us contributing according to our varied experience in anthropology, communications analysis, psychotherapy, psychiatry, and psychoanalysis. We have now reached common agreement on the broad outlines of a communicational theory of the origin and nature of schizophrenia; this paper is a preliminary report on our continuing research.

THE BASE IN COMMUNICATIONS THEORY

Our approach is based on that part of communications theory which Russell has called the Theory of Logical Types (17). The central thesis of this theory is that there is a discontinuity between a class and its members. The class cannot be a member of itself nor can one of the members be the class, since the term used for the class is of a different level of abstraction--a different Logical Type--from terms used for members. Although in formal logic there is an attempt to maintain this discontinuity between a class and its members, we argue that in the psychology of real communications this discontinuity is continually and inevitably breached (2), and that a priori we must expect a pathology to occur in the human organism when certain formal patterns of the breaching occur in the communication between mother and child. We shall argue that this pathology at its extreme will have symptoms whose formal characteristics would lead the pathology to be classified as a schizophrenia.

Illustrations of how human beings handle communication involving multiple Logical Types can be derived from the following fields:

1. The use of various communicational modes in human communication. Examples are play, non-play, fantasy, sacrament, metaphor, etc. Even among the lower mammals there appears to be an exchange of signals which identify certain meaningful behavior as "play," etc. 2) These signals are evidently of higher Logical Type than the messages they classify. Among human beings this framing and labeling of messages and meaningful actions reaches considerable complexity, with the peculiarity that our vocabulary for such discrimination is still very poorly developed, and we rely preponderantly upon nonverbal media of posture, ges-

---

2)A film prepared by this project, "The Nature of Play; Part I, River Otters, " is available.

ture, facial expression, intonation, and the context for the communication of these highly abstract, but vitally important labels.

2. Humor. This seems to be a method of exploring the implicit themes in thought or in a relationship. The method of exploration involves the use of messages which are characterized by a condensation of Logical Types or communicational modes. A discovery, for example, occurs when it suddenly becomes plain that a message was not only metaphoric but also more literal, or vice versa. That is to say, the explosive moment in humor is the moment when the labeling of the mode undergoes a dissolution and resynthesis. Commonly, the punch line compels a re-evaluation of earlier signals which ascribed to certain messages a particular mode (e. g., literalness or fantasy). This has the peculiar effect of attributing mode to those signals which had previously the status of that higher Logical Type which classifies the modes.

3. The falsification of mode-identifying signals. Among human beings mode identifiers can be falsified, and we have the artificial laugh, the manipulative simulation of friendliness, the confidence trick, kidding, and the like. Similar falsifications have been recorded among mammals (3, 13). Among human beings we meet with a strange phenomenon--the unconscious falsification of these signals. This may occur within the self--the subject may conceal from himself his own real hostility under the guise of metaphoric play--or it may occur as an unconscious falsification of the subject's understanding of the other person's mode-identifying signals. He may mistake shyness for contempt, etc. Indeed most of the errors of self-reference fall under this head.

4. Learning. The simplest level of this phenomenon is exemplified by a situation in which a subject receives a message and acts appropriately on it: "I heard the clock strike and knew it was time for lunch. So I went to the table." In learning experiments the analogue of this sequence of events is observed by the experimenter and commonly treated as a single message of a higher type. When the dog salivates between buzzer and meat powder, this sequence is accepted by the experimenter as a message indicating that "the dog has learned that buzzer means meat powder." But this is not the end of the hierarchy of types involved. The experimental subject may become more skilled in learning. He may learn to learn (1, 7, 9), and it is not inconceivable that still higher orders of learning may occur in human beings.

5. Multiple levels of learning and the Logical Typing of signals. These are two inseparable sets of phenomena--inseparable because

the ability to handle the multiple types of signals is itself a learned skill and therefore a function of the multiple levels of learning.

According to our hypothesis, the term "ego function" (as this term is used when a schizophrenic is described as having "weak ego function") is precisely the process of discriminating communicational modes either within the self or between the self and others. The schizophrenic exhibits weakness in three areas of such function: (a) He has difficulty in assigning the correct communicational mode to the messages he receives from other persons. (b) He has difficulty in assigning the correct communicational mode to those messages which he himself utters or emits nonverbally. (c) He has difficulty in assigning the correct communicational mode to his own thoughts, sensations, and percepts.

At this point it is appropriate to compare what was said in the previous paragraph with von Domarus' (16) approach to the systematic description of schizophrenic utterance. He suggests that the messages (and thought) of the schizophrenic are deviant in syllogistic structure. In place of structures which derive from the syllogism, Barbara, the schizophrenic, according to this theory, uses structures which identify predicates. An example of such a distorted syllogism is:

Men die.
Grass dies.
Men are grass.

But as we see it, von Domarus' formulation is only a more precise--and therefore valuable--way of saying that schizophrenic utterance is rich in metaphor. With that generalization we agree. But metaphor is an indispensable tool of thought and expression-- a characteristic of all human communication, even of that of the scientist. The conceptual models of cybernetics and the energy theories of psychoanalysis are, after all, only labeled metaphors. The peculiarity of the schizophrenic is not that he uses metaphors, but that he uses unlabeled metaphors. He has special difficulty in handling signals of that class whose members assign Logical Types to other signals.

If our formal summary of the symptomatology is correct and if the schizophrenia of our hypothesis is essentially a result of family interaction, it should be possible to arrive a priori at a formal description of these sequences of experience which would induce such a symptomatology. What is known of learning theory combines with the evident fact that human beings use context as a guide for mode discrimination. Therefore, we must look not for some specific traumatic experience in the infantile etiology but rather ior characteristic sequential patterns. The specificity for which we search is to be at an abstract or formal level. The sequences must have this characteristic: that from them the patient will acquire the mental habits which are exemplified in schizophrenic communication. That is to say, he must live in a universe where the sequences of events are such that his unconventional communicational habits will be in some sense appropriate. The hypothesis which we offer is that sequences of this kind in the external experience of the patient are responsible for the inner conflicts of Logical Typing. For such unresolvable sequences of experiences, we use the term "double bind."

THE DOUBLE BIND

The necessary ingredients for a double bind situation, as we see it, are:

1. Two or more persons. Of these, we designate one, for purposes of our definition, as the "victim." We do not assume that the double bind is inflicted by the mother alone, but that it may be done either by mother alone or by some combination of mother, father, and/or siblings.

2. Repeated experience. We assume that the double bind is a recurrent theme in the experience of the victim. Our hypothesis does not invoke a single traumatic experience, but such repeated experiences that the double bind structure comes to be an habitual expectation.

3. A primary negative injunction. This may have either of two forms: (a)"Do not do so and so, or I will punish you," or (b) "If you do not do so and so, I will punish you." Here we select a context of learning based on avoidance of punishment rather than a context of reward seeking. There is perhaps no formal reason for this selection. We assume that the punishment may be either the withdrawal of love or the expression of hate or anger--or most devastating--the kind of abandonment that results from the parent's expression of extreme helplessness. [3]

---

[3] Our concept of punishment is being refined at present. It appears to us to involve perceptual experience in a way that cannot be encompassed by the notion of "trauma."

4. <u>A secondary injunction conflicting with the first at a more</u> <u>abstract level, and like the first enforced by punishments or signals</u> <u>which threaten survival</u>. This secondary injunction is more difficult to describe than the primary for two reasons. First, the secondary injunction is commonly communicated to the child by nonverbal means. Posture, gesture, tone of voice, meaningful action, and the implications concealed in verbal comment may all be used to convey this more abstract message. Second, the secondary injunction may impinge upon any element of the primary prohibition. Verbalization of the secondary injunction may, therefore, include a wide variety of forms; for example, "Do not see this as punishment"; "Do not see me as the punishing agent"; "Do not submit to my prohibitions"; "Do not think of what you must not do"; "Do not question my love of which the primary prohibition is (or is not) an example"; and so on. Other examples become possible when the double bind is inflicted not by one individual but by two. For example, one parent may negate at a more abstract level the injunctions of the other.

5. <u>A tertiary negative injunction prohibiting the victim from</u> <u>escaping from the field</u>. In a formal sense it is perhaps unnecessary to list this injunction as a separate item since the reinforcement at the other two levels involves a threat to survival, and if the double binds are imposed during infancy, escape is naturally impossible. However, it seems that in some cases the escape from the field is made impossible by certain devices which are not purely negative, e.g., capricious promises of love, and the like.

6. Finally, the complete set of ingredients is no longer necessary when the victim has learned to perceive his universe in double bind patterns. Almost any part of a double bind sequence may then be sufficient to precipitate panic or rage. The pattern of conflicting injunctions may even be taken over by hallucinatory voices (14).

THE EFFECT OF THE DOUBLE BIND

In the Eastern religion, Zen Buddhism, the goal is to achieve Enlightenment. The Zen Master attempts to bring about enlightenment in his pupil in various ways. One of the things he does is to hold a stick over the pupil's head and say fiercely, "If you say this stick is real, I will strike you with it. If you say this stick is not real, I will strike you with it. If you don't say anything, I will strike you with it." We feel that the schizophrenic finds himself continually in the same situation as the pupil, but he achieves something like disorientation rather than enlightenment. The Zen pupil might reach up and take the stick away from the Master--who might accept this response, but the schizophrenic has no such choice since with him there is no not caring about the relationship, and his mother's aims and awareness are not like the Master's.

We hypothesize that there will be a breakdown in any individual's ability to discriminate between Logical Types whenever a double bind situation occurs. The general characteristics of this situation are the following:

1. When the individual is involved in an intense relationship; that is, a relationship in which he feels it is vitally important that he discriminate accurately what sort of message is being communicated so that he may respond appropriately.

2. And, the individual is caught in a situation in which the other person in the relationship is expressing two orders of message and one of these denies the other.

3. And, the individual is unable to comment on the messages being expressed to correct his discrimination of what order of message to respond to, i.e., he cannot make a metacommunicative statement.

We have suggested that this is the sort of situation which occurs between the pre-schizophrenic and his mother, but it also occurs in normal relationships. When a person is caught in a double bind situation, he will respond defensively in a manner similar to the schizophrenic. An individual will take a metaphorical statement literally when he is in a situation where he must respond, where he is faced with contradictory messages, and when he is unable to comment on the contradictions. For example, one day an employee went home during office hours. A fellow employee called him at his home, and said lightly, "Well, how did you get there?" The employee replied, "By automobile." He responded literally because he was faced with a message which asked him what he was doing at home when he should have been at the office, but which denied that this question was being asked by the way it was phrased. (Since the speaker felt it wasn't really his business, he spoke metaphorically.) The relationship was intense enough so that the victim was in doubt how the information would be used, and he therefore responded literally. This is characteristic of anyone who feels "on the spot," as demonstrated by the careful literal replies of a witness on the stand in a court trial. The schizophrenic feels so terribly on the spot at all times that he habitually responds with a defensive insistence on the literal level when it was quite inappropriate, e.g., when someone is joking.

Schizophrenics also confuse the literal and metaphoric in their own utterance when they feel themselves caught in a double bind. For example, a patient may wish to criticize his therapist for being late for an appointment, but he may be unsure what sort of a message that act of being late was--particularly if the therapist has anticipated the patient's reaction and apologized for the event. The patient cannot say, "Why were you late? Is it because you don't want to see me today?" This would be an accusation, and so he shifts to a metaphorical statement. He may then say, "I knew a fellow once who missed a boat, his name was Sam and the boat almost sunk, ... etc.," Thus he develops a metaphorical story and the therapist may or may not discover in it a comment on his being late. The convenient thing about a metaphor is that it leaves it up to the therapist (or mother) to see an accusation in the statement if he chooses, or to ignore it if he chooses. Should the therapist accept the accusation in the metaphor, then the patient can accept the statement he has made about Sam as metaphorical. If the therapist points out that this doesn't sound like a true statement about Sam, as a way of avoiding the accusation in the story, the patient can argue that there really was a man named Sam. As an answer to the double bind situation, a shift to a metaphorical statement brings safety. However, it also prevents the patient from making the accusation he wants to make. But instead of getting over his accusation by indicating that this is a metaphor, the schizophrenic patient seems to try to get over the fact that it is a metaphor by making it more fantastic. If the therapist should ignore the accusation in the story about Sam, the schizophrenic may then tell a story about going to Mars in a rocket ship as a way of putting over his accusation. The indication that it is a metaphorical statement lies in the fantastic aspect of the metaphor, not in the signals which usually accompany metaphors to tell the listener that a metaphor is being used.

It is not only safer for the victim of a double bind to shift to a metaphorical order of message, but in an impossible situation it is better to shift and become somebody else, or shift and insist that he is somewhere else. Then the double bind cannot work on the victim, because it isn't he and besides he is in a different place. In other words, the statements which show that a patient is disoriented can be interpreted as ways of defending himself against the situation he is in. The pathology enters when the victim himself either does not know that his responses are metaphorical or cannot say so. To recognize that he was speaking metaphorically he would need to be aware that he was defending himself and therefore was afraid of the other person. To him such an awareness would be an indictment of the other person and therefore provoke disaster.

If an individual has spent his life in the kind of double bind relationship described here, his way of relating to people after a psychotic break would have a systematic pattern. First, he would not share with normal people those signals which accompany messages to indicate what a person means. His metacommunicative system-- the communications about communication--would have broken down, and he would not know what kind of message a message was. If a person said to him, "What would you like to do today?" he would be unable to judge accurately by the context or by the tone of voice or gesture whether he was being condemned for what he did yesterday, or being offered a sexual invitation, or just what was meant. Given this inability to judge accurately what a person really means and an excessive concern with what is really meant, an individual might defend himself by choosing one or more of several alternatives. He might, for example, assume that behind every statement there is a concealed meaning which is detrimental to his welfare. He would then be excessively concerned with hidden meanings and determined to demonstrate that he could not be deceived--as he had been all his life. If he chooses this alternative, he will be continually searching for meanings behind what people say and behind chance occurrences in the environment, and he will be characteristically suspicious and defiant.

He might choose another alternative, and tend to accept literally everything people say to him; when their tone or gesture or context contradicted what they said, he might establish a pattern of laughing off these metacommunicative signals. He would give up trying to discriminate between levels of message and treat all messages as unimportant or to be laughed at.

If he didn't become suspicious of metacommunicative messages or attempt to laugh them off, he might choose to try to ignore them. Then he would find it necessary to see and hear less and less of what went on around him, and do his utmost to avoid provoking a response in his environment. He would try to detach his interest from the external world and concentrate on his own internal processes and, therefore, give the appearance of being a withdrawn, perhaps mute, individual.

This is another way of saying that if an individual doesn't know what sort of message a message is he may defend himself in ways which have been described as paranoid, hebephrenic, or catatonic. These three alternatives are not the only ones. The point is that he cannot choose the one alternative which would help him to discover what people mean; he cannot, without considerable help, discuss the messages of others. Without being able to do that, the human being is like any self-correcting system which has lost its governor, it spirals into never-ending, but always systematic, distortions.

A DESCRIPTION OF THE FAMILY SITUATION

The theoretical possibility of double bind situations stimulated us to look for such communication sequences in the schizophrenic patient and in his family situation. Toward this end we have studied the written and verbal reports of psychotherapists who have treated such patients intensively; we have studied tape recordings of psychotherapeutic interviews, both of our own patients and others; we have interviewed and taped parents of schizophrenics; we have had two mothers and one father participate in intensive psychotherapy; and we have interviewed and taped parents and patients seen conjointly.

On the basis of these data we have developed a hypothesis about the family situation which ultimately leads to an individual suffering from schizophrenia. This hypothesis has not been statistically tested; it selects and emphasizes a rather simple set of interactional phenomena and does not attempt to describe comprehensively the extraordinary complexity of a family relationship.

We hypothesize that the family situation of the schizophrenic has the following general characteristics:

1. A child whose mother becomes anxious and withdraws if the child responds to her as a loving mother. That is, the child's very existence has a special meaning to the mother which arouses her anxiety and hostility when she is in danger of intimate contact with the child.

2. A mother to whom feelings of anxiety and hostility toward the child are not acceptable, and whose way of denying them is to express overt loving behavior to persuade the child to respond to her as a loving mother and to withdraw from him if he does not. "Loving behavior" does not necessarily imply "affection"; it can,

for example, be set in a framework of doing the proper thing, instilling "goodness," and the like.

3. The absence of anyone in the family, such as a strong and insightful father, who can intervene in the relationship between the mother and child and support the child in the face of the contradictions involved.

Since this is a formal description we are not specifically concerned with why the mother feels this way about the child, but we suggest that she could feel this way for various reasons. It may be that merely having a child arouses anxiety about herself and her relationships to her own family; or it may be important to her that the child is a boy or a girl, or that the child was born on the anniversary of one of her own siblings (8), or the child may be in the same sibling position in the family that she was, or the child may be special to her for other reasons related to her own emotional problems.

Given a situation with these characteristics, we hypothesize that the mother of a schizophrenic will be simultaneously expressing at least two orders of message. (For simplicity in this presentation we shall confine ourselves to two orders.) These orders of message can be roughly characterized as (a) hostile or withdrawing behavior which is aroused whenever the child approaches her, and (b) simulated loving or approaching behavior which is aroused when the child responds to her hostile and withdrawing behavior, as a way of denying that she is withdrawing. Her problem is to control her anxiety by controlling the closeness and distance between herself and her child. To put this another way, if the mother begins to feel affectionate and close to her child, she begins to feel endangered and must withdraw from him; but she cannot accept this hostile act and to deny it must simulate affection and closeness with her child. The important point is that her loving behavior is then a comment on (since it is compensatory for) her hostile behavior and consequently it is of a different order of message than the hostile behavior--it is a message about a sequence of messages. Yet by its nature it denies the existence of those messages which it is about, i.e., the hostile withdrawal.

The mother uses the child's responses to affirm that her behavior is loving, and since the loving behavior is simulated, the child is placed in a position where he must not accurately interpret her communication if he is to maintain his relationship with her. In other words, he must not discriminate accurately between orders of message, in this case the difference between the expression of simulated feelings (one Logical Type) and real feelings (another Logical Type). As a result the child must systematically distort his perception of metacommunicative signals. For example, if mother begins to feel hostile (or affectionate) toward her child and also feels compelled to withdraw from him, she might say, "Go to bed, you're very tired and I want you to get your sleep." This overtly loving statement is intended to deny a feeling which could be verbalized as "Get out of my sight because I'm sick of you." If the child correctly discriminates her metacommunicative signals, he would have to face the fact that she both doesn't want him and is deceiving him by her loving behavior. He would be "punished" for learning to discriminate orders of messages accurately. He therefore would tend to accept the idea that he is tired rather than recognize his mother's deception. This means that he must deceive himself about his own internal state in order to support mother in her deception. To survive with her he must falsely discriminate his own internal messages as well as falsely discriminate the messages of others.

The problem is compounded for the child because the mother is "benevolently" defining for him how he feels; she is expressing overt maternal concern over the fact that he is tired. To put it another way, the mother is controlling the child's definitions of his own messages, as well as the definition of his responses to her (e.g., by saying, "You don't really mean to say that," if he should criticize her) by insisting that she is not concerned about herself but only about him. Consequently, the easiest path for the child is to accept mother's simulated loving behavior as real, and his desires to interpret what is going on are undermined. Yet the result is that the mother is withdrawing from him and defining this withdrawal as the way a loving relationship should be.

However, accepting mother's simulated loving behavior as real also is no solution for the child. Should he make this false discrimination, he would approach her; this move toward closeness would provoke in her feelings of fear and helplessness, and she would be compelled to withdraw. But if he then withdrew from her, she would take his withdrawal as a statement that she was not a loving mother and would either punish him for withdrawing or approach him to bring him closer. If he then approached, she would respond by putting him at a distance. The child is punished for discriminating accurately what she is expressing, and he is punished for discriminating inaccurately--he is caught in a double bind.

The child might try various means of escaping from this situation. He might, for example, try to lean on his father or some other member of the family. However, from our preliminary observations we think it is likely that the fathers of schizophrenics are not substantial enough to lean on. They are also in the awkward position where if they agreed with the child about the nature of mother's deceptions, they would need to recognize the nature of their own relationships to the mother, which they could not do and remain attached to her in the modus operandi they have worked out.

The need of the mother to be wanted and loved also prevents the child from gaining support from some other person i the environment, a teacher, for example. A mother with these characteristics would feel threatened by any other attachment of the child and would break it up and bring the child back closer to her with consequent anxiety when the child became dependent on her.

The only way the child can really escape from the situation is to comment on the contradictory position his mother has put him in. However, if he did so, the mother would take this as an accusation that she is unloving and both punish him and insist that his perception of the situation is distorted. By preventing the child from talking about the situation, the mother forbids him using the metacommunicative level--the level we use to correct our perception of communicative behavior. The ability to communicate about communication, to comment upon the meaningful actions of oneself and others, is essential for successful social intercourse. In any normal relationship there is a constant interchange of metacommunicative messages such as "What do you mean?" or "Why did you do that?" or "Are you kidding me?" and so on. To discriminate accurately what people are really expressing we must be able to comment directly or indirectly on that expression. This metacommunicative level the schizophrenic seems unable to use successfully (2). Given these characteristics of the mother, it is apparent why. If she is denying one order of message, then any statement about her statements endangers her and she must forbid it. Therefore, the child grows up unskilled in his ability to communicate about communication and, as a result, unskilled in determining what people really mean and unskilled in expressing what he really means, which is essential for normal relationships.

In summary, then, we suggest that the double bind nature of the family situation of a schizophrenic results in placing the child in a position where if he responds to his mother's simulated affection her anxiety will be aroused and she will punish him (or insist, to protect herself, that his overtures are simulated, thus confusing him about the nature of his own messages) to defend herself from closeness with him. Thus the child is blocked off from intimate and secure associations with his mother. However, if he does not make overtures of affection, she will feel that this means she is not a loving mother and her anxiety will be aroused. Therefore, she will either punish him for withdrawing or make overtures toward the child to insist that he demonstrate that he loves her. If he then responds and shows her affection, she will not only feel endangered again, but she may resent the fact that she had to force him to respond. In either case in a relationship, the most important in his life and the model for all others, he is punished if he indicates love and affection and punished if he does not; and his escape routes from the situation, such as gaining support from others, are cut off. This is the basic nature of the double bind relationship between mother and child. This description has not depicted, of course, the more complicated interlocking gestalt that is the "family" of which the "mother" is one important part (11, 12).

ILLUSTRATIONS FROM CLINICAL DATA

An analysis of an incident occurring between a schizophrenic patient and his mother illustrates the "double bind" situation. A young man who had fairly well recovered from an acute schizophrenic episode was visited in the hospital by his mother. He was glad to see her and impulsively put his arm around her shoulders, whereupon she stiffened. He withdraw his arm and she asked, "Don't you love me any more?" He then blushed, and she said, "Dear, you must not be so easily embarrassed and afraid of your feelings." The patient was able to stay with her only a few minutes more and following her departure he assaulted an aide and was put in the tubs.

Obviously, this result could have been avoided if the young man had been able to say, "Mother, it is obvious that you become uncomfortable when I put my arm around you, and that you have difficulty accepting a gesture of affection from me." However, the schizophrenic patient doesn't have this possibility open to him. His intense dependency and training prevents him from commenting upon his mother's communicative behavior, though she comments on his and forces him to accept and to attempt to deal with the complicated sequence. The complications for the patient include the following:

1. The mother's reaction of not accepting her son's affectionate gesture is masterfully covered up by her condemnation of him for

withdrawing, and the patient denies his perception of the situation by accepting her condemnation.

2. The statement "don't you love me any more" in this context seems to imply:

(a) "I am lovable."

(b) "You should love me and if you don't you are bad or at fault."

(c) "Whereas you did love me previously you don't any longer," and thus focus is shifted from his expressing affection to his inability to be affectionate. Since the patient has also hated her, she is on good ground here, and he responds appropriately with guilt, which she then attacks.

(d) "What you just expressed <u>was</u> <u>not</u> <u>affection</u>," and in order to accept this statement the patient must deny what she and the culture have taught him about how one expresses affection. He must also question the times with her, and with others, when he thought he was experiencing affection and when they <u>seemed</u> to treat the situation as if he had. He experiences here loss-of-support phenomena and is put in doubt about the reliability of past experience.

3. The statement, "You must not be so easily embarrassed and afraid of your feelings," seems to imply:

(a) "You are not like me and are different from other nice or normal people because we express our feelings."

(b) "The feelings you express are all right, it's only that <u>you</u> can't accept them." However, if the stiffening on her part had indicated "these are unacceptable feelings," then the boy is told that he should not be embarrassed by unacceptable feelings. Since he has had a long training in what is and is not acceptable to both her and society, he again comes into conflict with the past. If he is unafraid of his own feelings (which mother implies is good), he should be unafraid of his affection and would then notice it was she who was afraid, but he must not notice that because her whole approach is aimed at covering up this shortcoming in herself.

The impossible dilemma thus becomes: "If I am to keep my tie to mother I must not show her that I love her, but if I do not show her that I love her, then I will lose her."

The importance to the mother of her special method of control is strikingly illustrated by the interfamily situation of a young woman schizophrenic who greeted the therapist on their first meeting with the remark, "Mother had to get married and now I'm here." This statement meant to the therapist that:

1. The patient was the result of an illegitimate pregnancy.

2. This fact was related to her present psychosis (in her opinion).

3. "Here" referred to the psychiatrist's office and to the patient's presence on earth for which she had to be eternally indebted to her mother, especially since her mother had sinned and suffered in order to bring her into the world.

4. "Had to get married" referred to the shot-gun nature of mother's wedding and to the mother's response to pressure that she must marry, and the reciprocal, that she resented the forced nature of the situation and blamed the patient for it.

Actually, all these suppositions subsequently proved to be factually correct and were corroborated by the mother during an abortive attempt at psychotherapy. The flavor of the mother's communications to the patient seemed essentially this: "I am lovable, loving, and satisfied with myself. You are lovable when you are like me and when you do what I say." At the same time the mother indicated to the daughter both by words and behavior: "You are physically delicate, unintelligent, and different from me ('not normal'). You need me and me alone because of these handicaps, and I will take care of you and love you." Thus the patient's life was a series of beginnings, of attempts at experience, which would result in failure and withdrawal back to the maternal hearth and bosom because of the collusion between her and her mother.

It was noted in collaborative therapy that certain areas important to the mother's self-esteem were especially conflictual situations for the patient. For example, the mother needed the fiction that she was close to her family and that a deep love existed between her and her own mother. By analogy the relationship to the grandmother served as the prototype for the mother's relationship to her own daughter. On one occasion when the daughter was seven or eight years old the grandmother in a rage threw a knife which barely missed the little girl. The mother said nothing to the grandmother but hurried the little girl from the room with the words,

"Grandmommy really loves you. " It is significant that the grandmother took the attitude toward the patient that she was not well
enough controlled, and she used to chide her daughter for being
too easy on the child. The grandmother was living in the house
during one of the patient's psychotic episodes, and the girl took
great delight in throwing various objects at the mother and grandmother while they cowered in fear.

Mother felt herself very attractive as a girl, and she felt that
her daughter resembled her rather closely, although by damning
with faint praise it was obvious that she felt the daughter definitely
ran second. One of the daughter's first acts during a psychotic
period was to announce to her mother that she was going to cut off
all her hair. She proceeded to do this while the mother pleaded
with her to stop. Subsequently the mother would show a picture of
herself as a girl and explain to people how the patient would look
if she only had her beautiful hair.

The mother, apparently without awareness of the significance
of what she was doing, would equate the daughter's illness with not
being very bright and with some sort of organic brain difficulty.
She would invariably contrast this with her own intelligence as
demonstrated by her own scholastic record. She treated her daughter with a completely patronizing and placating manner which was
insincere. For example, in the psychiatrist's presence she prom-
ised her daughter that she would not allow her to have further shock
treatments, and as soon as the girl was out of the room she asked
the doctor if he didn't feel she should be hospitalized and given
electric shock treatments. One clue to this deceptive behavior a-
rose during the mother's therapy. Although the daughter had had
three previous hospitalizations the mother had never mentioned to
the doctors that she herself had had a psychotic episode when she
discovered that she was pregnant. The family whisked her away
to a small sanitarium in a nearby town, and she was, according
to her own statement, strapped to a bed for six weeks. Her family did not visit her during this time, and no one except her parents
and her sister knew that she was hospitalized.

There were two times during therapy when the mother showed
intense emotion. One was in relating her own psychotic experience; the other was on the occasion of her last visit when she accused the therapist of trying to drive her crazy by forcing her to
choose between her daughter and her husband. Against medical
advice, she took her daughter out of therapy.

The father was as involved in the homeostatic aspects of the intrafamily situation as the mother. For example, he stated that he had to quit his position as an important attorney in order to bring his daughter to an area where competent psychiatric help was available. Subsequently, acting on cues from the patient (e.g., she frequently referred to a character named "Nervous Ned") the therapist was able to elicit from him that he had hated his job and for years had been trying to "get out from under." However, the daughter was made to feel that the move was initiated for her.

On the basis of our examination of the clinical data, we have been impressed by a number of observations including:

1. The helplessness, fear, exasperation, and rage which a double bind situation provokes in the patient, but which the mother may serenely and un-understandingly pass over. We have noted reactions in the father that both create double bind situations, or extend and amplify those created by the mother, and we have seen the father passive and outraged, but helpless, become ensnared in a similar manner to the patient.

2. The psychosis seems, in part, a way of dealing with double bind situations to overcome their inhibiting and controlling effect. The psychotic patient may make astute, pithy, often metaphorical remarks that reveal an insight into the forces binding him. Contrariwise, he may become rather expert in setting double bind situations himself.

3. According to our theory, the communication situation described is essential to the mother's security, and by inference to the family homeostasis. If this be so, then when psychotherapy of the patient helps him become less vulnerable to mother's attempts at control, anxiety will be produced in the mother. Similarly, if the therapist interprets to the mother the dynamics of the situation she is setting up with the patient, this should produce an anxiety response in her. Our impression is that when there is perduring contact between patient and family (especially when the patient lives at home during psychotherapy), this leads to a disturbance (often severe) in the mother and sometimes in both mother and father and other siblings (10, 11).

CURRENT POSITION AND FUTURE PROSPECTS

Many writers have treated schizophrenia in terms of the most extreme contrast with any other form of human thinking and behavior. While it is an isolable phenomenon, so much emphasis on the differences from the normal--rather like the fearful physical segregation of psychotics--does not help in understanding the problems. In our approach we assume that schizophrenia involves general principles which are important in all communication and therefore many informative similarities can be found in "normal" communication situations.

We have been particularly interested in various sorts of communication which involve both emotional significance and the necessity of discriminating between orders of message. Such situations include play, humor, ritual, poetry, and fiction. Play, especially among animals, we have studied at some length (3). It is a situation which strikingly illustrates the occurrence of meta-messages whose correct discrimination is vital to the cooperation of the individuals involved; for example, false discrimination could easily lead to combat. Rather closely related to play is humor, a continuing subject of our research. It involves sudden shifts in Logical Types as well as discrimination of those shifts. Ritual is a field in which unusually real or literal ascriptions of Logical Type are made and defended as vigorously as the schizophrenic defends the "reality" of his delusions. Poetry exemplifies the communicative power of metaphor--even very unusual metaphor--when labeled as such by various signs, as contrasted to the obscurity of unlabeled schizophrenic metaphor. The entire field of fictional communication, defined as the narration or depiction of a series of events with more or less of a label of actuality, is most relevant to the investigation of schizophrenia. We are not so much concerned with the content interpretation of fiction--although analysis of oral and destructive themes is illuminating to the student of schizophrenia--as with the formal problems involved in simultaneous existence of multiple levels of message in the fictional presentation of "reality." The drama is especially interesting in this respect, with both performers and spectators responding to messages about both the actual and the theatrical reality.

We are giving extensive attention to hypnosis. A great array of phenomena that occur as schizophrenic symptoms--hallucinations, delusions, alterations of personality, amnesias, and so on--can be produced temporarily in normal subjects with hypnosis. These need not be directly suggested as specific phenomena, but can be the "spontaneous" result of an arranged communication sequence. For example, Erickson (4) will produce a hallucination by first inducing catalepsy in a subject's hand and then saying, "There is no conceivable way in which your hand can move, yet when I give the signal, it must move." That is, he tells the subject his hand will remain in place, yet it will move, and in no way the subject can consciously conceive. When Erickson gives the signal, the subject hallucinates the hand moved, or hallucinates himself in a different place and therefore the hand was moved. This use of hallucination to resolve a problem posed by contradictory commands which cannot be discussed seems to us to illustrate the solution of a double bind situation via a shift in Logical Types. Hypnotic responses to direct suggestions or statements also commonly involve shifts in type, as in accepting the words "Here's a glass of water" or "You feel tired" as external or internal reality, or in literal response to metaphorical statements, much like schizophrenics. We hope that further study of hypnotic induction, phenomena, and waking will, in this controllable situation, help sharpen our view of the essential communicational sequences which produce phenomena like those of schizophrenia.

Another Erickson experiment (12) seems to isolate a double bind communicational sequence without the specific use of hypnosis. Erickson arranged a seminar so as to have a young chain smoker sit next to him and to be without cigarettes; other participants were briefed on what to do. All was ordered so that Erickson repeatedly turned to offer the young man a cigarette, but was always interrupted by a question from someone so that he turned away, "inadvertently" withdrawing the cigarettes from the young man's reach. Later another participant asked this young man if he had received the cigarette from Dr. Erickson. He replied, "What cigarette?", showed clearly that he had forgotten the whole sequence, and even refused a cigarette offered by another member, saying that he was too interested in the seminar discussion to smoke. This young man seems to us to be in an experimental situation paralleling the schizophrenic's double bind situation with mother: An important relationship, contradictory messages (here of giving and taking away) and comment blocked--because there was a seminar going on, and anyway it was all "inadvertent." And note the similar outcome: Amnesia for the double bind sequence and reversal from "He doesn't give" to "I don't want."

Although we have been led into these collateral areas, our main field of observation has been schizophrenia itself. All of us have worked directly with schizophrenic patients and much of this case material has been recorded on tape for detailed study. In addition, we are recording interviews held jointly with patients and their families, and we are taking sound motion pictures of mothers and disturbed, presumably preschizophrenic, children. Our hope is that these operations will provide a clearly evident record of the continuing, repetitive double binding which we hypothesize goes on steadily from infantile beginnings in the family situation of individuals who become schizophrenic. This basic family situation, and the overtly communicational characteristics of schizophrenia, have been the major focus of this paper. However, we expect our concepts and some of these data will also be useful in future work on other problems of schizophrenia, such as the variety of other symptoms, the character of the "adjusted state" before schizophrenia becomes manifest, and the nature and circumstances of the psychotic break.

THERAPEUTIC IMPLICATIONS OF THIS HYPOTHESIS

Psychotherapy itself is a context of multi-level communication, with exploration of the ambiguous lines between the literal and metaphoric, or reality and fantasy, and indeed, various forms of play, drama, and hypnosis have been used extensively in therapy. We have been interested in therapy, and in addition to our own data we have been collecting and examining recordings, verbatim transscripts, and personal accounts of therapy from other therapists. In this we prefer exact records since we believe that how a schizophrenic talks depends greatly, though often subtly, on how another person talks to him; it is most difficult to estimate what was really occurring in a therapeutic interview if one has only a description of it, especially if the description is already in theoretical terms.

Except for a few general remarks and some speculation, however, we are not yet prepared to comment on the relation of the double bind to psychotherapy. At present we can only note:

1. Double bind situations are created by and within the psychotherapeutic setting and the hospital milieu. From the point of view of this hypothesis we wonder about the effect of medical "benevolence" on the schizophrenic patient. Since hospitals exist for the benefit of personnel as well as--as much as--more than--for the patient's benefit, there will be contradictions at times in sequences where actions are taken "benevolently" for the patient when actually they are intended to keep the staff more comfortable. We would assume that whenever the system is organized for hospital purposes and it is announced to the patient that the actions are for his benefit, then the schizophrenogenic situation is being perpetuated. This kind of deception will provoke the patient to respond to it as a double bind situation, and his response will be "schizophrenic" in the sense that it will be indirect and the patient will be unable to comment on the fact that he feels that he is being deceived. One

vignette, fortunately amusing, illustrates such a response. On a ward with a dedicated and "benevolent" physician in charge there was a sign on the physician's door which said "Doctor's Office. Please Knock." The doctor was driven to distraction and finally capitulation by the obedient patient who carefully knocked every time he passed the door.

2. The understanding of the double bind and its communicative aspects may lead to innovations in therapeutic technique. Just what these innovations may be is difficult to say, but on the basis of our investigation we are assuming that double bind situations occur consistently in psychotherapy. At times these are inadvertent in the sense that the therapist is imposing a double bind situation similar to that in the patient's history, or the patient is imposing a double bind situation on the therapist. At other times therapists seem to impose double binds, either deliberately or intuitively, which force the patient to respond differently than he has in the past.

An incident from the experience of a gifted psychotherapist illustrates the intuitive understanding of a double bind communicational sequence. Dr. Frieda Fromm-Reichmann (5) was treating a young woman who from the age of seven had built a highly complex religion of her own replete with powerful Gods. She was very schizophrenic and quite hesitant about entering into a therapeutic situation. At the beginning of the treatment she said, "God R says I shouldn't talk with you." Dr. Fromm-Reichmann replied, "Look, let's get something into the record. To me God R doesn't exist, and that whole world of yours doesn't exist. To you it does, and far be it from me to think that I can take that away from you, I have no idea what it means. So I'm willing to talk with you in terms of that world, if only you know I do it so that we have an understanding that it doesn't exist for me. Now go to God R and tell him that we have to talk and he should give you permission. Also you must tell him that I am a doctor and that you have lived with him in his kingdom now from seven to sixteen--that's nine years--and he hasn't helped you. So now he must permit me to try and see whether you and I can do that job. Tell him that I am a doctor and this is what I want to try."

The therapist has her patient in a "therapeutic double bind." If the patient is rendered doubtful about her belief in her god then she is agreeing with Dr. Fromm-Reichmann, and is admitting her attachment to therapy. If she insists that God R is real, then she must tell him that Dr. Fromm-Reichmann is "more powerful" than he--again admitting her involvement with the therapist.

The difference between the therapeutic bind and the original double bind situation is in part the fact that the therapist is not involved in a life and death struggle himself. He can therefore set up relatively benevolent binds and gradually aid the patient in his emancipation from them. Many of the uniquely appropriate therapeutic gambits arranged by therapists seem to be intuitive. We share the goal of most psychotherapists who strive toward the day when such strokes of genius will be well enough understood to be systematic and commonplace.

REFERENCES

1. Bateson, G. Social planning and the concept of "deutero-learning". Conference on Science, Philosophy, and Religion, Second Symposium. Harper, New York, 1942.
2. Bateson, G. A theory of play and fantasy. Psych. Res. Rep., 2:39-51, 1955.
3. Carpenter, C. R. A field study of the behavior and social relations of howling monkeys. Comp. Psychol. Monogr., 10:1-168, 1934.
4. Erickson, M. H. Personal communication, 1955.
5. Fromm-Reichmann, F. Personal communication, 1956.
6. Haley, J. Paradoxes in play, fantasy, and psychotherapy. Psych. Res. Rep, 2:52-58, 1955.
7. Harlow, H. F. The formation of learning sets. Psychol. Rev., 56:51-65, 1949.
8. Hilgard, J. R. Anniversary reactions in parents precipitated by children. Psychiatry, 16:73-80, 1953.
9. Hull, C. L., et al. Mathematico-deductive Theory of Rote Learning, Yale Univ. Press, New Haven, 1940.
10. Jackson, D. D. An episode of sleepwalking. J. Amer. Psychoanal. Assn., 2:503-508, 1954.
11. Jackson, D. D. Some factors influencing the Oedipus complex. Psychoanal. Quart., 23:566-581, 1954.
12. Jackson, D. D. The question of family homeostasis. Psychiat. Quart. Suppl., 31, Part 1: 79-90, 1957. (See p. 1, this volume.)
13. Lorenz, K. Z. King Solomon's Ring, Crowell, New York, 1952.
14. Perceval, J. A Narrative of the Treatment Experienced by a Gentleman during a State of Mental Derangement, Designed to Explain the Causes and Nature of Insanity, etc. Effingham Wilson, London, 1836 and 1840.
15. Ruesch, J. and Bateson, G. Communication: The Social Matrix of Psychiatry, Norton, New York, 1951.

16. von Domarus, E.   The specific laws of logic in schizophrenia.
    In J.S. Kasanin (Ed.), Language and Thought in Schizo-
    phrenia,   Univ. of California Press, Berkeley, 1944.
17. Whitehead, A.N. and Russell, B.   Principia Mathematica,
    Cambridge Univ. Press, Cambridge, 1910.

A NOTE ON THE
DOUBLE BIND--1962

Gregory Bateson, Don D. Jackson
Jay Haley and John H. Weakland

Because of the reaction in the literature to the concept of the
double bind as presented in our joint article "Toward a Theory
of Schizophrenia," it secms appropriate to state briefly the research context of that article, to clarify what we consider most
significant about our work generally, and to describe the further
developments in our research since 1956.

Prior to the 1956 paper the research project had investigated
a variety of phenomena from the communication point of view--the
nature of metaphor, humor, popular films, ventriloquism, training of guide dogs for the blind, the nature of play, animal behavior,
the formal nature of psychotherapy and the communicative behavior
of individual schizophrenics (1, 2, 30). All communication involves the use of categories and classes, and our focus of interest
was on the occurrence in classification systems of combinations
which generate paradox; a particular interest was in the ways two
or more messages--meta-messages in relation to each other--may
qualify each other to produce paradoxes of Russellian type.

Originally the idea of the double bind was arrived at largely de-
ductively: given the characteristics of schizophrenic communica-
tion--a confusion of message and meta-message in the patient's
discourse--the patient must have been reared in a learning context which included formal sequences where he was forced to respond to messages which generated paradox of this type. In this
sense the double bind hypothesis was initially a conjecture about
what must have happened granted the premises of the theoretical

Reprinted from FAMILY PROCESS, 2, No. 1:154-161 (March
1963). Copyright, The Mental Research Institute of the Palo Alto
Medical Research Foundation and the Family Institute.
Reproduced by permission.

approach and the observations of the schizophrenic individual's way of communicating. By 1956 this conjecture was beginning to be supported by empirical observation of mothers and their disturbed children.

However, although our investigations thus involved various fields of phenomena, and the particular concept of the double bind was a striking one--as attested by the specific attention that both we and others have given it--neither these specific subject-matters nor this specific concept has been the real core of our work as we see it. This point needs special attention, as it seems that a number of existing criticisms or misunderstandings of our statements rest on a lack of clarity at just this level.

A COMMUNICATIONAL APPROACH TO THE STUDY OF BEHAVIOR

What is more important in our work, and may not have been sufficiently emphasized or clear in our 1956 paper, is a general communicational approach to the study of a wide range of human (and some animal) behavior, including schizophrenia as one major case. The present and future status of the more specific double bind concept can appropriately be considered only within this, its more general and inclusive framework. This communicational approach might be described or characterized in various ways, as it has been in other of our publications. It will suffice here to note that we are always concerned when examining the activity of people (or other organisms) to consider how this behavior may be in response to observable communications from others, and how it in turn itself is communicative. Especially, we have been concerned with the importance of attending adequately to the complexity of communication. That is, there is never "a message" singly, but in actual communication always two or more related messages, of different levels and often conveyed by different channels--voice, tone, movement, context, and so on. These messages may be widely incongruent and thus exert very different and conflicting influences. This approach seems to us to be helpful when we try to examine and conceptualize many sorts of social or psychological problems, and we have continued to pursue and extend its application.

Since 1956 when "Toward a Theory of Schizophrenia" appeared, the project members have published papers on a variety of areas of investigation. These papers are listed here with reference numbers referring to items in the bibliography at the end of this article. The publications are arranged roughly by subject matter although many of them included overlapping subjects.

1. Schizophrenic Communication and the Nature of Schizophrenia
   The distortions of schizophrenic communication were discussed (6), a subjective account of a psychosis was presented (16) and schizophrenic behavior was described in terms of levels of communication (34).

2. The Family Context as an Etiologic Factor and a Subject of Study Itself
   The etiology of schizophrenia was discussed in terms of the mother as a factor (27), trauma vs. patterns (45), and there was a description of the immediate circumstances of a schizophrenic episode (65).

   The families of schizophrenics were described in terms of feedback and calibration patterns (15), the family was described as a cybernetic system (35, 36), guilt and its relation to maternal control was discussed (50), and letters of mothers to their schizophrenic children were described (70).

   Family organization and dynamics were discussed with reference to incest (9), patterns (15), family homeostasis (52), three-party interaction in double bind communication (66), the relationship between an anxiety syndrome and a marital relationship (28), experimentation with families (41) and family therapy as an arena for research (69).

3. Therapy
   A report on investigating therapy was given (15), the detailed study of a therapeutic interview was provided (22), psychoanalysis was described in communications terms (31, 33), transference was discussed in terms of paradox (63), brief psychotherapy was described (38) as well as psychotherapy with schizophrenics (39) and family therapy (40, 52, 56, 58, 59, 64).

4. Hypnosis in Communication Terms
   A description of the interaction of hypnotist and subject was made (32), an analysis was done of a verbatim trance induction (23), the relief of fear with hypnosis was discussed (37), and hypnosis was discussed as a model for describing psychotherapy (38).

5. Wider Studies of Communication and Organization
   Various general areas of investigation included studies of hos-

pital wards (7, 15), wider social spheres (5, 10, 20), a detailed analysis of an interview segment (22), levels of learning (17, 18), the theory of games was discussed (11, 13, 15) and evolution was described in terms of communication and double bind patterns (12).

The research project terminated in 1962 after ten years of association. A summary statement of the group agreement about the double bind at the time of termination would include the following: I. The double bind is a class of sequences which appear when phenomena are examined with a concept of levels of communication. II. In schizophrenia the double bind is a necessary but not sufficient condition in explaining etiology and, conversely, is an inevitable by-product of schizophrenic communication. III. Empirical study and theoretical description of individuals and families should for this type of analysis emphasize observable communication, behavior, and relationship contexts rather than focusing upon the perception or affective states of individuals. IV. The most useful way to phrase double bind description is not in terms of a binder and a victim but in terms of people caught up in an ongoing system which produces conflicting definitions of the relationship and consequent subjective distress. In its attempts to deal with the complexities of muti-level patterns in human communications systems, the research group prefers an emphasis upon circular systems of interpersonal relations to a more conventional emphasis upon the behavior of individuals alone or single sequences in the interaction.

REFERENCES

1. Bateson, G. A theory of play and fantasy. Psychiat. Res. Rep., 2:39-51, 1955.
2. Bateson, G. The message "this is play." In Second Conference on Group Processes, Josiah Macy Jr. Fnd., New York, 1956.
3. Bateson, G., Jackson, D. D., Haley, J. and Weakland, J. H. Toward a theory of schizophrenia. Behavioral Sc., 1:251-264, 1956. (See p. 31, this vol.)
4. Bateson, G. Language and psychotherapy, Frieda Fromm-Reichmann's last project. Psychiatry, 21:96-100, 1958.
5. Bateson, G. Naven, 2nd edition with a new chapter, Stanford Univ. Press, 1958.
6. Bateson, G. Schizophrenic distortion of communication. In Psychotherapy of Chronic Schizophrenic Patients, C. Whitaker (Ed.), Little, Brown & Co., Boston, 1958.
7. Bateson, G. Analysis of group therapy in an admission ward.

In Social Psychiatry in Action, H. A. Wilmer (Ed.), Thomas, Springfield, Ill., 1958.

8. Bateson, G. Anthropological theories. Science, 129:334-349, 1959.

9. Bateson, G. Panel review. In Individual and Familial Dynamics, J. H. Masserman (Ed.), Grune & Stratton, New York, 1959.

10. Bateson, G. Cultural problems posed by a study of schizophrenic process. In Schizophrenia, an Integrated Approach, A. Auerback (Ed.), A. P. A. Symposium 1958, Ronald Press, New York, 1959.

11. Bateson, G. The New Conceptual Frames for Behavioral Research. Proceedings of the Sixth Annual Psychiatric Institute, Princeton, 1958.

12. Bateson, G. Minimal requirements for a theory of schizophrenia. Arch. Gen. Psychiat., 2:477-491, 1960.

13. Bateson, G. The group dynamics of schizophrenia. In Chronic Schizophrenia: Explorations in Theory and Treatment, L. Appleby, J. M. Scher, and J. Cumming (Eds.), Free Press, Glencoe, Ill., 1960.

14. Bateson, G. Discussion of "Families of schizophrenic and of well children; method, concepts and some results," by Samuel J. Back, Amer. J. Psychiat., 30:263-266, 1960.

15. Bateson, G. The biosocial integration of behavior in the schizophrenic family. And, The challenge of research in family diagnosis and therapy, summary of panel discussion: I. Formal research in family structure. Both in Exploring the Base for Family Therapy, N. W. Ackerman, F. L. Beatman, and S. Sanford (Eds.), Family Service Assoc., New York, 1961.

16. Bateson, G. (Ed.) Perceval's Narrative, A Patient's Account of His Psychosis, 1830-1832, Stanford Univ. Press, 1961.

17. Bateson, G. Structure and the Genesis of Relationship, Frieda Fromm-Reichmann Memorial Lecture, Psychiatry (in press).

18. Bateson, G. Exchange of Information about Patterns of Human Behavior. Symposium on Information Storage and Neural Control, Houston, Texas, 1962, (in press).

19. Bateson, G. Communication theories in relation to the etiology of the neuroses. Symposium on the Etiology of the Neuroses, Society of Medical Psychoanalysis, New York, 1962 (in press).

20. Bateson, G. Problems of Credibility and Congruence in Applying Computational Methods to Problems of Peace. Delivered at the Spring Joint Computer Conference, Amer-

ican Federation of Information Processing Societies, San Francisco, 1962.

21. Bateson, G. The Prisoner's Dilemma and the Schizophrenic Family. (To be published)

22. Bateson, G., Brosin, H.W., Birdwhistell, R., and McQuown, N. The Natural History of an Interview. (Mimeo).

23. Erickson, M.H., Haley, J., and Weakland, J.H., A transcript of a trance induction with commentary. Am. J. Clin. Hyp., 2:49-84, 1959.

24. Fry, W.F. The use of ataractic agents. Calif. Med., 98: 309-313, 1958.

25. Fry, W.F. Destructive behavior on hospital wards. Psychiat. Quart. Suppl., 33: Part 2, 197-231, 1959.

26. Fry, W.F. and Heersema, P. Conjoint family therapy: a new dimension in psychotherapy. In Topic. Prob. Psychother., V. 4, 147-153, Karger, Basel and New York, 1963.

27. Fry, W.F. The schizophrenogenic who? Psychoan. and Psychoan. Rev., 49:68-73, 1962.

28. Fry, W.F. The marital context of an anxiety syndrome. Fam. Proc., 1:245-252, 1962.

29. Fry, W.F. Sweet Madness: A Study of Humor, Pacific Books, Palo Alto, Calif., 1963.

30. Haley, J. Paradoxes in play, fantasy, and psychotherapy. Psychiat. Res. Rep., 2:52-58, 1955.

31. Haley, J. The art of psychoanalysis. Etc., 15:190-200, 1958.

32. Haley, J. An interactional explanation of hypnosis. Am. J. Clin. Hyp., 1:41-57, 1958.

33. Haley, J. Control in psychoanalytic psychotherapy. Progress in Psychotherapy, 4:48-65, Grune & Stratton, New York, 1959.

34. Haley, J. An interactional description of schizophrenia. Psychiatry, 22:321-332, 1959. (See p. 151, this vol.)

35. Haley, J. The family of the schizophrenic: a model system. Am.J.Nerv.Ment.Dis., 129:357-374, 1959.(See p.171, this vol.)

36. Haley, J. Observation of the family of the schizophrenic. Am. J. Orthopsychiat., 30:460-467, 1960.

37. Haley, J. Control of fear with hypnosis. Am. J. Clin. Hyp., 2:109-115, 1960.

38. Haley, J. Control in brief psychotherapy. Arch. Gen. Psychiat., 4:139-153, 1961.

39. Haley, J. Control in the psychotherapy of schizophrenics. Arch. Gen. Psychiat., 5:340-353, 1961.

40. Haley, J. Whither family therapy? Fam. Proc., 1:69-100, 1962.

41. Haley, J. Family experiments: a new type of experimentation. Fam. Proc., 1:265-293, 1962. (See p. 264, this vol.)

42. Haley, J. Marriage therapy. Arch. Gen. Psychiat., (in press).
43. Haley, J. Strategies of Psychotherapy, Grune & Stratton, New York, (in press).
44. Jackson, D. D. Countertransference and psychotherapy. In Progress in Psychotherapy, F. Fromm-Reichmann and J. L. Moreno (Eds.), 1:234-238, Grune & Stratton, 1956.
45. Jackson, D. D. A note on the importance of trauma in the genesis of schizophrenia. Psychiatry, 20:181-184, 1957. (See p. 23, this vol.)
46. Jackson, D. D. The psychiatrist in the medical clinic. Bull. Am. Assoc. Med. Clinics, 6:94-98, 1957.
47. Jackson, D. D. The question of family homeostasis. Psychiat. Quart. Suppl., 31:79-90, part 1, 1957. (See p. 1, this vol.)
48. Jackson, D. D. Theories of suicide. In Clues to Suicide, E. Shneidman and N. Farberow (Eds.), McGraw-Hill, New York, 1957.
49. Jackson, D. D. The family and sexuality. In The Psychotherapy of Chronic Schizophrenic Patients, C. Whitaker (Ed.), Little-Brown, Boston, 1958.
50. Jackson, D. D. Guilt and the control of pleasure in schizoid personalities. Brit J. Med. Psychol., 31: part 2, 124-130, 1958. (See p. 12, this vol.)
51. Jackson, D. D., Block, J., and Patterson, V. Psychiatrists' conceptions of the schizophrenogenic parent. Arch. Neur. Psychiat., 79:448-459, 1958.
52. Jackson, D. D. Family interaction, family homeostasis and some implications for conjoint family psychotherapy. In Individual and Familial Dynamics, J. Masserman (Ed.), Grune & Stratton, New York, 1959.
53. Jackson, D. D. The managing of acting out in a borderline personality. In Case Studies in Counseling and Psychotherapy, A. Burton (Ed.), Prentice-Hall, New York, 1959.
54. Jackson, D. D. and Weakland, J. H. Schizophrenic symptoms and family interaction. Arch. Gen. Psychiat., 1:618-621, 1959.
55. Jackson, D. D. (Ed.) The Etiology of Schizophrenia, Basic Books, New York, 1960.
56. Jackson, D. D. The monad, the dyad, and the family therapy of schizophrenics. In Psychotherapy of the Psychoses, A. Burton (Ed.), Basic Books, New York, 1961.
57. Jackson, D. D., Satir, V., and Riskin, J. A method of analysis of a family interview. Arch. Gen. Psychiat., 5: 321-339, 1961. (See p. 230, this vol.)
58. Jackson, D. D. and Satir, V. Family diagnosis and family therapy. In Exploring the Base for Family Therapy,

N. Ackerman, F. Beatman, and S. Sherman (Eds.), Family Service Assoc., New York, 1961.

59. Jackson, D.D. and Weakland, J.H. Conjoint family therapy, some considerations on theory, technique, and results. Psychiatry, 24: Suppl. to No. 2, 30-45, 1961.

60. Jackson, D.D. Action for mental illness--what kind? Stanford Med. Bull., 20:77-80, 1962.

61. Jackson, D.D. Interactional psychotherapy. And,Family therapy in the family of the schizophrenic. In Contemporary Psychotherapies, M.I. Stein (Ed.), Free Press, Glencoe, Ill., 1962.

62. Jackson, D.D. Psychoanalytic education in the communication processes. In Science and Psychoanalysis, J. Massermann (Ed.), Grune & Stratton, New York, 1962.

63. Jackson, D.D. and Haley, J. Transference revisited. J. Nerv. Ment. Dis., 137:363-371, 1963.

64. Jackson, D.D. and Watzlawick, P. The acute psychosis as a manifestation of growth experience. A.P.A. Res. Reports, 16:83-94, 1963.

65. Weakland, J.H. and Jackson, D.D. Patient and therapist observations on the circumstances of a schizophrenic episode. Arch. Neur. Psychiat., 79:554-574, 1958. (See p.87, this vol.)

66. Weakland, J.H. The "double bind" hypothesis of schizophrenia and three-party interaction. In The Etiology of Schizophrenia, D.D. Jackson (Ed.), Basic Books, New York, 1960.

67. Weakland, J.H. The essence of anthropological education. Am. Anth., 63:1094-1097, 1961.

68. Weakland, J.H. Review of E.H. Schein, I. Schnier and C. H. Barker, Coercive Persuasion, Norton, New York, 1961, J. Asian. Studies, 21:84-86, 1961.

69. Weakland, J.H. Family therapy as a research arena. Fam. Proc., 1:63-68, 1962.

70. Weakland, J.H. and Fry, W.F. Letters of mothers of schizophrenics. Am. J. Orthopsychiat., 32:604-623, 1962. (See p.122, this vol.)

A REVIEW OF THE
DOUBLE BIND THEORY

Paul Watzlawick

In 1956, Bateson, Jackson, Haley, and Weakland reported on a
research project which they had undertaken to formulate and test
a new view on the nature of schizophrenic communication. This
report was entitled "Toward a Theory of Schizophrenia" (97), and
postulates the concept of the double bind.

The present paper has the purpose of reviewing the literature
of the last five years (1957-1961 inclusive) and assessing the attention the concept has found in psychiatric thinking.

This review is based on a search of 37 American and European
periodicals and of other pertinent publications in the field of psychiatry and of the behavioral sciences in general. It should, therefore, be reasonably comprehensive.

At the outset it may be useful to state once more the definition
of a double bind, as contained in the original paper:

The necessary ingredients for a double bind situation, as we
see it, are:

1. Two or more persons. Of these, we designate one, for
purposes of our definition, as the "victim." We do not assume
that the double bind is inflicted by the mother alone, but that it
may be done either by mother alone or by some combination of
mother, father, and/or siblings.

2. Repeated experience. We assume that the double bind is a
recurrent theme in the experience of the victim. Our hypothesis

Reprinted from FAMILY PROCESS, 2, No. 1:132-153 (March
1963). Copyright, The Mental Research Institute of the Palo Alto
Medical Research Foundation and the Family Institute; reproduced
by permission.

does not invoke a single traumatic experience, but such repeated experience that the double bind structure comes to be an habitual expectation.

3. A primary negative injunction. This may have either of two forms: (a) "Do not do so and so, or I will punish you," (b) "If you do not do so and so, I will punish you." Here we select a context of learning based on avoidance of punishment rather than a context of reward seeking. There is perhaps no formal reason for this selection. We assume that the punishment may be either the withdrawal of love or the expression of hate or anger--or most devastating--the kind of abandonment that results from the parent's expression of extreme helplessness. (Our concept of punishment is being refined at present. It appears to us to involve perceptual experience in a way that cannot be encompassed by the notion of "trauma.")

4. A secondary injunction conflicting with the first at a more abstract level, and like the first enforced by punishments or signals which threaten survival. This secondary injunction is more difficult to describe than the primary for two reasons. First, the secondary injunction is commonly communicated to the child by nonverbal means. Posture, gesture, tone of voice, meaningful action, and the implications concealed in verbal comment may all be used to convey this more abstract message. Second, the secondary injunction may impinge upon any element of the primary prohibition. Verbalization of the secondary injunction may, therefore, include a wide variety of forms; for example, "Do not see this as punishment"; "Do not see me as the punishing agent"; "Do not submit to my prohibitions"; "Do not think of what you must not do"; "Do not question my love of which the primary prohibition is (or is not) an example"; and so on. Other examples become possible when the double bind is inflicted not by one individual but by two. For example, one parent may negate at a more abstract level the injunctions of the other.

5. A tertiary negative injunction prohibiting the victim from escaping from the field. In a formal sense it is perhaps unnecessary to list this injunction as a separate item since the reinforcement at the other two levels involves a threat to survival, and if the double binds are imposed during infancy, escape is naturally impossible. However, it seems that in some cases the escape from the field is made impossible by certain devices which are not purely negative, e.g., capricious promises of love, and the like.

6. Finally, the complete set of ingredients is no longer necessary when the victim has learned to perceive his universe in double
bind patterns. Almost any part of a double bind sequence may then
be sufficient to precipitate panic or rage. The pattern of conflicting injunctions may even be taken over by hallucinatory voices
(98a).

References to the theoretical aspects of the double bind are
relatively few in number. Two brief references can be found in
the American Handbook of Psychiatry; one by Ruesch (66) in his
contribution to the "General Theory of Communication in Psychiatry, " and the second by Cobb (22) in the chapter on Neurology.
Cobb points to the fact that nervous and mental disorders are
phenomena of such complexity that different conceptual frame-
works can be used for their study without necessarily conflicting
with one another. One of the examples he uses in support of this
fact is schizophrenia which, according to the approach chosen, can
be viewed as genogenic, histogenic, chemogenic, or psychogenic.
As an explanatory principle for this latter category he mentions
the double bind theory.

The general attitude towards the communicational approach to
the problems of mental illness is well summarized by Mora (56)
in his contribution to the American Handbook of Psychiatry, even
though he does not specifically refer in it to the double bind theory:

Outside the realm of psychoanalysis, but more in line
with the American emphasis on the value of symbolic logic,
of language, of interactional systems amd the like, are
the theoretical formulations by Jurgen Ruesch and Gregory
Bateson of communication as the "social matrix of psychiatry." Although these formulations are still too recent to allow any historical judgment, they seem to be
an expression of the "operationalistic" tendencies largely
diffused in psychological quarters. As such, they are
subjected to the same type of criticism leveled against
conditioned reflex theory--namely, a lack of understanding of the basic inner condition of the patient. So far,
they have met, if not open resistance, an attitude of
caution.

Very few of the references to the double bind theory deal with
what its originators consider the essential concept, i.e., the
Theory of Logical Types. The reason for this is not clear. In
the first place, it would appear that it is due to a rather widely

though tacitly shared belief that a basic science like logic has no place in the behavioral sciences. Logic is not infrequently thought of as a dry abstraction too remote from the complexities of life to be of any help. Another possible reason is that rather unusual subjective difficulties oppose themselves to an awareness of the complex structure of the logical types. This is not too surprising once it is realized that one of the primary functions of the ego is to avoid a confusion of logical levels in all its dealings with outer and inner reality, and to protect the mind from the potential dangers of this confusion. Not unlike the resistance to the lifting into consciousness of unconscious emotional material, attempts at gaining introspection into the vital ego-function which normally guarantees proper dealing with the complexities and paradoxes of logical typing in everyday life and especially human communication, are likely to encounter similar difficulties. Anybody who has tried to tamper with the Pandora box of logical levels can attest to these formidable resistances. It is, therefore, difficult to appreciate Ostow's (58) sweeping statement that the double bind theory is "an example of ... mathematico-logical pseudo-psychologizing." He goes on to say:

> In the journal Behavior (sic) one can find many attempts
> to apply... general systems theory to psychologic and
> psychiatric problems. I have yet to see such an attempt
> which has made a real contribution to our understanding.
> The reason for this failure is not that the theory is in-
> correct, nor even that it is essentially inapplicable to
> human behavior. In my opinion, the reason is that those
> who try to apply the theory, in general, refuse to deal
> with the ultimate variables of human behavior, as ex-
> pressed in psychoanalytic metapsychology, and postulate
> their own variables based solely on naive, a priori, and
> invalid assumptions. Such assumptions, no matter how
> elegant the theory applied to them, can yield only naive
> and invalid conclusions.

Even an otherwise sympathetic reviewer of the double bind theory like Laing (47) has evident difficulty in seeing why the Theory of Logical Types should be invoked. "The authors," he writes,

> seem in doubt about what "frames of reference" to em-
> ploy or develop in casting their theory. They use the
> potentially fruitful though at present vague expression
> "modes of communication," but they try to develop
> this formulation in terms of Logical Types. But it is

doubtful if the Logical Type theory they employ is any longer viable.

The author does not elaborate further on the reasons for his doubt.

Again, it may be helpful to quote here from the original paper:

We hypothesize that there will be a breakdown in any individual's ability to discriminate between Logical Types whenever a double bind situation occurs. The general characteristics of this situation are the following:

1. When the individual is involved in an intense relationship; that is, a relationship in which he feels it is vitally important that he discriminate accurately what sort of message is being communicated so that he may respond appropriately.

2. And, the individual is caught in a situation in which the other person in the relationship is expressing two orders of message and one of these denies the other.

3. And, the individual is unable to comment on the messages being expressed to correct his discrimination of what order of message to respond to, i.e., he cannot make a metacommunicative statement.

Specific mention of Russell and Whitehead's Theory of Logical Types and its application to the double bind theory is made by Szasz (82) in connection with his game-playing model of human behavior:

...It was not until 1922, however, that Russell explicitly applied the principles of the theory of types to the logic of languages. This led to establishing hitherto unexpected connections between mathematics, logic, linguistics, philosophy, and finally psychiatry and the study of social behaviour...I believe Bateson (94) was the first to call attention to the significance of Russell's theory of types for psychiatry. Defining psychiatry as the study of (human) behaviour, he emphasized the need to distinguish various levels of communications (i.e., communication and metacommunication). In a recent essay,

Bateson et al. (97) again made use of Russell's theory of logical types, applying it to the elucidation of the communications which the schizophrenic patient and his significant objects characteristically exchange with one another.

Logical typing of signals and multiple levels of learning were considered in the original paper inseparable sets of phenomena-- "inseparable because the ability to handle the multiple types of signals is itself a learned skill and therefore a function of the multiple levels of learning." As ten thousands of pages of psychological journals bear evidence, learning theory and learning experiments have received more attention than probably any other psychological phenomenon. However, while the vast majority of these papers are traditionally concerned with the acquisition of a single and isolated skill only, the learning theory approach proposed here differs from them by taking into account the complexities of discontinuous and multiple levels of learning.[1] During the period under review at least two papers were published which deal with schizophrenia and learning theory and also refer to the double bind concept. One is by Mednik (54) who acknowledges the double bind concept as a theoretical explanation of the schizophrenic thinking disorder, but does so within a framework of escalating drive and anxiety patterns.

The other paper is by Rashkis and Singer (62) and is paradigmatic of a frequent misunderstanding of the double bind theory. In the part of their paper dealing with learning theory, these authors state:

> Liddell has described an experiment in which a hungry rat is fed when he sees a circle but not when he sees an ellipse. The ellipse is then gradually made more circular and the circle more elliptical until the rat can no longer differentiate between them. This type of learning is usually referred to as DR, or "discrimination response," and in the experiment described by Liddell is seen the breakdown of such a learned reaction. Here, as the discrimination is made successively

---

[1]The postulation of these levels of learning preceded the double bind theory by many years and was independently investigated by Hull, et al. (46) in 1940, by Bateson (93) in 1942 and by Harlow (40) in 1949.

more difficult, there is, to be sure, at first an improved differentiation, but this then levels off, becomes
worse, and finally disappears altogether; the rat no
longer acts as though he could distinguish circles from
ellipses. The outcome is what has been referred to as
an experimental neurosis, or, better, psychosis.

What Bateson has called the "double bind, " and what in
Lewinian terms we have called a conflict of avoidances,
may now be seen more sharply in terms of a failure in
discrimination.

We hold that this conclusion is erroneous. The double bind is
not a failure in discrimination, nor is this experiment itself con-
clusive of such a phenomenon. Weakland and Jackson (102) pointed
out the non-Pavlovian aspects of these discrimination experiments
and recently Bateson (98) has stated:

> In the well-known experiments in which an animal sub-
> ject is reduced to psychotic behavior by first training
> the subject to discriminate e. g. between an ellipse and
> a circle and then making the discrimination impossible,
> the "trauma" is not as is commonly stated, the "break-
> down of discrimination" but is the breakdown of that
> pattern of complex contingencies which the experiment-
> er had previously taught to the animal. As I see it,
> what happens at the climax of the experiment is that
> the animal is penalized for following a deeply uncon-
> scious and abstract pattern which the psychologist pre-
> viously rewarded. It is not that the animal cannot dis-
> criminate, it is that the animal is put in error when
> he thinks that this is a context for discrimination. [2]

---

[2] Animal experiments have also shown that an untrained animal, exposed from the very beginning to a universe in which discrimination is impossible because all events are made by the experimenter to occur at random, will adapt to this kind of contingency pattern and will not exhibit the specific pathology described
above.

It would appear, however, that not any breaking of a previously
established contingency pattern leads to pathology. In the course
of his life an individual is again and again confronted with situations for which neither past experience nor the present context
offer an adequate explanation. These situations can be extremely
stressful and anxiety-producing, but are certainly not pathogenic

There is considerable discrepancy of opinion as to the pathogenicity of the double bind. In this connection it may be helpful to repeat here the view of the authors expressed in their original paper:

> If our formal summary of the symptomatology is correct and if the schizophrenia of our hypothesis is essentially a result of family interaction, it should be possible to arrive a priori at a formal description of these sequences of experience which would induce such a symptomatology. What is known of learning theory combines with the evident fact that human beings use context as a guide for mode discrimination. Therefore, we must look not for some specific traumatic experience in the infantile etiology but rather for characteristic sequential patterns. The specificity for which we search is to be at an abstract or formal level. The sequences must have this characteristic: that from them the patient will acquire the mental habits which are exemplified in schizophrenic communication. That is to say, he must live in a universe where the sequences of events are such that his uncon-

___

per se. After all, millions of people grow up, resolve the problem of becoming independent while still remaining emotionally attached to their parents, adapt to different cultural patterns and somehow bridge similar paradoxes without turning schizophrenic. But in most of these typical situations, the individual can either remove himself physically, comment on the inconsistency of the injunctions imposed upon him, reject or modify them, leave the field in some other way or--most important of all--maintain his basic premises and at the same time expand them so as to include the new contingencies. This is not to imply that we are blind to the high incidence of schizophrenia in all phases of life involving the breaking-up of an old pattern. But we do suggest that the individuals who cannot master these situations are the ones who in their early experiences were threatened with punishment if they tried to leave the field or even show that they were aware of the paradox imposed upon them--in other words: who had been double-bound. (Cf. in this context also Leder (48), Stierlin (79) and Lu (52).) It is on these grounds that we doubt the specificity of Devereux' Sociological Theory of Schizophrenia (28), proposed in 1939, of which--according to him (29)--the double bind theory is an independent rediscovery.

ventional communicational habits will be in some sense
appropriate. The hypothesis which we offer is that
sequences of this kind in the external experience of
the patient are responsible for the inner conflicts of
logical typing. For such unresolvable sequences of
experiences, we use the term "double bind."

The existence of these sequential patterns in schizophrenia is
denied by Singer (76) and Sanua (68) in very brief references. It
must be reiterated, however, that these patterns occur on an abstract level and are usually of a very subtle nature. [3] Arieti
(7, 8), Ackerman (2, 3), and Bruch (14, 16), while validating the
usefulness of the double bind concept, question the pathogenicity
on different grounds, and seem to overlook what in the original
paper was defined as the tertiary negative injunction prohibiting
the victim from escaping from the field. Arieti, for instance,
points out that

...all of us would agree that our schizophrenic
patients have been repeatedly exposed to this
double-bind situation. But I think we would also
agree that many neurotics were exposed, and many
normal people, and we, too.

However, while this is undoubtedly correct, the long-lasting exposure to double binds which is part and parcel of the family life
of schizophrenics or of other schizophrenogenic life situations,
and the impossibility of the victim's leaving the field and seeking
corrective experiences and identifications outside the family, is
not sufficiently accounted for by these authors. As Foudraine (36),
in taking issue with Arieti's view, points out:

This double-bind hypothesis, attempting to explain in
terms of a learning-theory, the serious communicational
disorders of the schizophrenic patient which drive him
to a state of progressive isolation, is certainly very

---

[3] May it here suffice to point out that specific double bind sequences have been unfailingly present in the approximately 50
families so far studied both by the Bateson Group (Project for
the Study of Schizophrenic Communication) and the staff of the
Mental Research Institute. An anthology tape of typical interchanges is being prepared and should be available in the not too
distant future. [Paul Watzlawick, An Anthology of Human Communication, Science & Behavior Books, Inc., Palo Alto, 1964.]

fascinating. Arieti, in a critical comment, considers the mechanisms of the double-bind non-specific for schizophrenia or neurosis. According to him human beings are constantly exposed to these double or multiple-bind situations. He compares the situation with that of divided loyalty and believes that the mechanism is not pathological in itself, but rather in the way the parents make use of it. I doubt whether Arieti does justice to the double-bind theory. [4)]

Laing (47) refers to the same phenomenon by stating:

> The situation is sealed off for the "victim" by a further unavowed injunction forbidding him or her to get out of the situation, or to dissolve it by commenting on it. The "victim" is thus in an "untenable" position. He cannot make a single move without evoking a threatened catastrophe...

and Schwartz (72) by pointing to "the distortion or absence of a social environment which facilitates appropriate discriminative responses." Alanen (4) also emphasizes "the intensive and enduring 'pseudo-mutuality' in the family relations of many schizophrenics, described by Wynne et al., as well as the double bind situation..." Symonds (81) sees in the double bind situation one of the sources of the schizophrenic process but does not believe that it accounts for the entire disorder. Also, Rosenthal (65), in a study on identity confusion in twins, refers to the double bind concept as one of the patterns of mother-child relationship leading to this confusion. Clausen and Kohn (21), Rioch (63), Meyers and Goldfarb (55), Goldfarb (38), Varley (85), and Spiegel and Bell (78) concur in the specificity of the double bind situation in the families of schizophrenics.

With regard to the effect of a double bind on the victim, the original paper suggests that

> ...he must deceive himself about his own internal state in order to support mother in her deception. To sur-

---

[4)] However, in the _American Handbook of Psychiatry_, Arieti (6) does suggest a higher frequency of double bind situations in the childhood of schizophrenics than of other people and sees in it one of the possible factors responsible for the general state of anxiety that eventually leads to the disorder.

vive with her, he must falsely discriminate his own internal messages as well as falsely discriminate the messages of others.

While this point seems to have been overlooked by Symonds (81), it is emphasized by Bruch (13, 14), McReynolds (53), and Weigert (88).

References to the specific family structure which is conducive to double bind situations are relatively numerous, though brief (1, 10, 12, 21, 35, 37, 39, 45, 50, 61, 64, 83, 85, 89, 90, 91, 92). By and large, these authors agree that the mother is the dominant parent whose pathological influence on the child is not sufficiently counteracted by the typically rather weak or withdrawn father.

The role of the mother is treated in the original paper in detail and the repercussions of the patient's improvement either on the mother or on other family members (e. g., a sibling) are discussed. Bruch (13) concurs with this aspect of the mother-patient relationship and states:

It is also in line with the observation that the mother, or some other person, who was interacting with the patient in this (i. e., a double bind) pattern may become severely disturbed when the patient no longer responds in the accustomed way.

However, what the original paper omitted to mention more specifically (but what has since been dealt with in detail by Weakland (103)) is the fact that a double bind always binds both parties and that, strictly speaking, there is no "binder" and "bound," but rather two victims. This fact is most clearly stated by Laing (47):

... One must constantly remember, of course, that the child from babyhood may put his parents into untenable positions. This may occur in the early baby-mother interaction where the baby cannot be satisfied. It cries "for" the breast. It cries when the breast is presented. Its crying is intensified when the breast is withdrawn. A mother unable to "click with" or "get through" to such a baby may become intensely anxious, and feel hopeless as a mother. She then withdraws from the baby in one sense, while becoming over-solicitous in another sense. Double binds are usually mutual.

The mutuality of the interaction between mother and child and especially the child's reaction to the mother is seen somewhat differently by Searles (73, 74, 75) who criticizes the purely negative role ascribed to the mother in the original paper. He claims that

> ...an even more powerful reason for the continuance of
> the symbiosis into the offspring's chronological adult-
> hood, resides in his basically loving and loyal sacrifice
> of his own individuality in order to preserve the mother's
> unstable personality-equilibrium. He senses that his
> own sick personality-functioning dovetails with hers in
> such a way as to keep her head above water. (75)

Searles further draws attention to the playful quality which according to him exists in this interaction:

> Moreover, while Bateson et al. brilliantly describe the com-
> plexity of the incessant jockeying for position that goes on
> between patient and mother, they seem unaware that this
> jockeying can involve an element of covert, but intensely
> and mutually pleasurable, playfulness with this endlessly
> fascinating, complex "game," as I have repeatedly dis-
> covered with my patients, relatively late in the course of
> therapy. The authors dwell upon this as being solely in
> the nature of anguished, conflictual, desperate related-
> ness. (73)

However, from the above it is not quite clear whether Searles refers here to the actual mother-child interaction in a double bind situation, or to the particular game-like quality of that later stage of a successful psychotherapy of a schizophrenic which is, for instance, described by Scheflen (71) in his extensive report on John Rosen's direct analysis and the deliberate use of therapeutic double binds by that therapist. In another paper Scheflen (70) refers to the occurrence of double binds in regressive one-to-one relationships in general and not only in the classic mother-child symbiosis. The mutuality of double-binding is also recognized by Ackerman (2), Perr (60), and Boszormenyi-Nagy (9), whereas Hoffer and Callbeck (43) question the validity of the double bind theory on the assumption that the

> ...basic fault may be within the illness and not be a
> result of faulty transmission. The error may be a
> faulty receiver. It is difficult to understand why a
> schizophrenic person should be so perceptive of
> mother's faulty signals and be so unaware of his own.

The authors, unfortunately, do not elaborate, and especially their
statement about the patient's unawareness remains unclear. How
skilled the schizophrenic usually is in manipulating his environment is, on the other hand, borne out by Arieti (7): "At times the
psychotic masters the situation by shifting to the metaphoric field;
more often, he becomes an expert in setting double bind situations."

What is the relationship of the double bind theory to the classic
concept of ambivalence? It will be remembered that ambivalence
in Bleuler's sense is the simultaneous presence of mutually contradictory "psychisms"--in particular love and hate (emotional
ambivalence)--and that Bleuler thinks of it as a manifestation of
schizophrenia and not as a pathogenic factor. Furthermore, it is
described as a purely intrapsychic phenomenon and not as an interactional pattern. Arieti (7) considers the double bind "a special
ambivalence, inasmuch as it is not merely indecision between
possible alternatives, but a circular process, or a feedback mechanism." Cornelison (25) feels that the reader might consider the
double bind concept "as a warmed-over version of ambivalence,"
while the original paper presents it as a communicational experience which, Cornelison suggests, is "an added dimension to the
idea of ambivalence." However, once the idea of the multiplicity
of levels in human communication is accepted, it will be seen that
feelings like love and hate, hope and fear, wanting and not wanting,
can share the same more abstract premises and do not, therefore,
necessarily contradict each other at that (meta-) level.

It is suggested in the original paper that anybody caught in a
double bind situation will feel "on the spot" and that his ability for
correct discrimination of logical types will be impaired. It is also
pointed out that the schizophrenic feels so terribly on the spot at
all times that he habitually responds with defensive maneuvers involving shifts in the levels of communication, e.g. between the
literal and the metaphorical. As the original paper puts it:

> His (the schizophrenic's) metacommunicative system--
> the communications about communication--would have
> broken down, and he would not know what kind of mes-
> sage a message was. If a person said to him, "What
> would you like to do today?" he would be unable to
> judge accurately by the context or by the tone of voice
> or gesture whether he was being condemned for what
> he did yesterday, or being offered a sexual invitation,
> or just what was meant.

The defensive maneuvers employed by the schizophrenic in this area, i. e. , his shifts between the literal and the metaphorical, the use of unlabelled metaphor, disqualifications of self and others, the continuous incongruity between what is said and how it is qualified, the blocking of spontaneous comments, the phenomenon of symbolic language--these typically schizophrenic ways of communicating are referred to in more or less detail by several authors in relation to the double bind theory (7, 11, 13, 20, 30, 36, 75, 81). In particular Ferreira (32) has examined the characteristics of schizophrenic language in terms of the basic assumptions of the theory.

Turning now to the double bind and its relation to the therapy of schizophrenia, mention should first be made of an interesting contribution by Urquhart and Forrest (84) to the old controversy of biochemical versus psychological therapy. They report on an unsuccessful clinical trial of acetylpromazine and promazine hydrochloride in chronic schizophrenics. In the course of this trial, however, they noticed that the patients responded to the intensified attention they received from the doctors, and they suggest:

> The apparent benefit derived from weekly interviews, though based on a small number of patients, seems to be the most significant observation of this trial. From the historical standpoint we are in process of rediscovering what was known 150 years ago, namely that chronic patients are responsive to friendly interest and encouragement. But to be effective such interest must be directed within a conceptual framework regarding the nature of schizophrenia itself. If we believe in the psychogenesis of schizophrenia then clearly a psychotherapeutic approach is appropriate, though not necessarily effective. Such work has been reported by Bateson and his co-workers at Palo Alto (1956).

Several papers (2, 19, 59, 64) dealing with the treatment of the family as a unit, contain specific references to the double bind theory and its relevance in this type of therapeutic approach to psychosis.

J. H. Smith (77), Hora (44) and Savage (69) warn of the subtle and yet very real danger of a double bind which the therapist may unwittingly impose on his psychotic patients. Savage, in particular, points out that:

The inordinate investment of time and energy coupled with the scant return often reinforce the analyst's tendency to obtain narcissistic gratification at the patient's expense, by reason of the patient's helpless dependence on him; he may unconsciously need the patient to remain sick, and, while consciously enjoining him to growth and development, may, unconsciously, not welcome it at all. These conflicting conscious and unconscious messages to the patient that he both grow up and remain a child at the same time place the patient in the pathogenic "double-bind" situation described by Bateson, Jackson et al.

The problem of the resolution of a pathogenic double bind and of the use of therapeutic double binds has been dealt with by a number of authors. Reference must here again be made to Scheflen's rather extensive treatment of the subject (70). Pointing out that John Rosen uses double-binding techniques in a highly intuitive and often not conscious way, the author states:

The schizophrenic problems of symbiosis and the symbolic defect are probably related in mutual simultaneous causation. The fear of dying cements the symbiotic dependency and the training to remain symbiotic makes abstraction impossible. Theoretically, then, psychotic episodes of schizophrenia might be terminated by the formation of apparent symbiosis. Possibly this is a first stage in all successful interpersonal methods. Modification of schizophrenia itself, however, would require the repudiation of the infantile one-to-one phantasy or at least of the literal expectation of living in symbiosis.

The matter could be formulated in the language of the "double bind" by postulating that the basic implicit instruction of the schizophrenogenic parent is: "Remain symbiotically related to me." The explicit instruction, "Move away," is the aspect of parental rejection which Rosen and others have thought to be the whole communication. Rosen's portrayal and cues to non-literality are out-of-awareness just as were the parental instructions to remain attached. He thus tries to supply the missing metacommunication about the literality of remaining attached to a parent.

Some observations seem to strengthen these specula-
tions. Those patients who appeared to comprehend
that the idealizations were not to be taken literally,
often showed rapid clinical improvements of psychosis.
The "maturational spurts" mentioned above often accompanied Rosen's role-playing in which he contrasted
sexual and parental roles and in which he offered evident metacommunications about their literality. Such
patients developed a humorous, playful, game-like
relationship with Rosen and at the same time they began to show pleasure, affection, and reduced anxiety.
Such patients kidded with Rosen about faithfulness,
sexuality, dependency and his professed maternalness.
They teased him about his "trickery and deception" as
if they understood it was somehow for their benefit.
On the other hand the two patients who had the poorest
result took every interchange with complete and serious
literality. The suggestion that these simultaneous occurrences may be causally related is sufficient to war-
rant further study.

In another report from the Institute of Direct Analysis, English
(31) reviews the double bind concept, but both his examples and his
conclusions seem to miss the essential problem of a double bind.
The boy who is able to convey to his mother the message that he
had to go fishing without telling her, because otherwise he would
have had to submit to her disapproval and stay home or defy her
disapproval and feel guilty, is precisely not in a double bind. Similarly, in the example chosen by English from a therapy session,
Rosen simply confronts the patient with the painful fact that the
patient's family does not care for her, but nowhere in this interchange does Rosen resort to therapeutic double-binding techniques.
Burton (18), Hayward (41) and Hill (42) have presented extensive
clinical case descriptions in the light of the double binds involved
and the author's attempts at their resolution. They concur that the
double bind theory opens up a new dimension to the understanding
of schizophrenic behavior.

It may seem from the foregoing that it is sometimes extremely
difficult to decide where the line between pathogenic and therapeutic double binds is to be drawn. While it is certainly true that "for
successful psychotherapy, communication between therapist and
patient must be clear and congruent" (Fine, (34)), or that successful teachers of emotionally disturbed children create an atmosphere which "appears to be singularly free from 'double bind' en-

tanglements" (Bruch and Rosenkotter (15)), the use of a therapeutic double bind always implies a certain element of trickery. Haley has shown that any kind of trance induction is a double bind phenomenon (101), and the double binds inherent in humor, play, fantasy, etc. have been investigated by Bateson (95, 96), Haley (100) and Fry (99). Indeed, it would be impossible to imagine any emotional involvement, such as for instance courtship, in which double-binding does not constitute a core element.

Still on the subject of the resolution of double binds in the treatment situation, mention must be made to various articles briefly dealing with different aspects of the problem, i.e., Novey (57), Cohen (23), Varley (85), Lichtenberg and Pao (49), and Ruesch (67).

In a paper on delinquency and the rather suggestive similarities between the dynamics of schizophrenic and delinquent families, Ferreira (33) postulates the "split double-bind" as a characteristic pattern of interaction. According to him, the source of the messages is split and the victim is caught in a bipolar message emanating from father and mother separately. Furthermore, Ferreira claims, there is no tertiary negative injunction in the split double-bind, i.e., the victim can not only leave the field, but is often actually "pushed" out of it. The concept of the split double-bind is taken up by Coodley (24) in a paper on delinquency and addiction.

Brief references to double binds observable in psychiatric training can be found with Appel et al. (5), Curran (27) and especially Coser (26) who deals with the plight of the psychiatric resident who must assume the role of a student with his seniors and a professional, non-student role with his patients.

Further extensions of the theory to non-schizophrenogenic stress situations are suggested by Arieti (7) with regard to loyalty problems, and the field of art and esthetics in general. The specific double bind situation inherent in an individual's position vis-a-vis society is formulated by Watts (87, cf. also 86):

> Here, then, is a major contradiction in the rules of the social game. The members of the game are to play as if they were independent agents, but they are not to know that they are just playing as if! It is explicit in the rules that the individual is self-determining, but implicit that he is so only by virtue of the rules. Furthermore, while he is defined as an independent agent, he must not be so independent as not to submit

to the rules which define him. Thus he is defined as
an agent in order to be held responsible to the group
for "his" actions. The rules of the game confer independence and take it away at the same time, without
revealing the contradiction.

An appraisal of the double bind theory in the light of existentialism
is presented by Burton (17) who contends

> ...that the problem of schizophrenia mirrors the prob-
> lems of all people--that it represents one mode of exist-
> ence among the many that can be chosen. It is one way
> of eluding the Absurd--that is, reality. The problem of
> schizophrenia has been called nothing more and nothing
> less than the problem of reality. The hypothesis of the
> "double bind," if removed from the limiting and situa-
> tional context in which its authors place it, seems to be
> the problem of Absurd in the larger sense. The Absurd
> is the double bind par excellence and the model for all
> others.

Except for the United Kingdom, the double bind theory seems to
have found little attention in Europe. [5] This is not surprising when
one bears in mind that psychiatric thinking in Europe is traditionally oriented either along strictly organistic lines or else has an
intrapsychic orientation based on the principles of monadic, but not
interactional psychology. Incidentally, even the translation of the
term "double bind" into other languages is difficult. Thus, the
best translation a bilingual author like Stierlin (80) has come up
with in German is "Beziehungsfalle" (relationship trap). The
German author Loch (51), in a report on the pathogenesis and meta-
psychology of a case of schizophrenia, translates the term with
"Zwickmühle," i.e. double mill.

REFERENCES

1. Ackerman, N.W. The Psychodynamics of Family Life, Basic
   Books, New York, 1958.
2. Ackerman, N.W. Family-focused therapy of schizophrenia.
   In The Out-Patient Treatment of Schizophrenia, S.C. Sher
   and H.R. Davis (Eds.), Grune & Stratton, 1960.
2a. Ackerman, N.W. The schizophrenic patient and his family
   relationships, a conceptual basis for family focused therapy

---

[5]It was introduced in the European literature by Bruch (13).

of schizophrenia. In <u>Mental Patients</u> in <u>Transition, Step</u>
in Hospital-Community <u>Rehabilitation</u>, M. Greenblatt, D.J.
Levinson and G.L. Klerman (Eds.), Thomas, Springfield,
Ill., 1961.

3. Ackerman, N.W. Discussion of Hasting's paper "Professional
Staff Morale." In <u>The</u> <u>Out-Patient</u> <u>Treatment</u> <u>of</u> <u>Schizo-</u>
<u>phrenia</u>, S.C. Sher and H.R. Davis (Eds.), Grune & Stratton,
New York, 1960.

4. Alanen, Y. Some thoughts on schizophrenia and ego development in the light of family investigations. <u>Arch. Gen.</u>
<u>Psychiat.</u>, 3:650-656, 1960.

5. Appel, K.E., Goodwin, H.M., Wood, H.P., and Askren, E.L.
Training in psychotherapy, the use of marriage counseling in
a university teaching clinic. <u>Am. J. Psychiat.</u>, 117:709-
711, 1961.

6. Arieti, S. Schizophrenia: the manifest symptomatology, the
psychodynamic and formal mechanisms. In <u>American Handbook of Psychiatry</u>, S. Arieti (Ed.), Basic Books, New York,
1959, Chapter 23.

7. Arieti, S. Recent conceptions and misconceptions of schizophrenia. <u>Am. J. Psychoth.</u>, 14:3-29, 1960.

8. Arieti, S. Discussion of Ackerman's paper "Family-Focused
Therapy of Schizophrenia." In <u>The</u> <u>Out-Patient</u> <u>Treatment</u>
<u>of</u> <u>Schizophrenia</u>, S.C. Sher and H.R. Davis (Eds.), Grune
& Stratton, New York, 1960.

9. Boszormenyi-Nagy, I. The concept of schizophrenia from the
perspective of family treatment. <u>Fam. Proc.</u>, 1:103-113,
1962.

10. Bowen, M. A family concept of schizophrenia. In <u>The</u>
<u>Etiology of Schizophrenia</u>, D.D. Jackson (Ed.), Basic Books,
New York, 1960.

11. Brady, J.P. Language in schizophrenia. <u>Am. J. Psychoth.</u>,
12:473-487, 1958.

12. Brody, E.B. Social conflict and schizophrenic behavior in
young adult Negro males. <u>Psychiatry</u>, 24:337-346, 1961.

13. Bruch, H. Studies in schizophrenia: psychotherapy with
schizophrenics. <u>Acta Psychiat. Scand.</u>, 34 (Suppl. 130),
28-48, 1959.

14. Bruch, H. Transformation of oral impulses in eating disorders: a conceptual approach. <u>Psychiat. Quart.</u>, 35:458-
481, 1961.

15. Bruch, H. and Rosenkotter, L. Psychotherapeutic aspects of
teaching emotionally disturbed children. <u>Psychiat. Quart.</u>
34:648-657, 1960.

16. Bruch, H. and Palombo, S. Conceptual problems in schizo-

phrenia. J. Nerv. Ment. Dis., 132:114-117, 1961.

17. Burton, A. Schizophrenia and existence. Psychiatry, 23: 385-394, 1960.

18. Burton, A. The quest for the golden mean: a study in schizophrenia. In Psychotherapy of the Psychoses, A. Burton (Ed.), Basic Books, New York, 1960.

19. Carroll, E.J. Treatment of the family as a unit. Penn. Med. J. 63:57-62, 1960.

20. Chapman, L.J. Confusion of figurative and literal usages of words by schizophrenics and brain-damaged patients. J. Abn. Soc. Psychiat., 60:412-416, 1960.

21. Clausen, J. and Kohn, M.L. Social relations and schizophrenia: a research report and a perspective. In The Etiology of Schizophrenia, D.D. Jackson (Ed.), Basic Books, New York, 1960.

22. Cobb, S. Neurology. In American Handbook of Psychiatry, S. Arieti (Ed.), Basic Books, New York, 1959. Part 12, Chapter 81.

23. Cohen, R.A. The hospital as a therapeutic instrument. Psychiatry, 21:29-35, 1958.

24. Coodley, A.E. Current aspects of delinquency and addiction. Arch. Gen. Psychiat., 4:632-640, 1961.

25. Cornelison, F.S. Review of C. Whitacker (Ed.) "Psychotherapy with Chronic Schizophrenics." In Psychosom. Med. 21:84-85, 1959.

26. Coser, R.L. Laughter among colleagues. Psychiatry, 23: 81-95, 1960.

27. Curran, C.A. Counseling skills adapted to the learning of foreign languages. Bull. Menn. Clin., 25:78-93, 1961.

28. Devereux, G. A sociological theory of schizophrenia. Psychoanal. Rev., 26:315-342, 1939.

29. Devereux, G. The nature of the bizarre: a study of a schizophrenic's pseudo slip of the tongue. J. Hillside Hosp., 8: 266-278, 1959.

30. Dittman, A.D. and Wynne, L.C. Linguistic techniques and the analysis of emotionality in interviews. J. Abn. Soc. Psychiat., 63:201-204, 1961.

31. English, O.S. Clinical observations in direct analysis. In Direct Analysis and Schizophrenia, Clinical Observations and Evaluation, O.S. English, et al., (Eds.), Grune & Stratton, New York, 1961.

32. Ferreira, A.J. The semantics and the context of the schizophrenic's language. Arch. Gen. Psychiat., 3:128-138, 1960.

33. Ferreira, A.J. The "double-bind" and delinquent behavior. Arch. Gen. Psychiat., 3:359-367, 1960.

34. Fine, L.J. Nonverbal aspects of psychodrama. In Progress in Psychotherapy, J. M. Masserman and J. L. Moreno (Eds.) Grune & Stratton, New York, 1959.

35. Fleck, S. Family dynamics and origin of schizophrenia. Psychosom. Med., 22:333-344, 1960.

36. Foudraine, J. Schizophrenia and the family, a survey of the literature 1956-1960 on the etiology of schizophrenia. Acta Psychotherapeutica, 9:82-110, 1961.

37. Garmezy, N., Clarke, A.R. and Stockner, C. Child rearing attitudes of mothers and fathers as reported by schizophrenic and normal parents. J. Abn. Soc. Psychiat., 63:178-182, 1961.

38. Goldfarb, W. The mutual impact of mother and child in childhood schizophrenia. Am. J. Orthopsychiat., 31:738-747, 1961.

39. Grotjahn, M. Trends in contemporary psychotherapy and the future of mental health. Brit. J. Med. Psychol., 33:263-267, 1960.

40. Harlow, H. F. The formation of learning sets. Psychol. Rev., 56:51-65, 1949.

41. Hayward, M. L. Schizophrenia and the "double-bind." Psychiat. Quart. 34:89-91, 1960.

42. Hill, L. B. Psychotherapy of a schizophrenic. Am. J. Psychoanal., 17:99-109, 1957.

43. Hoffer, A. and Callbeck, M. J. Drug-induced schizophrenia. J. Ment. Sci., 106:138-159, 1960.

44. Hora, T. Epistemological aspects of existence and psychotherapy. J. Indiv. Psy., 15:166-173, 1959.

45. Hora, T. Ontic perspectives in psychoanalysis. Am. J. Psychother., 19:134-142, 1959.

46. Hull, C. L., Hovland, C. L., Ross, R. T., et. al., Mathematico-Deductive Theory of Rote Learning: A Study in Scientific Methodology, Yale University Press, 1940.

47. Laing, R. D. The Self and Others, Further Studies in Sanity and Madness, Tavistock Publ., London, 1961.

48. Leder, H. H. Acculturation and the "Double-Bind," M. A. Thesis, Dept. of Anthropology, Stanford University, 1959.

49. Lichtenberg, J. D. and Pao, Ping-Nie. The prognostic and therapeutic significance of the husband-wife relationship for hospitalized schizophrenic women. Psychiatry, 23:209-213, 1960.

50. Lidz, T., Cornelison, A., Terry, D. and Fleck, S. Intrafamilial environment of the schizophrenic patient: VI. The transmission of irrationality. Arch. Neur. Psychiat., 79:305-316, 1958.

84

51. Loch, W. Anmerkungen zur Pathogenese und Metapsychologie einer schizophrenen Psychose. Psyche, (Berl.), 15:684-720, 1961.
52. Lu, Y.C. Contradictory parental expectations in schizophrenia. Arch. Gen. Psychiat., 6:219-234, 1962.
53. McReynolds, P. Anxiety, perception and schizophrenia. In The Etiology of Schizophrenia, D.D. Jackson (Ed.), Basic Books, New York, 1960.
54. Mednik, S.A. A learning theory approach to research in schizophrenia. Psychol. Bull., 55:316-327, 1958.
55. Meyers, D.I. and Goldfarb, W. Studies of perplexity in mothers of schizophrenic children. Am. J. Orthopsychiat., 31:551-564, 1961.
56. Mora, G. Recent American psychiatric developments (since 1939). In American Handbook of Psychiatry, S. Arieti (Ed.), Basic Books, New York, 1959.
57. Novey, S. The outpatient treatment of borderline paranoid states. Psychiatry, 23:357-364, 1960.
58. Ostow, M. Discussion of Arieti's "Recent Conceptions and Misconceptions of Schizophrenia." Am. J. Psychoth., 14: 23-29, 1960.
59. Parloff, M.B. The family in psychotherapy. Arch. Gen. Psychiat., 4:445-451, 1961.
60. Perr, H.M. Criteria distinguishing parents of schizophrenic and normal children. Arch. Neur. Psychiat., 79:217-224, 1958.
61. Query, J.M.N. Pre-morbid adjustment and family structure: a comparison of selected rural and urban men. J. Nerv. Ment. Dis., 133:333-338, 1961.
62. Rashkis, H.A. and Singer, R.D. The psychology of schizophrenia. Arch. Gen. Psychiat., 1:406-416, 1959.
63. Rioch, D. McK. The sense and the noise. Psychiatry, 24: 7-18, (Suppl. to No. 2), 1961.
64. Rosenbaum, C.P. Patient-family similarities in schizophrenia. Arch. Gen. Psychiat., 5:2, 120-126, 1961.
65. Rosenthal, D. Confusion of identity and the frequency of schizophrenia in twins. Arch. Gen. Psychiat., 3:297-304, 1960.
66. Ruesch, J. General theory of communication in psychiatry. In American Handbook of Psychiatry, S. Arieti (Ed.), Basic Books, New York, 1959.
67. Ruesch, J. Therapeutic Communication, Norton, New York, 1961.
68. Sanua, Victor D. Sociocultural factors in families of schizo-

phrenics; a review of the literature. Psychiatry, 24:246-265, 1961.

69. Savage, C. Countertransference in the therapy of schizophrenics. Psychiatry, 24:53-60, 1961.

70. Scheflen, A. E. Regressive one-to-one relationships. Psychiat. Quart., 34:692-709, 1960.

71. Scheflen, A. E. A Psychotherapy of Schizophrenia: Direct Analysis, Thomas, Springfield, Ill., 1961.

72. Schwartz, D. P. The integrative effect of participation. Psychiatry, 22:81-86, 1959.

73. Searles, H. F. Positive feelings in the relationship between the schizophrenic and his mother. Int. J. Psychoanal., 39:569-586, 1958.

74. Searles, H. F. The effort to drive the other person crazy--an element in the aetiology and psychotherapy of schizophrenia. Brit. J. Med. Psy., 32:1-18, 1959.

75. Searles, H. F. Integration and differentiation in schizophrenia: an over-all view. Brit. J. Med. Psy., 32:261-281, 1959.

76. Singer, R. D. Organization as a unifying concept in schizophrenia. Arch. Gen. Psychiat., 2:61-74, 1960.

77. Smith, J. H. The metaphor of the manic-depressive. Psychiatry, 23:375-383, 1960.

78. Spiegel, J. P. and Bell, N. W. The family of the psychiatric patient. In American Handbook of Psychiatry, S. Arieti (Ed.), Basic Books, New York, 1959.

79. Stierlin, H. The adaptation to the "stronger" person's reality, some aspects of the symbiotic relationship of the schizophrenic. Psychiatry 22:143-152, 1959.

80. Stierlin, H. Report on the Hawaiian Divisional Meeting of the A. P. A., May 1958, Psyche (Berl.), 13:843-845, 1959/60.

81. Symonds, A. Discussion of Arieti's "Recent Conceptions and Misconceptions of Schizophrenia." Am. J. Psychoth., 14:21-23, 1960.

82. Szasz, T. S. The Myth of Mental Illness, Foundations of a Theory of Personal Conduct, Hoeber-Harper, New York, 1961.

83. Titchener, J. and Emerson, R. Some methods for the study of family interaction in personality development. Psychiat. Res. Report No. 10, 72-88, 1958.

84. Urquhart, R. and Forrest, A. D. Clinical trial of promazine hydrochloride and acetylpromazine in chronic schizophrenic patients. J. Ment. Sci., 105:260-264, 1959.

85. Varley, B. K. "Reaching out" therapy with schizophrenic patients. Am. J. Orthopsychiat., 29:407-416, 1959.

86. Watts, A. W. Nature, Man and Woman, Pantheon Books, New

York, 1958.

87. Watts, A.W. Psychotherapy East and West, Pantheon Books, New York, 1961.

88. Weigert, E. Loneliness and trust--basic factors of human existence. Psychiatry, 23:121-131, 1960.

89. White, R.B. The mother-conflict in Schreber's psychosis. Int. J. Psychoanal., 42:55-73, 1961.

90. Will, O.A. Human relatedness and the schizophrenic reaction. Psychiatry, 22:205-223, 1959.

91. Wolman, B.B. The fathers of schizophrenic patients. Acta Psychother., 9:193-210, 1961.

92. Wynne, L.C., Ryckoff, I.M., Day, J. and Hirsch, S.I. Pseudo-mutuality in the family relations of schizophrenics. Psychiatry, 21:205-220, 1958.

93. Bateson, G. Social planning and the concept of "deutero-learning." Science, Philosophy, and Religion, Second Symposium (Conference on Science, Philosophy and Religion), New York, 1942.

94. Bateson, G. and Ruesch, J. Communication: The Social Matrix of Psychiatry, Norton, New York, 1951.

95. Bateson, G. A theory of play and fantasy. Psychiat. Res. Rep., 2: 39-51, 1955.

96. Bateson, G. The message "this is play." In Second Conference on Group Processes, Josiah Macy Jr. Fnd. New York, 1956.

97. Bateson, G., Jackson, D.D., Haley, J. and Weakland, J.H. Toward a theory of schizophrenia. Behav. Sci., 1:251-264, 1956. (See p.31, this vol.)

98. Bateson, G. Exchange of Information about Patterns of Human Behavior. Symposium on Information Storage and Neural Control, Houston, Texas, 1962, (To be Published).

98a. Bateson, G. (Ed.) Perceval's Narrative, A Patient's Account of His Psychosis, 1830-1832, Stanford Univ. Press, 1961.

99. Fry, W.F. Sweet Madness: A Study of Humor, Pacific Books, Palo Alto, 1963.

100. Haley, J. Paradoxes in play, fantasy, and psychotherapy. Psychiat. Res. Rep, 2:52-58, 1955.

101. Haley, J. An interactional explanation of hypnosis. Am. J. Clin. Hyp., 1:41-57, 1958.

102. Weakland, J.H. and Jackson, D.D. Patient and therapist observations on the circumstances of a schizophrenic episode. Arch. Neur. Psychiat., 79:554-574, 1958. (See p.87, this vol.)

103. Weakland, J.H. The "double bind" hypothesis of schizophrenia and three-party interaction. In The Etiology of Schizophrenia, D.D. Jackson (Ed.), Basic Books, New York, 1960.

PATIENT AND THERAPIST OBSERVATIONS
ON THE CIRCUMSTANCES OF A
SCHIZOPHRENIC EPISODE

John H. Weakland and Don D. Jackson

"Now see that noble and most sovereign reason,
Like sweet bells jangled, out of tune and harsh."
— Hamlet

Bateson, Jackson, Haley, and Weakland (1) have recently outlined a theory of schizophrenia in rather general terms. This paper consists of the verbatim transcript of the major portion of a psychotherapeutic interview with a schizophrenic patient, with accompanying analytic comments based on the concepts presented in the earlier article. Thus their theory is here shown in relation with basic psychiatric data, the actual interpersonal communication of a patient, including the messages of the other party, which heretofore have too often been neglected.

This particular interview is focused on the circumstances of the patient's psychotic break (his second). Apart from acute psychotic states during military service, there has been a paucity of data available in the literature about the factors surrounding the onset of a schizophrenic psychosis, although this period of remarkably rapid and extensive change of behavior is of great practical and theoretical importance.

This is especially true if one includes as relevant data the examination of those others immediately playing significant roles in the patient's breakdown. These data are often neglected, or their significance is denied. For example, it was the reading of one of

Reprinted from the A. M. A. ARCHIVES OF NEUROLOGY & PSYCHIATRY, 79:554–574 (May 1958). Copyright, American Medical Association, Chicago; reproduced by permission.

the early papers on the psychotherapy of schizophrenia by Laforgue (2) that led one of us (D. D. J.) to become interested in the concept of family homeostasis. (3) Laforgue mentioned that at a significant point in his female patient's therapy her sister (with whom she lived) became severely depressed. He attributed the sister's difficulty to a manifestation of the same unfortunate genetic structure that had caused his patient's schizophrenia. He did not note that the sister's depression was coincident with a sudden improvement in his patient.

Obviously, if schizophrenia is prejudged a hereditary disorder, the therapist's view of the data available to him, including precipitating factors, will be limited. Such a bias may be present when it is reported that an examination of the circumstances surrounding the onset of a schizophrenic psychosis demonstrates that there were no stressful factors operating and thus the disorder must have been physiologically (constitutionally) caused. (4) It is our opinion that stress is a private matter and cannot be evaluated from a so-called normogenic viewpoint. That is to say, we hold that what is stressful to any individual depends on its meaning or significance in relation to his life history. It is well known, for example, that a success of some kind can play a crucial role in the onset of some depressions and in suicides, and is responsible for the onset of acute anxiety states in some neurotics. Particularly in the obscure matter of the precipitation of psychosis, we have a situation for empirical inquiry, not for a priori judgments from oversimplified assumptions. This need not mean that each case is unique and isolated; uniformities may be found at the level of personal significance. It is well to recall that even in the area of clearly organic disease what seems "enough stress" depends on prior life experience, and, even more, upon the state of medical knowledge. Thus, microscopic organisms were once considered an insufficient etiological explanation of organic disease, whereas the notion of "bad humors" and "vapors" was widely accepted as sufficient, though these could not be observed at all. [1]

THEORETICAL VIEWPOINT ON FAMILY INTERACTION

Bateson, Jackson, Haley, and Weakland (1) postulated that part of the etiology of schizophrenia is a communication sequence they labeled "a double bind." A double-bind relationship, most simply, can be described as a hostile dependent involvement where one of the parties insists on a response to multiple orders of messages

---

[1] For further discussion of this matter, see Jackson. (5)

which are mutually contradictory, and the other (the schizophrenic patient-to-be) cannot comment on these contradictions or escape from the situation. Obviously, a double-bind relationship can exist only within a special family or group relationship, since, for example, a child could break out of a double-bind situation with his mother if his father were capable of handling such contradictory multi-leveled messages and thus setting an example and offering support to the child.

For purposes of description, we speak of the child's being in a double-bind relationship with the mother, and yet the mother is as much a victim caught up in a morass of her own maneuvers as the child is. In a real sense, she needs the child for her own mental economy. Evidence for this viewpoint can be found in observing what happens to the family interrelations when a schizophrenic patient makes a successful recovery while living within the family framework. (3) Similarly, the siblings or spouse of the patient can be one factor in the double-bind situation and yet to the casual clinical observer may appear as the healthy one. The person who has culturally sanctioned motives and attitudes will have obvious advantages over the other partner. Such a person may be severely crippled, for example, by inflexible righteousness and morality, and yet never come near the confines of a psychiatrist's office. This whole question of "Who the kept and who the keeper?" which is central in the interview and discussion to follow, is a complex and important matter, which needs further study.

THE PATIENT AND HIS FAMILY SITUATION

X. is in his middle 30's. He was born, one of several brothers, in Eastern Europe and was brought to the United States as a young child. His father died when he was an infant, and he was raised by his mother and an angry, violent stepfather, now also dead. The mother, who is a member of a reformist Orthodox sect, X. describes as inordinately prideful, stingy, and retaining her old-country ways. X. seems to have been somewhat solitary as a child, but there is no evidence he had any incapacitating difficulties, mental or physical. He completed high school successfully, and shortly afterward went into the Army. He had about two years of service in the United States and the Pacific areas as a laboratory technician. Two weeks before the end of the war, he had an especially good letter from his favorite brother, stating they should get closer together after the war. A few days later X. learned that his brother had been killed in action, and shortly after had a psychotic attack, of unstated nature. He was hospitalized, was returned to the United States, and three months later was discharged "in partial remission." X. now appears to minimize this episode, saying he was not so much "crazy" as afraid he'd be killed like his brother and desirous of getting home.

After discharge he entered college, taking a pre-medical curriculum. However, in three years he had completed only two years' work, and in three more years he had done one year's work. He then left school and began to work at a variety of minor technical or clerical jobs, changing every year or so and repeatedly getting into difficulties with employers and other employees.

In 1950 he married a girl whose family came from a geographical and religious background similar to his own. Her mother had died when she was a young child, and at first she was reared by her father and his sister, but later was sent by her father to a Catholic school. Catholicism and her relationship to the nuns remain very important to her. Mrs. X. has moderately severe epilepsy. At the time of the patient's second psychotic episode, which is discussed in the recorded interview, he and his wife and two small children lived in an apartment building owned by her suspicious, irascible, and aging father. His mother lived nearby and, despite being a source of friction between the patient and his wife, was a frequent visitor in the home, partly because she was available as a baby sitter. There were frequent arguments among the various family members over religion and finances. Finally, as described in the following interview, X. again broke down and was hospitalized, with a diagnosis of "acute schizophrenic reaction, paranoid type" and "schizo-affective psychosis."

INTERVIEW AND COMMENTS

This interview took place four months after the patient's break. He had then been seeing the therapist in three hourly interviews a week for 10 weeks. There had also been several joint interviews with the patient and his wife. All of these interviews were tape-recorded, with the knowledge of all parties. The first third of this transcribed interview, before discussion became focused on the circumstances of the break, is here excerpted and summarized to cover certain points importantly related to the later material or to our basic theory. The final two-thirds is given verbatim, with no editing except concealment of names. Our ideas and comments developed subsequently are interspersed, in parentheses:

X.: Could you help me get out of here?--I mean--within a month or so?

T.: Well, I told your ward--I don't want to do anything to hinder you getting out of here--

X.: Well, that isn't positive--I mean that's--didn't give me a push--I have to get a little help, to get out--

(X. opens by asking for specific help. This is a realistic request in that the therapist might be able to influence an administrative decision, but X. also shows his own feelings of helplessness, which appear more fully later on in the interview.)

Then X., in explanation of why the therapist should give him a push, starts to develop two themes of concern about staying in the hospital: 1. The present ward doctor, a woman, is about to leave, and whoever takes over might leave him in for months. 2. He is uncertain about going home and asks the therapist to take a stand.

X.: ...I'd either stay here completely or go home completely--if you gather what I mean--

T.: Why do you suppose you might have a feeling like that?

X.: ...Well I don't know--why I might I mean it's the--as if it's the same question--in a small way it's as if why, uh, why did I have the nervous breakdown in the first place--it's just about the same question--and if I knew, I'm not saying I could do anything about it--but at least I could--at least I could--understand--what it was--

(X. states he must either stay in or get out--a black or white viewpoint. This is almost immediately related to the psychotic break as "the same question" as that of why he broke down in the first place. X. also deals with the question in terms of the "illusion of alternatives," a concept to be developed in the discussion.)

T.: Has it got something, maybe, to do with changing what you're adjusting to--back and forth? That you sort of adjust to being home and then adjust to being here--or something like that?

X.: It might be, that might be it--(pause) Well, I wonder if it really would do me good to, to stay away from my mother more, like B. (his wife) seems to want--maybe it would help, uh--less, uh, it would cause less conflicts; I'm not sure of it myself; but it might, might be part, it might be true; in other words it's a--(pause)

T.: This, again, is sort of around the topic--should you stay in one place, or can you live with more than one sort of thing at a time--

<u>X.</u>: Well, in that case it seems as though B. --B. would be disturbed if I would see mother too much, or she more or less demands, to know every single thing we say, and then she'd notice whether it was disturbing <u>me</u> or whether it would disturb <u>her</u>-- (pause)

(When the therapist essays a general statement about X.'s "this or that" problem, originally about home or hospital, X. shifts to mention a similar conflict around "wife or mother," emphasizing his keeping away from mother more as possibly being helpful, though he lives with his wife, and the transactions immediately preceding his break mainly concern his wife. He is covertly asking how the therapist feels about his leaving or staying, and if there is a disagreement with the female administrator.)

<u>X.</u> then shifts back to difficulties about getting out of the hospital--could his wife help?--and especially the change of doctors; maybe the new one will think differently about him than the old one. The therapist ties these several situations, and feelings of helplessness, together, then comments:

<u>T.</u>: (It looks as if) you are afraid that one person will say one thing, and another person will say another thing, and you won't know what to do about it.

<u>X.</u>: Well, that's--that's right; in other words, all I can do is just--uh--take the general opinion--in other words, it's a--it's sort of a coming together of the minds--like--well, in one respect if I should compare--uh--coming together of the mind of my mother and B.--well, and if I compare that with, say, coming together in my mind of you and the (ward) doctor--if you and the doctor had the same opinion of each other as B. and my mother have of each other, well, they'd never be a coming of the mind together--there never would--but, thank God, there isn't <u>that</u> particular situation; there isn't an enmity between you and the doctor over me--see--

<u>T.</u>: Um hmn.

<u>X.</u>: Such as there is between my mother and B.--so, of course, I imagine there is more hope of getting out--than, uh--than that.

(X. now overtly connects the therapist and ward doctor with the mother and wife but does so by utilizing denial. It is not certain how much grounds for fearing such a conflict he had in reality, though it can be said that if one existed, it would probably have been mainly covert, therefore all the more difficult for him. (6) There may have been a repetition of his childhood situation, as covert or tangential maternal-paternal conflict seems common in the families of schizophrenics. (7)

There is then some further discussion of X.'s feelings of helplessness, which he contrasts with opening his mouth and saying how he feels. But if he does, his wife, for example, would get angry. She might even get a divorce.

(Why does he feel helpless? As X. sees it, it is because if he should assert himself by voicing his feelings, he might be abandoned. But the situation is actually more complex than the mere alternative of keeping quiet or speaking up. It later becomes evident that also if he keeps quiet his wife is angry and implies he is only a "mother's boy" or a "weakling," which she does not want. Thus, the apparent alternative of keeping quiet or taking a stand does not offer a real choice--the two possibilities lead to the same outcome, the threat of abandonment. The question, then, becomes one of why he cannot see and comment on the fact that whatever he does he is blamed. This situation is the center of his helplessness.)

Then X. says that sometimes he does try to get his way, and speaks of getting his wife to promise not to go out to church alone at night, because she once had an epileptic attack on the way; she told him about the fit, showed her bruises, but said, "Don't worry." (X. mentioned his wife's "spells" very briefly and obliquely in his previous remarks about having to avoid angering her. He seems to feel caught: If he is assertive, she might have a seizure--thus abandoning him, as well as increasing her "control by helplessness." If he is compliant, she goes out alone at night, and may have a seizure, too. He also allows himself to be trapped by the way she exhibits her epilepsy but then rejects his concern about it.

An earlier fear that his mother might be hurt by his violent stepfather, and he be helpless about it, expressed in other interviews, may underlie these current concerns. As a child, he learned there was a high value placed on his protective concern toward his mother.)

The therapist inquired about possibilities of argument or discussion between X. and his wife.

X.: Well, I'll say that these years we've been married, we've argued quite a lot--quite a bit--

T.: Uh huh--

X.: and we--I guess she'd call them discussions; I call them ar-
guments--over religion, over finances, over things she planned to
do, and I've always tried to--well to me to take the more cautious--

T.: Uh huh--

X.: Attitude, and as far as religion, well her--her religion is
all--is all right, it's just the one and I try to--to show that, well
in a way, I didn't quite agree with that, and, uh, I don't know--she
seems to like to--I know she said she's had a lot of discussions
about religions, and she defended Catholicism and nobody could
beat her down on it, nobody could. She took pride in that--and I
found out later that--even with my utmost reasoning and; uh, whatever I could do, I never could, uh--just like she'd say, I never
could beat her down; she'd never agree. It's just like, uh, she--an
extreme case I was going to mention; she gave me her promise not
to go to this church at night, and yet she went without telling me--
and then she said, "Well, that's not deception," because it's a good
thing she was doing, and you only practice deception when you're
doing an evil thing. Well, of course, what can--you see there's a
definition that--how can you fight a person when they set their own
definition?--that isn't playing the ball.

(When he tries to discuss things, his wife defeats him by sticking to one extreme position, though one that also has strong cultural sanction.

But if he does manage to seem in the right, despite his usual
tentativeness, she shifts from one extreme to another, by redefining everything at a higher level of interpretation, which she
controls. She deceives him about not going out to church, but
because she is going to church, this deception isn't deception.
X. is thus involved with a person who overtly gives him contradictory messages, and denies that this is so. It is our impression that preschizophrenics are particularly blind to
changes of context as a controlling device by others. This difficulty in handling contradictions appears more fundamental
than X.'s somewhat similar difficulty in handling opposing influences from two different persons.)

There is some more discussion of arguing. X. reemphasizes
with another example that if someone shifts definitions, you not
only can't win; there's no getting together. He didn't think arguing
was disturbing until he had this breakdown. People take advantage
of others in arguments; but if you do, they may resent it and pay
you back--(From here on is verbatim unbroken sequence.)

<u>T.</u>: So that this sort of brings up some things we were talking about before--a couple of times you were on your way to getting your own way--and then you begin to feel sort of uneasy about it-- even with B. a couple of times you were arguing with her about something, looked like she was giving in to you; you sort of then said: "Well, go do it your own way."

<u>X.</u>: Well, I did that a couple of times, here--yeah--only before, when I used to argue with her, I'd never do that; I--I, uh--I wouldn't give in that way. Uh--I imagine, uh, I'm getting back to where I could argue more now, but, uh--I'm thinking that the-- maybe that isn't the best thing to--to argue, I know--all--the only-- sort of a clue--that I have--it's, just before I had my nervous breakdown, I had an argument with my--father-in-law, and I was kind of arguing with B. in a way, although she didn't think it was much of an argument--but I got very disturbed over it--only I know this was the week where I wasn't feeling well. And I even woke up--from a dream that was very uncomfortable, I couldn't--I don't know what the dream was, just sort of an uncertainty, just that's all I can describe it, an uncertainty, and, uh, when, uh--another thing--we stayed out a little late there--it was on account of B. that I did that--I--I, that's why I'm kind of blaming her, for the occasion, and my father-in-law really raised the roof--and he seemed to despise us so much, and it hurt me; in other words, that attitude in his--it seemed to hurt me, and I could see that my mother was siding with my father-in-law--and that hurt me also-- I tried to explain, but they wouldn't accept the explanation.

(X. recalls having a horrible dream the week he got sick: He can only say it was about "uncertainty." But uncertainty is a main theme of the whole interview, and he goes on at once to mention one of the situations it is related to--being caught be- tween two other people; the other being concealed or denied con- tradictory messages from one person.

And he can't resolve the uncertainty, because no matter what he tries--argument or explanation--he is rejected. All these mat- ters are mentioned in close connection with his psychotic break.)

<u>T.</u>: What was this about?

<u>X.</u>: Well, we went out to buy him some apples, and we--we stopped in at his apartment house and got some information for him, and B. and I went shopping, and we spent quite a lot of time in the store, and where she likes to go and--we went out to change a wrist watch for her--and it was way on the other side of the city-- and then she wanted to stop in at the convent--at the, the M--High

School, and she spent quite a little while there with the nun, and we were talking, and uh, fi--finally, I went home, but I phoned into the postoffice that--that I was ill, and, uh--I really wasn't too ill; I just couldn't make it on time they--they have a ruling--if you don't make it on time they--especially for subs, like me, they could just send you home, see--without working--

T.: Uh huh.

X.: That's your punishment. And so I phoned in, and, that's--that's when my father-in-law got so disturbed, because he knew I'd missed the work--see, I missed work; I said: "Well, it's not fatal; I haven't done anything wrong. They know I am not coming!" and, uh, yet he, he just seemed so upset over it; and my mother told me: "He's been upset now for about three hours, waiting for you people to come home, you know--you--you've been gone all day."

(He was doing things for his wife and her father; this made him late, and he was blamed for it. Again, it probably appears to him that if he is "good," he may be accepted; but this is illusory.

It seems that X. is afraid to face openly even the possibility of a clear rejection--in this instance at the job--another uncertainty arising largely from an apparent "wife-or-job" alternative--and has to deal with this evasively by saying he's sick and thereby lowering his self-esteem.)

T.: What upset him so much about this?

X.: Well, because we should have returned so much sooner--according to his mind-- and what--what it, he thought we'd gone out here to Palo Alto to B., B.'s aunt; that's what he thought, or else we took a trip somewhere--and, uh, in other words, it just wasn't right for us to do that--that's what.

T.: I find it a little difficult to understand what he was so disturbed about, particularly since just Wednesday afternoon B. was talking about how lenient he was about her coming and going before she was married.

X.: Well, uh--that's true, but this case of her--her aunt, see--she never, she never tells when she visits the aunt--he had a misunderstanding with her--and he doesn't like B. to visit her, although now she says finally that he has agreed to that, to her visiting her aunt--but he still--he still doesn't want to have anything to do with that aunt, and, uh, I don't know--he didn't know that we went to the aunt--which, we didn't go--but he thought that we had taken a trip, and he was disturbed that--uh--

T.: It looks like he thought--you might have?

X.: Well, we might have, but that didn't seem to be the thing that was bothering him--the thing that bothered him was that I should've been to work on time; in other words, it's so important--to get to work on time and--and see--see the work is <u>very</u> important as far as he is concerned--

(X.'s difficulties again force him to be caught in the middle. The father-in-law is probably angry with his daughter for deceiving him and for irresponsibly keeping her husband away from his work. However, he takes it out on the patient, who accepts the full blame; he can neither point out the father-in-law's contradictions about an agreement that wasn't agreement (as daughter's deception wasn't deception) nor get together with him to blame her jointly for being irresponsible.

By his accepting being the scapegoat, perhaps X. escapes, temporarily, from facing problems of contradictions, mixed feelings, and deception, with the father-in-law and with his wife.)

<u>T.</u>: What importance does that--does it have to him?
<u>X.</u>: Well, that I should have a good job, and keep the job, and not--not dillydally with it. Of course, I--I always--I know I said always--be punctual, and I always try to work good--and just--for my own, it's my own nature--and not just his--I know that--
<u>T.</u>: Although what it strikes me, is that he certainly seems to take a very powerful concern--
<u>X.</u>: Yes, it's a paternal attitude--very, very interested in and--and, uh, in a way, I--I always wanted to cultivate his good will, like I told you all along; in this case I could see that--that we just had that argument and then, this happened--you see--it just sort of added fuel on the fire--
<u>T.</u>: And, in this argument about you, uh--should have been there on time to go to work--your mother also got into this and--?
<u>X.</u>: Oh, yes, she jumped in both feet--and, "Where have you been?" and she didn't say too much to B.; but she was really digging into me there, and, uh, well, I--I just told them: "Simmer down; simmer down," you know; "Everything is all right; there's nothing to get excited about."
<u>T.</u>: Were you all together at this time?
<u>X.</u>: Yeah; she was home looking at the kids.
<u>T.</u>: Uh huh.
<u>X.</u>: When we go on a trip like this, I'd usually try to get my m--my mother to look after the children; it's one of the reasons I always like to have my mother in good terms with B. so--just for that purpose--
<u>T.</u>: So that really everybody--just before you had your break

then, everybody was on good enough terms--so that--

X.: Oh yes--

T.: You were all gathered together--in the house.

X.: Yes, definitely--yes.

T.: So that the great d--I mean regardless of some of these previous disagreements--

X.: Yeah--

T.: Uh--

X.: Still--

T.: The real thing didn't blow up until you got sick--

X.: That's right--that's very true--yeah.

T.: I mean, this in spite of--

X.: Yes, in--

T.: In spite of what I heard about before--

X.: That's right--(overlapping)

T.: About the time B. was so upset--by hearing what your mother was saying and--

X.: Sure--that's right; in other words, this finally was enough of a--of an occasion to cause a permanent--or it looks like it's a permanent cleavage--in other words, he's--when he's getting now to the point where you'd--he calls my mother a snake--and he's so vicious against her, and B.'s thr--threatening divorce, I want--well, you see this is, they're just playing it--pretty tough now--

(X. accepts his father-in-law's control and interprets it as benevolent, a paternal attitude, to which he responds with an effort at "goodness" again; he aims "to cultivate his good will." Yet everyone is jumping on X.; how does he himself invite this? Perhaps just by his "goodness."

He fears that everything will fall apart and that he will be completely abandoned, left without anyone. A similar fear seems implicit in his statement that he wants his wife and mother to get along so that the children will be cared for. This fear seems extreme, but his childhood situation has given him real cause to be concerned about the solidarity of the home.

It is perhaps also relevant to this abandonment theme that his first psychotic episode occurred shortly after the news that his favorite brother had been killed.)

T.: Um hm.

X.: That's it; that's all I could say--

T.: But this--this situation when you got home then; it seems like you must have felt like everybody was jumping on you for something that wasn't even really your doing--and--

X.: Well--

T.: I mean, as you recounted it--

X.: Well, I felt--(overlapping)

T.: It was mainly B. was going from here to there, and taking a lot of time about it.

X.: I felt that way because, whenever I go with B. it takes so much, uh, time. In other words, I always--the time--try to hurry her up. "Hurry-hurry-hurry up" and, uh--seems--she isn't the hurrying type. And no doubt we, we stopped in, uh, a drive-in and had something to eat, and, uh, all I know is that B. wanted to go to this, uh--convent; and I blew up, and I said: "No, you're not going; we're not going; we got to get home." See--I knew I had to get home; I thought I'd make it in time for work, and then, uh--I felt, then I had just this nagging--what it was--I--I know I wasn't feeling too well--and, I told her--"Well, look, you're driving me nuts." Well, I really didn't blame her--I wasn't really blaming her for it --I said; "I don't feel well; I can only do one thing at a time"--I know I said--but this's actually the way I felt--

T.: Um hm.

X.: I couldn't seem to--to just be relaxed--I had to just--keep my mind on one track--and I said: "Well, if--if you'd like to go, to go to the convent, it's all right with me." So she said, "O.K."

T.: You mean you changed around--

X.: Yeah, I changed, I changed around--I know I'd done that a couple of times before, but not too often, 'cause--maybe I felt sorry for her or somethin'--I knew this was an opportunity for her to see this nun she loves so much--and, uh--she always praised her so much and everything--she's just like a mother to her, and the one person in the world in whom she has complete faith, and all that sort of rot--well to me, you know, it's--to me it's rot; maybe to her it isn't.

T.: Why didn't she take care of going to see the nun? Instead of getting you to do it for her and miss your job?

X.: Well, uh, in a way I guess she knew that I, I probably could call in, uh, late, and, uh--so that's what happened--we--

T.: And what did B. say when this argument developed when you got home?

X.: She didn't have much to say about it--she was rather kind of quiet--

T.: And she just left you to take it?

X.: Well--she went in with the children, and I think she might have said a couple of things--uh--uh, but we did not mention the fact we stopped in at the, at the convent--I don't think I mentioned it--to my father-in-law.

(When the therapist puts some of the blame on the patient's wife, X. rises to the occasion and agrees: He had told her: "You're driving me nuts," a comment on her communications. But he soon backs down again; as the interview goes on, in general he minimizes and excuses her part in the situation, and emphasizes difficulties with her father. This relative protection of her seems related to attitudes around "mother." Mrs. X. went to the convent to see a nun who was "like a mother to her"; her leaving X. to face the music later was excused by her going in to be a mother to their children, and so on. X. also tends to minimize his own mother's part in the attack on him.

X.'s emphasis on the father-in-law and minimization of any maternal part in his difficulties are similar to the situation we have observed in other families of schizophrenics: The father is rather like one of the children, and he collaborates with them—often by engaging in manifest, but unessential, conflicts—in screening the mother's activities from view.)

T.: Why was that?

X.: Well—I don't know—he, he may have thought that wasn't exactly a good excuse—you know that—if't been a flat tire, or, something wrong with the car, well, you see, that would've been a good excuse; but just going to the convent, I don't imagine that it would have been such a good excuse, and then my mother, I know she wouldn't agree with that—

T.: Well, neither, neither one of them would have accepted this—

X.: That excuse—

T.: As any reason.

X.: Yes, and I told them—

T.: Even, even though your father-in-law was the one who put B. in charge of the Catholic nuns in the first place.

X.: Yes, that's right—and my mother had disagreed with him like that as though he had committed a crime—I know—she, she'd mentioned it to him: "Why did you do that—why did you put your daughter, and make her a Catholic," and all that, uh. As far as she is concerned, see, she showed her intolerance to the Catholic Church right there—and many other times—so finally, you see, she's—she did work herself so that—that is why I don't blame myself—myself for—anything that happened: I know I did open my mouth, in a few vital spots, such as to Father H., and—

(It seems that only something practical and accidental would serve to excuse his lateness—something extraneous. Anything relevant, especially personal desires and feelings, would bring up all the old differences they seem unable really to resolve, such as that between X.'s father-in-law and wife over the convent and the aunt; X. seems very eager to avoid such conflicts.)

T.: Well, I still think about this particular time, which seems pretty important--and it looks like so you must have felt that you were sort of standing there all alone, everybody giving you hell for something that wasn't your fault--

X.: Well, uh, I just took it--

T.: Why should you take it?

X.: Well, I don't know--that's a good question--I, I don't know; it's a good--maybe I, I should have blown up and let off steam; maybe that would have helped--

T.: Why couldn't you just say, "B. insisted on going to the convent"?

X.: Well, you see--it's sort of a mixed-up affair--I, I'd say that, and then what, what would I get from B., see? You understand?

T.: Well, didn't B. insist on it?

X.: Well, no, she didn't insist on it; that's just it--she, she asked; and then I blew up and told her "no"--

T.: Yeah--

X.: And then I changed my mind and said: "Well, would you like to? All right"--see--

T.: So partly you, you went along with it--

X.: See, I went along with it--

T.: Well, then, we get back to the question: Why did you go along with it?

X.: Well, that's a good question, too; like I said, I felt sorry for her and thought, well, she, if't means so damn much to her, well let her have--uh, let her, let her have her way--I know she wanted to see her--she, mn--I had a feeling if we wouldn't go, she'd be--s. . .

T.: She'd make you suffer for it.

X.: (overlapping): She'd be pouting down her nose, yes; she'd be pouting down on her nose--

T.: O.K.; so in a way you feel she did make you go--

X.: In a way, yes--it's in other words it's ah--I--I'd the experience before, and I sort of learned that--in other words, if I--if I'd agree to her wishes--you see it'd be easier on me--she'd have a better attitude; she'd have a happier attitude. I don't know why-- that affected me so much when she had the--nasty attitude, and there'd sort of be of tension on me--for a long time; maybe it would last a day or two--

(Here X. also shows again how he, too, can't settle on anything. Just as he is about to take a definite stand of his own, he backs down, again under the illusion that he can buy acceptance.)

T.: Yeah, she would sort of hold a grudge on you--
X.: Yeah, she'd hold a grudge and--
T.: Make you know it--
X.: Yeah, and I thought: "Well what the hell! See 'em and"--uh--and on the other hand, it turned out the other way--those two were waiting for me with a--might say a loaded shotgun, I mean, that is emotionally; that's what it was--they just blasted into us and, uh--well, I thought, I didn't think much of it--then, the next day, I didn't think anything untoward, I said, well-uh, I slept late, as is my custom, and, uh, went to work, and then after a couple of hours, I started to feel funny--
T.: Uh huh--
X.: I, I didn't know why I--I but--first I thought the--the supervisor was watching me--and, sure enough, I kind of thought they were watching me--so, "Well, am I doing something wrong?" and, then, I--I had the feeling that there was tension in me--and, and if I could only last out until--well, until lunch time, or last out until, uh, a couple of hours, I'd be all right, it would pass--
T.: Uh huh.
X.: Well, seems though there was just a little too much tension just to pass that lightly; so--that's all I can say--it seemed to build up more.
T.: Um hm.
X.: And, uh--I got sort of a befuddled state, where I couldn't seem to--my simple task was to separate long letters from short letters, see? It's very simple; I mean there's nothing simpler than that, and then I started getting confused--
T.: Uh huh--
X.: I seemed to pay too much attention to the in-between letters. Couldn't decide whether they go with the long or the shorts.

(The problem of decision versus terrible uncertainty has been a theme throughout. It has appeared in relation to dealing with differences of opinion between two other people, and dealing with contradictory messages from one person. Here, as X. nears his break, it reappears in a bare, almost diagrammatic form. [2] This instance is without manifest interpersonal context; however, it can certainly be related to the patient's own tendency to be an "in-between," and his need to please and conciliate everyone, all the time, by "doing right.")

T.: Uh huh--
X.: So, well, I felt, I felt that was kind of funny: I talked a little to the guy who worked on the other side--and, then, I--I couldn't seem to give the right answers; I was--I seemed to be too critical of myself. I don't know why. I thought the best thing would be to shut up--and yet I couldn't seem to shut up--
T.: Uh huh.
X.: The best thing would be to just keep quiet; and if I could have kept quiet that would have been fine; but I--I didn't. I seemed to talk with the--uh--then I just get disturbed and wonder: "Am I saying the right thing?"--then I asked one of the guys, I said: "Well, I just don't feel right; what shall I do?" "If you don't feel right, why don't you go home?" I said: "Well that's a good thing--I mean--I don't--this would be the first time I'd have to go home in a year and a half"--and I went up and asked--and, uh, well, later George told me--he said--"Well, your face was white, just white"; so you see it really was evidently...
T.: Uh huh.
X.: The autonomic system, or something, wasn't working right--the blood was drained from my face, uh; something was wrong; so, when I went home, I took a jitney, and I just kept quiet all the way, just trying to think: "Well, how could I explain this to my--father-in-law or to B. or to mother?"
T.: Uh huh-- sort of like things would be back where they were the night before?
X.: Yeah, that's right--
T.: Uh huh.
X.: I thought well, well; then I started to get disturbed--sort of like in a trap or something--
T.: Like there didn't seem to be any way out--
X.: There's no way out, that's right; and when I got in, I just started crying--then when I was crying like I told you, I felt in a way: "This will punish the old bastard!" You know what I mean?

---

[2] X.'s collapse over inability to discriminate between long and short letters sounds much like Pavlov's production of experimental neurosis in dogs by setting them a circle-ellipse discrimination problem, which was eventually made too difficult by changing the ellipse nearer and nearer to circular form. (8)

104

(X. is more and more concerned with "rightness"--"Am I doing
right; am I talking right; am I even functioning right physically?"
--but how can he find out? Desperate as he is, he feels it is also wrong to ask about it, or leave work; and if he goes home, it
will be like the night before; so he's trapped.

In our view of schizophrenia, the trap is real, and centers on
the fact that the child must not bring it out if he does feel bad or
upset, because this is to his mother an accusation that she is not
a "good mother," and she cannot stand this. So the line of communication for possible correction of difficulties is blocked.)

T.: Uh huh.
X.: The old man. And this way, of course, I wouldn't talk with
him or anything, and he--just sat around for a while, then after th--
minute you see, B. manged to, take me to the--uh--hospital, but
actually, you see, now that I look at it, nothing actually--st--uh--
started, started me wrong--didn't happen--until I--I, in fact when
I was in L. Hospital for a while, for a few hours, and they couldn't
agree where to send me, or--I wanted to go home--see? I told B.:
"Well, let's go home; let's take a taxi and go home, or something,"
"No, let's wait a while," and then when they finally decided to, to
take me to M. Hospital, I had the idea that this, uh, was one of the
aides dressed up as a cab man--
T.: Uh huh.
X.: And I thought: "Well, they're just testing me out"; see, al-
ready I was imagining things--

(X. has a delusion involving deception but explains it away, much
as his wife explained away her deceiving him--"It's for a good
purpose.")

T.: Uh huh--
X.: And then, uh--the funny thing is that that darned meter
seemed to spin fast, you know, real fast--and then it slowed down;
it almost stopped just--just--when, actually you know darn well
that the meter just has one constant speed.
T.: Uh huh--
X.: So then that confused me; so I says: "Well, is the meter
rigged?"; you know--
T.: Uh huh.
X.: For this--and then I was getting very upset; I--I was saying:
"Well, you're going the wrong way"; I'd say: "Well, B., you should
go this way"; then finally, after a while: "Well, you're going the
right way; looks to me like I know part of the city" and, uh, finally

I mean I kept this up until the doctor at M.--M.--I don't remember the first night how I slept, but I sure got very upset for the next few days--

T.: I wonder if we go back a minute again, to the night where the argument went on--uh--what did you do--while they were--while your father-in-law and your mother were telling you this was all so terrible?

X.: Well, I know he was in no condition even to just talk to. He just s--stalked off, sullen, and I thought: "Well, I better let him cool off for a while."

T.: He just sort of gave you hell and then walked away?

X.: Yeah, and with her, I just tried to tell her, but she just, you know--mother was saying: "Well, you're wrong, you're wrong: you know you, you shouldn't have done that," uh--

T.: And you mean nobody even gave you a chance to talk back to them?

X.: That's right--I couldn't reason with her; she's, uh, all in his favor, I mean, and, so, I didn't say much to B.; I know I was-- but I don't know whether that was actually what caused it--

T.: Well, I'm just trying to get a clearer picture of the circumstances--

X.: That's what happened, though--

T.: So you didn't really say much to anybody?

X.: No--so, uh, well, it's hard to just keep, keep something in you, in--n; just keep it in you, uh, and be to blame for it--I mean-- that's--

T.: Sure.

X.: Then I realized--you see, this was such a small item actually; this was a very small item. The thing that I really, I raised a fuss over, like I say, was when he accused me of not even paying the interest on the--this property--damn property, I--it's not worth over $10,000 or $12,000; he paid $17,000 for it, and, uh, it is such an inconvenience after he bought it in, and then so many disadvantages--

T.: How come you--when--after they all told you, you were all in the wrong about this--you didn't say anything to B. either?

X.: Well, I felt that B. knew the circumstance, and that she-- she was with me all day, and--uh--(pause) I kind of felt that she sympathized with me in a way; you know what I mean? I mean, she didn't have much to say but--I knew that she wasn't against me--

T.: Was she there at all when they were giving you the devil?

X.: Yes, she was right there--

T.: Um. But she didn't speak up?

X.: Well--I don't know--uh--whether she spoke up or not; if she did, I didn't pay much attention to it.

T.: But, at any rate, you don't have any recollection of her saying anything about: "Well, I wanted to go to the convent," or anything of that sort?

X.: No; no, she didn't--I don't think she--(pause) Later, I think I told mother that we went to see this nun, and she says: "Oh, that's it:"you know--it's B.'s fault, you know--I think I told mother that-- she jumped on B., as she usua--she usually does; she usually does blame B. for everything, see? As far as mo--mother is concerned, everything is B.'s fault, and, uh--so, uh--

T.: "Later" when do you mean by "later on"? You mean that evening? or

X.: Yeah, she--that evening--yeah, I--I mentioned it to her-- then again; well, it's true, one thing, mother knew a lot about our life, a lot of things--I, I'd tell her--uh--you know, in other words, uh, confidences, you might say--uh--not about our very personal life but, you know, things like, like the--handling of the children-- things like that--so--uh, now I feel calmed down to the extent that, us, I feel like I could go back to work--

(X. is again protecting his wife, by taking the blame instead of accusing her of making him late. However, this also enables him to interpret her silence as sympathy; if he doesn't take the blame, he fears losing this "sympathy." This is made clearer when he tentatively accuses her to his mother, and mother totally takes his side, denying anything positive with his wife-- "everything is B.'s fault." At this, X. seems fearful that things have gone too far the other way, that his tie with B. is being destroyed, perhaps because of the intensity of his own unresolved feelings that this arouses.)

T.: You seem to have there some sort of a special feeling there about, uh, mentioning that your mother knows a lot about things-- about your life with B.

X.: Well, my feeling is this--see, B.'s--B. was accusing me of being a mother's boy; that's one of her--things that she will not stand for, one of the reasons she didn't marry another person she met before she met me--how--to her it's despicable, and she got me to the extent where I admitted that I was a mother's boy; I mean she'd just badgered me--

T.: Made you--

X.: "The hell with you--I am a mother's boy, then, if you--"

T.: You just said this to get some peace, really?

X.: Yeah, in a way, that's right--and, uh, finally, when she did grab that and then really started, I said: "Well, damn you; I am no mother's boy; if you think that--that I am," I said, "I am a human being, and I have my own opinions. I know I was raised by my mother, but what the hell am I supposed to be? Killed for that? Or what?" You know, "What can you hold against me for being raised by my mother? I didn't have a father"; so, uh, so I knew that--I had, uh--that was when she was talking about getting a trustee for the children--which I don't know anything about--I mean, I don't know how that could be arranged--

T.: It seems like you had a special--

X.: Yeah--

T.: Kind of a--you had a feeling--I got an idea from the way you looked when you were telling me about--how your mother knew a good bit about... the family, and I was just wondering what that feeling was--it seemed to mean something then.

X.: Well, I don't know, uh--well, I don't know what that would be except I thought if Mother didn't know too much, she wouldn't have stuck her nose in so much that--she--to get it burned, so to speak, by B.--

T.: Uh huh.

X.: And her father.

T.: Maybe some sort of--

X.: She stuck her nose into (too?) personal affairs, such as-- uh, oh, the way I do this and that--and, uh, and, uh, you see B. knew it and, uh, and, that's part of the reason why she--she's against her, because, uh--

T.: I was wondering if there was some feeling there that when you did bring up the matter of--it wasn't all your fault that you were late, that it had something to do with what B. wanted, that, in a way, this made trouble, too. Like there, again, there wasn't any way out for you--

X.: Well--uh--

T.: Like your mother seized on this not really to understand you or your situation, but--to stir things up between you and B. again.

X. (pause): That's right; that's it; maybe I didn't realize it, but I know that; I knew she has been stirring things up between me and B. for a long time, if you put it that way--you know--she'd, uh, pass these comments about how incapable she was, and--and this and that--so--

(If X. turns to his mother, she uses _what_ he says to attack his relationship with his wife. This increase of the conflict there obviously weakens him and makes him feel more dependent on mother. At the same time, his wife uses the _fact_ that he goes to his mother, regardless of why or about what, to characterize him as a "mother's boy," although she is pushing him that way by putting so much off on him herself. It is a sort of double bind involving his relationship with two people, each focusing on only one level of his behavior, in the way least favorable to him, and rejecting his efforts to say there is something more to the situation, which they ignore.)

T.: Well, it sure seems like (here X. interrupts)--

X.: With B., on the other hand, always saying: "We have to get closer together closer, and our love has to grow," and this and that--well, I start getting confused; I don't see how I can meet those conditions unless--I couldn't see--in other words, she-- lately she's been saying, that, that, that, uh, it depends on our love; it depends on--I don't mean intercourse; on other words, love, whatever it might, I can't even define the kind of love she means--

T.: It's not really clear what she is really talking about.

X.: Well--

T.: When she says this--

X.: That we have to understand each other, and love one another, and, uh, become two bodies in one soul; and, uh, well, you see that's kind of hard--uh--that, that's setting up a pretty rigid--uh-- qualification.

T.: (pause): Maybe you feel that has a little bit of flavor, that she wants you just to go along with her in everything--

X.: Yes, and I imagine that's what I finally, finally concluded; I've been fighting it for years--I always wanted to have my own way--and that's why I always told her that if I decided to go to church, I might go to a Methodist church; I always wanted that out for myself, because I never, never would agree--completely; I said: "I might become a Catholic, but don't count on it--when mother dies"; y' know, they knew mother was against it. And so all--all that she's gotten, she's got from this, hate from my moth- er--I imagine I--without meaning to, I'd--nurtured it, I'd given reason for that hate; in other words she thought if she could get mother out of the way--who knows, then--then I'd swing to her, actually I--I didn't think so; I felt the most important thing was to keep a job, make sure the children had enough to be brought up on, and, uh--ourselves, com-comfortable--you know--

(The wife emphasizes more and more that he must not be a "mother's boy"--she quit going with one before; so the threat of abandonment is there--while making it almost impossible to be otherwise: If he turns directly to mother, he is one, ac- cording to her, regardless of conditions. If he turns to her, since she says they should get closer, she has laid out all the specifications; she would be dominant, making him a mother's boy. He tries to be a man by working, but she keeps him away from the job; so everyone thinks him inadequate as a man there, too.

All this time, she, as mentioned earlier, has various sources of support in religion--father, fine phrases, like "closeness," and so on, that are culturally acceptable, or that she can put over by skillful definition as "good," while all his needs are defined as "weakness"--so successfully that he increasingly accepts this; perhaps his illness may itself be seen as a resolution by accepting such accusations even more.)

T.: Uh, well, as I--I think over what you tell me about--that night, it sure sounds like although you may have been involved in it to the extent of saying, "O.K., we'll stop at the convent, and you can talk to the nun," it sure does seem that once that was done, when you got home, everybody was--was giving you the devil and leaving you standing all alone, and the thing that you couldn't see any way out of at all--

X.: Yes, but that really shouldn't have disturbed me; I mean-- that's one thing I can't understand, because--

T.: Why shouldn't it?

X.: Why should it? It's such a small item--

T.: Your father-in-law gives you hell and walks off; your mother gives you hell and won't listen; your wife stands there and lets them give you hell and doesn't say: "I wanted to go to the convent, and that's why we're so late," and she walks off then--

X.: Well, possibly--

T.: I mean, you're getting hell from all sides and being left alone, to boot; it's a pretty rough situation.

X.: Well, I didn't look at it; I mean I know I'd--I felt it strongly, I know that; in other words, you know, sort of, sort of a surprise, it happened so quickly; well, what the hell is going on, you know-- and then-- (overlapping and indistinct here)

T.: Yeah, must have been pretty confusing, to--having all this just sort of fall down on me.

X.: It was a little confusing, but then I just thought: "Well, the hell with them!" That's what I thought; I just said; "Well, the hell with"--that's the way they feel--it shouldn't; I didn't think it'd bother me, but there is something deeper than that--uh, it's--it seemed to--been a delayed reaction--in other words, I wasn't feeling good, even on that trip--

T.: Uh huh.

X.: In other words, I--I know I--I was having this feeling of confusion--so that was even before that argument--

T.: Just this may have been added on to--

<u>X.</u>: That's right--

<u>T.</u>: Something else, but at least it gives us a--a picture of how you were in a difficulty with that, and we can talk some more then on what may have preceded it--

<u>X.</u>: Yeah--

<u>T.</u>: Well, I'm glad you were able to tell me about that today--

<u>X.</u>: Well, I thought I told you this once before--

<u>T.</u>: No, I never had anything like this clear a picture of it--

<u>X.</u>: Well, I don't think it was--<u>the</u>--I--mean I wasn't sure-- like I say, I didn't feel well before that even--

<u>T.</u>: Well, we don't have to say this situation is the cause of any- thing, if this gives a picture of a difficulty you were in--O.K., X., I'll see you Monday. Hope you have a nice weekend.

<u>X.</u>: Thank you.

COMMENT

We would like to review and emphasize several aspects of the material that seem to us to have particular relevance to the life situation in which X. developed a psychosis, and to the therapeutic situation in which he reviews these matters.

<u>Pattern</u> <u>of</u> X.'s <u>Life</u> <u>Situation</u>--We have mentioned above our concept of the double bind as a situation 1) in which a person is faced with contradictory messages, 2) which are not readily visible as such because of concealment or denial or because the messages are on different levels, and 3) in which he can neither escape nor notice and effectively comment on the contradictions. We have tried to point out in our comments that X. is repeatedly involved in such situations with the people most important to him. His father-in-law sends him out on errands and his wife delays him further, but when he is attacked by the old man for not behaving like a responsible person, X. can only see the criticism as a "paternal" interest in his welfare. X.'s mother in this same con- text, even though she does not get along well with the father-in-law, berates X. for upsetting his father-in-law; X. attempts to handle the situation by saying it is unimportant. X.'s wife, after making him late, retires from the scene, leaving him to face the blame; he <u>imagines</u> she is "sympathetic" and had to leave in order to care for their children. In other examples, he appears caught in simi- lar binds by the joint behavior of two persons--as between wife and mother on the "mother's boy" issue, or even by one person's bla- tant contradictions, as when his wife successfully insists that de- ception was not deception because it involved the church.

It is evident in the interview what strain and difficult situations of this sort recurrently produced for X., even though he is still trying hard to minimize or deny this. Denial is his usual, though ineffective, technique for handling them.

However, as mentioned earlier, the double bind is not a simple one-way relationship but is an interaction in which both (or all) parties tend to be sharing important similarities of behavior, at least for relationships that persist over some time. This is rather clearly illustrated by the instance--not a unique example--in which X., when just succeeding in refusing his wife's unreasonable request to visit the nun, suddenly reverses and gives in, pseudo-benevolently, if she "would like to." Clearly, X. does not fully want to get free.

This poses rather sharply the problem, "Why did X. and not his wife break down?" Since they were both caught up in a similar family situation, what visible difference in their handling of affairs might account for her continued social functioning and his failure and eventual psychotic break?

Who the Kept and Who the Keeper? Mrs. X.'s Transactions. --
It would be a simple matter to postulate that X. is genetically more disposed to schizophrenia than his wife, and hence was the logical one to break down under the stress of an unhappy marriage. However, there are other considerations which might be offered as data relevant to Mrs. X.'s being in the more emotionally fortunate position.

1. She has fairly severe epilepsy and is "entitled" to the kind of consideration that the husband longs for. It is possible, additionally, that her disorder offers other psychological gains; e.g., it will be recalled that shock therapy for schizophrenia arose out of the observation that schizophrenia and epilepsy were relatively incompatible.

2. She was actively religious and able to use her religion as a strong lever to get "one-up" on her husband, who appeared to be a religious renegade but was not completely free. Her religious activities additionally provided certain positive figures both in reality and in fantasy for her emotional support.

3. Her inadequacies as a wife and mother could be justified from the standpoint of her illness and from the fact that her own mother was dead. That she exploited the latter fact is revealed in

her attitude toward the patient's relations with his mother. He was criticized for being a "mother's boy"; yet her dependent relationship to her aunt and to the nuns was accepted, and indeed sanctioned, by the patient.

4. The cultural concept of "a mother" carried a good deal of weight for the patient and caused him, his wife, and his father-in-law to be acutely aware of his responsibilities toward her. [3] The "mother" concept further provided a dilemma for the patient in that he was torn between his duty to his own mother and to the mother of his children.

Because of the conventional validity and unimpeachability of her rationalizations, and the similarity of her maneuvers to those of his own mother, the patient was almost totally unable to spot the contradictions in the wife's communications. Yet, of course, she was equally helpless to get much satisfaction from her relationship either with her husband or with her children; she was "successful" negatively rather than positively.

The concepts mentioned above are only a few related to observable features of the actual relationship that might be reviewed in reconsidering the problem of relative "ego strength" of the patient and of his wife. They suffer additionally from the fact that they are presented alone rather than in some stratified fashion, layered with the husband's and other relatives' own personality problems and interpersonal behavior. That is, in considering the nature of psychogenic stress and its relevance to the onset of a schizophrenic psychosis, it is necessary to review the type of perduring or predominant transactions that are occurring between the patient and the significant others in his immediate environment and their

---

[3] Perhaps it is relevant to note that statistics of hospital admissions for schizophrenia reveal that it is not until 40 years of age that the admission rate for women exceeds that of men. Additionally, prior to age 40 a sizable percentage of female admissions are unmarried or childless women. It is possible that more is involved in these statistics than the simple fact that the female schizophrenic-to-be does not marry or, if she does, does not tend to bear children. Some such women may find a protective component, mental-health-wise, in being a mother of young children, either in the positive cultural sanctions and values accorded motherhood as such, or in the children's absorbing the most malignant aspects of the interpersonal difficulties.

relation to the patient's early past. Domination by weakness can
be especially effective as a means of controlling the definition of
the relationship if the person doing the defining is ill, female, or
operates in a matriarchal environment. Thus, the patient's wife
related to her father in such a manner as to appear submissive,
like a good daughter; at the same time she was actively controlling
him.[4] It is important also to note that the concept of a "good
daughter" has a positive cultural evaluation, while the patient's being a "good boy" vis-a-vis his mother has a negative connotation.
Although the wife's father made difficulties for her by his seclu-
siveness, irritability, and weak health, he was also busy catering
to her needs and asked no more from her than the husband did.
Who can say what might have eventuated if her father had died just
prior to her marriage to the patient, and she had been robbed of
the prototype for her dealings with her husband, as well as losing
an ally in her marital struggles?

The Illusion of Alternatives: X.'s Transactions. -- One aspect
of being an American that receives attention from the public press
is the freedom to do what one wants and to tell the other fellow to
"go to hell." Americans, by reputation, are their own bosses and
resent being told what to do. The stereotype is familiar, and in
some ways resembles an attitude manifested by Patient X. and by
a number of schizophrenics we have studied. Overlooking the actual circumstances of concealed contradictory influences, the patient particularly feels as if he is the master of his fate, and hence
holds himself responsible for making wrong specific choices or decisions and is haunted by obsessive doubts as to what choice to
make. Actually, there is only an illusion of alternatives, since
by the very nature of the double-bind situation, the patient will
be "damned if he does and damned if he doesn't."

For example, one of the major points in the interaction described
by X. is his feeling that he must take the blame for his wife's making them late and that by doing so he minimizes the possibility of a
fight between B. and his mother. He states that B. can't stand a

---

[4]A dramatic picture of the apparently submissive daughter who
gets her own way, while placing responsibility for her behavior on
the parental figures to whom she is "obedient," appears in Ann
Whitefield, Shaw's heroine in "Man and Superman." It should be
noted, though, that Ann is perhaps aware of her manipulations, and
to that extent responsible, in contrast to Mrs. X.'s irresponsible
unawareness and denial of control.

mother's boy; yet by covering up for her, he becomes a "mother's boy." Additionally, she had told him that she had stopped going with a former suitor because she discovered he was a "mother's boy." She wants to get closer to X. --in her words, "to become two bodies in one soul"--but this means to X. a suffocating closeness in which she is the "one soul" and he is the "lost soul." He turns to his mother when he feels B. is suffocating him, but this only reawakens the same problem with his mother and allows B. to taunt him. That he feels caught between B. and his mother is clear in the statement: "I might become a Catholic when mother dies." His work makes him feel more like a man, but he accepts a situation that B. sets up, in which he is forced to choose between her and his work. His defaulting in her favor increases his father-in-law's contempt for him, and so the possibility of the two men sticking together fades. It is not adequate to see that S. has no satisfactory relationship within the family. Rather it is noteworthy how, for him, a troubled relationship begets further troubled relationships.

There is ample evidence that X. sees himself as weak and helpless, and, on the other hand, as a good guy, who tries hard and who suffers from being "too nice." He would like some babying, but he marries a woman who despises weakness and utilizes helplessness to gain interpersonal power. He notes neither this contradiction in her nor its reciprocal in himself. Indeed, so long as X. accepts denials and concealments he is offered and acts according to the illusion of alternatives--as, of course, he is encouraged to do--the more the situation will tend to deteriorate. He tries to adapt to opposing manifest demands at different moments instead of dealing with the over-all contradictions embodied. But as these varying apparent problems are at best merely tangential aspects of the real ones, X. does not succeed in satisfying the others who make the demands, does not achieve acceptance and satisfaction, and is progressively more involved in fluctuating and contradictory behavior himself. This only reinforces the reciprocal double-bind involvements between them all.

We are primarily concerned here not with why X. follows this unsatisfactory course and is unable to break out of it but, rather, with its nature and outcome. However, we may say, on the basis of additional interview material with X. and with other patients, that we assume that X. had countless experiences in his childhood, when his real dependency needs were great, that were prototypically related to the pattern described in this interview.[5] One such sequence from a nonpsychotic patient is described below because it was studied shortly after its inception and is probably more reliable than an adult patient's report of events in his childhood. The example appears as different only in degree from Patient X.'s experience.

A young adolescent who had a problem in not feeling like one of the boys, and who wanted to please his ineffectual father by becoming popular, returned home later than usual one day because he had been out with the gang. His enthusiasm for his new-found manliness was somewhat dampened when his mother greeted him with an underplayed "I was worried to death about you" approach. There was an unpleasant feeling in his stomach, and an old ghost reminded him that he was capable of worrying mother and that she would be free from worry if it were not for him. This feeling was a kind of unconscious heroin for him because, though sickening, it produced grandiosity and a special sense of preciousness. As a consequence of the incident with mother, he renounced the pleasure of roaming the streets with the fellows and came home promptly for the next few days; but then one night mother announced at the dinner table that there hadn't been as many phone calls for him lately. He resented her doing this in front of father, but the signal from his stomach announced: "I am worrying her again." At this point he still attempted to solve the dilemna in terms of alternatives. These alternatives, stated roughly, were: "Should I spend more time at home or more time with the boys?"

Being still unsure, he returned home promptly the next day, only to find that mother had gone uptown and had left a note telling him so. Here was an opportunity to break the bind they were in, but it is in the nature of these reverberating cyclic sequences that he could not pull out. Instead, he stayed around the house and surprised mother when she returned by having started dinner. There was some mutual uneasiness about the "pansy" implications of his cooking dinner, but this was handled (as so many things had been in the past) by a covert agreement not to mention it to dad. And so the cycle was perpetuated.

The Psychotic Break. -- While we are unable to state at what precise point a psychosis eventuates in X. or any other patient, it

---

[5]Some consideration of the general etiology of such double-bind involvement is given by Bateson, Jackson, Haley, and Weakland. (1)

does seem to relate to the frequency, intensity, and timing of double-bind sequences. Constitutional factors, external stresses, and the experience of a previous psychosis are also possible contributory factors. We shall consider here the question of what sort of change in response pattern is X.'s development of psychosis, and what factors one can see that appear to have been temporarily related to it.

X.'s way of alternating conciliatory "good behavior" with occasional and abortive rebellious assertion does not gain him any control in his relationships, and indeed produces the opposite result. We can assume that his inability to deal with his wife's control through helplessness may have produced a covert competition with her that becomes manifest and explicit when he becomes psychotic. This is not to say that X. deliberately becomes psychotic to get attention. Rather, viewing the matter in terms of communication, as X. more desperately and unsuccessfully attempts to gain some control and satisfaction in his relationships, but fails with ordinary verbal means, his level of communication shifts. Thus, when he cannot separate the letters, he does not feel talking will help any, but he pales and a fellow worker notices he looks sick. [6] Yet X. goes even further, into psychosis. Several factors may be significant for this ultimate development.

1. X. escaped his job problem by illness but felt his family problems remained, just as they did after feigned illness the day before.

2. It seemed, though, that some fortuitous, unplanned change at the level of physical objects, e.g., an auto breakdown, might alleviate the family struggle. Hallucination at least subjectively fits this specification.

3. He had already had an experience of a psychotic break; so this path was to some extent marked out for him. [7]

---

[6] This shift may be compared with an example of culturally different levels of communication in social excuses pointed out by Margaret Mead: A Russian would not excuse himself from a party he did not wish to attend by reporting a non-existent headache, about which he might then feel guilty. This is more characteristic of an American; a Russian would just have the headache! (9)

[7] It is striking to notice that if X.'s retrospective account is accurate, his psychotic break involves at least three specific instances

Becoming psychotic does put X. at once in a position of maximum helplessness, because he is crazy and unable to do anything, while at another level it also gives him much more control. If he is more helpless than his wife and others, they must now take care of him. It is evident that as he becomes psychotic, the family members alter their behavior toward him, a change which he could not get them to make before.

Accompanying this alteration of relationships, and paralleling it in important respects, is a great alteration in X.'s perceptions and conceptions. This is the aspect of psychosis that has received the most attention from investigators. However, it is essential to see, as this interview illustrates, that X., in becoming psychotic, does not shift from perceiving correctly to "distorting reality." X.'s observations and communications are distorted before his break, and are differently distorted afterward.

Prior to his psychosis, X. is maintaining a very special view of the world in his illusion of alternatives, an "either-or" way of regarding relationships. Particularly, he is distorting perceptions of his social world, the most fundamental "reality" for human beings. He is oriented to the material world and to limited transactions, but not to contradiction between levels or modes of behavior. When he hopes for an accident to the car to provide him with an excuse for being late, he is on the slippery edge beyond which the material world gets distorted to provide hoped-for interpersonal gain.

When he becomes psychotic, he distorts material "reality," as with the taximeter, and more limited social situations, as in his feeling watched at work. These distortions are more easily recognizable by the rest of us. Yet at the same time he sees certain feelings and relationships more clearly than in his prepsychotic state. A patient who has felt guilty because he is not a good enough son and who, when he becomes psychotic, expresses concern over mother's suicide potential is not just expressing hostility but is acknowledging mother's depressive tendency.

Such insights are a mixed blessing, however. The patient can see and speak important truths because he is "sick" and out of the situation. But these perceptions are difficult to integrate because,

---

of idea and realization. He claims illness, then gets sick. He wishes for something wrong with the car, then sees the peculiar taximeter. He tells his wife "You're driving me crazy," then breaks.

since he is crazy, they do not count and others do not respond to his communications as messages to them. The so-called "social recovery" is the prime example of a person who manages to disregard a whole class of percepts by labeling them as his previously crazy self.

As mentioned earlier, it is not possible to establish with certainty the specific nature and circumstances of X.'s psychotic break. However, the available evidence suggests that after a long build-up of stress there was a fairly sudden and sharp break into overt psychosis. This seems to have occurred at a time when X.'s existing practice of denial and distortion of interpersonal realities was becoming inadequate to avoid choice and action, or, put with a different emphasis, when he was closer to being able to see his true situation, but not able to face it. Thus, on the day before his break, all of those most significant to him were attacking him in ways which must have made their contradictions especially blatant and hard to overlook, while simultaneously making it impossible to turn from one of them to another, as before, for even temporary support. Other available data also suggest that, despite his difficulties, X. recently had been making some progress in his job. Just at this point his wife attacks this by making him late. Was it becoming so clear that she did not want him to succeed that he could not, short of psychosis, fail to see this?

Then came the last straw, the matter of sorting the letters. This situation is an incredible parallel to X.'s dealings with interpersonal problems by the illusion of alternatives, as the problem with the letters is to make a correct choice between two polar alternatives. X. does not see that his personal alternatives are not real ones, or that there are not really two distinct kinds of letters but only arbitrary definitions. With the letters he must make a choice and cannot use the denial-and-avoidance techniques he employs with people. This appears to be that point at which he shifts from attempting to "solve his problems" to becoming "sick," whereby he is admitting he cannot solve them. He describes the sequence beautifully.

1. He felt they were watching him, as if waiting for him to make a mistake. (Later he produces something--paleness--and they do watch him.)

2. An apparently simple task separating the long letters from the short ones turned out to be impossible because of the in-betweens. In-betweens are not allowed.

3. He became increasingly critical of himself. This had worked to some extent in relating to people; it was ineffective with the letters.

4. The turning point was an involuntary behavior, which others noticed, and responded to. He became visibly ill and was told: "If you don't feel right, why don't you go home?"

5. Even the shift into the frame of illness was not enough, because all the way home he worried: "How can I explain this to them?"

6. Psychotic delusions allowed him to free himself of decision making. For example, the cab driver is a hospital attendant in disguise. There is no problem in "home" vs. "hospital"; it has been resolved.

The Interview Situation and Psychotherapy. --It is perhaps unexpectedly rewarding to raise the question: "Why did this interview centering on X.'s break take place just when it did?" --what were its circumstances? In no previous interview had he discussed this matter in any such detail, and in this one it was not brought up deliberately as a topic. Rather, the therapist merely followed up with some persistence the patient's early remark that his current difficulties about leaving the hospital are "just about the same question" as "why did I have the nervous breakdown in the first place?" The parallel situation in the present is his attempting to make a sharp choice between staying in the hospital or going home, while feeling helpless to do so. He fears that his fate really may be controlled by conflicts between others--the therapist and the ward doctor, and, beyond them, his wife and his mother again. He feels like a pawn in their games, but he now trusts the therapist enough to bring up his concern. Talking about his psychotic episode, although promoted by emotional and relational similarities, seems also to depend on at least three current differences from the old situation. 1. There is some real difference in the persons immediately involved and their behavior. The therapist and ward doctor at least present him with less concealed contradictions than his family members did. 2. Beyond this, also, the situation is less crucial for him; it is more limited and the persons involved less important. 3. He believes in doctors and accepts to a large extent that they are trying to help him. By talking about his hospital situation, he is working through an "artificial" psychosis, similar to the real one but more manageable. A parallelism with the Freudian idea of "transference neurosis" is evident here; however, analytic thinking usually plays down the role of the actual therapeutic situation.

We feel that the similarity of circumstances between original significant events and their re-creation, review, and reworking in therapy is crucial, and is not confined to the session presented here. Especially, although detailed exposition and evidence must await later publications, we believe that something resembling the "double bind" must often be instituted on the patient by the therapist to obtain therapeutic change. This "therapeutic bind," however, must also differ in such a way as to require not the distortion, denial, or unawareness of the nature of vital interpersonal relationships, of the patient but, rather, increased awareness of their true nature. Such awareness stands in contrast to both X.'s private distortions and Mrs. X.'s special manipulation of public stereotypes. It may not always be necessary. For example, in stable social contexts habitual patterns of behavior may serve to establish and regulate relationships in a reasonably satisfactory way. Thus, ordinary everyday relationships among "normal" people often do not involve much conscious awareness of their nature as such. But unsatisfactory relationships, with no mutually fitting behavior and views in important situations, may arise from social changes, cultural contacts, and individual idiosyncrasies. Then increased awareness may be an important means of locating interpersonal dissatisfaction and making adaptive changes in relationships.

CONCLUSION

We present a transcribed interview in which Patient X., recovering from a schizophrenic episode, is describing the circumstances surrounding his psychotic break. We attempted to demonstrate that, despite the absence of any horrendous or earth-shaking occurrences, X., because of the circumstances of his rearing and current living, was under a very great stress. He was caught up in a series of self-perpetuating transactions, which we label "binds" because they inflexibly involve two people in a dissatisfying amalgam. X. attempted to solve his interpersonal difficulties as though they were solvable if he could but make the right choice. This method, the illusion of alternatives, developed out of his inability to comment upon (notice) mutually contradictory multilevel communication sequences. His subsequent psychosis we see as restitutive, since his being "sick" encloses his attempts to form relationships within a new frame and allows him to view what he has been avoiding.

It is important to restate that we do not see X. as having gotten "sick" (psychotic) in order to break the bind. The change is not

voluntary, and the psychotic state and the being "sick" create a
new set of problems as formidable in some ways as the previous
ones. X. starts the interview by indicating that all is not well with
his hospitalized self. He fears the re-creation of the problems
that drove him to the hospital in the first place. Fortunately, because of the therapeutic relationship, he can voice his doubts and
fears and make some sense of them. The old ties are still operating, and X. must also face another failure (his job and having to
be hospitalized), so that he pays dearly for his new insights. He
tells the therapist in effect: "What is a man profited, if he shall
gain the whole world, and lose his own soul?"

REFERENCES

1. Bateson, G., Jackson, D. D., Haley, J., and Weakland, J.
H. Toward a theory of schizophrenia. Behav. Sci., 1:251-264,
1956. (See p. 31, this vol.)
2. Laforgue, R. A contribution to the study of schizophrenia.
International J. Psycho-Analysis, 17:147-162, 1936.
3. Jackson, D. D. The question of family homeostastis. Psychiat.
Quart. (Suppl.) 31:79-90, 1957. (See p. 1, this vol.)
4. Kant, O. The problem of psychogenic precipitation in schizophrenia. Psychiat. Quart. 16:341-350, 1942.
5. Jackson, D. D. A note on the importance of traumia in the
genesis of schizophrenia. Psychiatry, 20:181-184, 1957. (See
p. 23, this vol.)
6. Stanton, A. H., and Schwartz, M. S. The Mental Hospital: A
Study in Institutional Participation in Psychiatric Illness and Treatment. p. 342, Basic Books, New York, 1954.
7. Block, J., Patterson, V., and Jackson, D. D. A study of the
parents of schizophrenic children. Psychiatry, to be published.
8. Pavlov, I. P. Lectures on Conditioned Reflexes, pp. 342,
359, translated by W. H. Gantt, International Publishers, New
York, 1928.
9. Transactions of the Third Group Process Conference (1956),
B. Schaffner (Ed.), University Seminar on Communications,
Columbia University, New York, Josiah Macy, Jr. Foundation,
to be published.

LETTERS OF MOTHERS OF SCHIZOPHRENICS

John H. Weakland and William F. Fry, Jr.

Several letters to schizophrenic patients from their mothers
are presented verbatim as raw communicational data. These
letters are examined, microscopically and macroscopically,
for characteristic formal patterns of expression. It is found
that: 1) While the letters vary greatly in details of content,
style, etc., they exhibit similar pervasive and highly influential patterns of incongruent communication. 2) These
letters agree with another schizophrenic's characterization
of such letters generally. 3) The observed pattern fits prior
general statements of the author's research group about the
"double bind" and incongruent communication in schizophrenia.

This paper presents some primary data on the nature and etiology of schizophrenia, consisting of several selected letters to
schizophrenic patients from their mothers, and one patient's verbatim general characterization of such letters, and examines these
data for characteristic and significant patterns.

Before presenting this material, however, it is important to
clarify our view of its general relevance to the study of schizophrenia. There are still many different competing notions, both organic and psychological, about the nature and etiology of this disorder.

Thus, while all of these various approaches involve general
scientific problems of collecting data as sources of theoretical

Reprinted from THE AMERICAN JOURNAL OF ORTHOPSY-
CHIATRY, 32, No. 4:604-623 (July 1962). Copyright, The American
Orthopsychiatric Association, Inc., New York; reproduced by
permission.

ideas and presenting selected parts of them to support the ideas, the sort of data that are appropriate and their relationship to theory vary with the chosen focus of investigation and line of approach. Our own theory (2, 7, 10), which will appear in more detail later, is generally concerned with schizophrenia as a form of adaptive communicative behavior, learned and maintained over time in relation to continuing patterns of family interaction and communication, which in spite of their importance may be unobtrusive.[1] This is quite different not only from an intrapersonal orientation as to "thought disorders," but even from the sort of interpersonal view that looks for some kind of early, sharp, and dramatic trauma as likely to be particularly significant.[2]

Data relevant to our approach then must provide information on such matters as the nature of family communication patterns and the patient's involvement in them, in sufficient detail to detect subtleties, since we do not posit gross and manifest traumatic events; on the persistence and pervasiveness of any patterns believed pathogenic, and so on. Moreover, examining actual communication for previously undefined subtleties presents special problems in getting or giving a sample of data that is adequate yet manageable. Examination tends to be lengthy and summarization difficult. The choice of a bounded unit in the ongoing continuity of communication is very difficult. And when dealing with schizophrenia, the usual problems of objectivity and reliability of data are not simplified--though sometimes this seems to have excused oversimplifying, as when patients' statements have been assumed necessarily false or valueless as evidence.

The use of letters as data appears particularly suited to handling certain of these requirements and difficulties. A letter is a permanent and "objective" piece of data; as a sample of communication it can be examined repeatedly, closely, and by various individuals. Also, it is a simpler piece of communication than an equally "objective" tape recording or sound film in that it is more purely verbal; there are no vocal, facial, or gestural messages to consider though there remain various verbal levels, handwriting, spatial organization, and the context to take into account. A letter is also unitary; it is a piece of communication with definite bound-

---

[1] This approach is also evident in the work of Bowen (3), Lidz, (4), Wynne (12) and their colleagues.

[2] This major difference is discussed further in a note by Jackson (8).

aries. Letters also often are relatively brief yet rich; they are
condensed communication samples. And it is important that such
restriction, delimitation, and condensation have been done by the
sender of the message himself, not by its analyst. It is therefore reasonable to assume that while a letter, in comparison with
ordinary speech, is a form easier for analytic study, it remains
typical of the sender's communicative habits in major respects,
and indeed may highlight these because of the selectivity the writer
has exercised.

Further, having actual letters from several mothers plus a
patient's statement about such letters in general allowed important
comparisons. The actual letters provide a check on the patient--
after all, if schizophrenic, he may be presenting a false or distorted view. On the other hand, the patient's involvement and
sensitivity may promote seeing real but subtle or hidden aspects
of the actual letters.

Certain problems do accompany the use of such materials:
1) The danger of isolation or overemphasis of the mother, and her
messages; 2) the related problem of the context of any specific
letters examined; and 3) problems concerning the choice of particular letters for presentation. On these we can only explicitly
clarify our position. Our fundamental point of view is toward considering interaction in a family system; the communication of the
patient, and of the father, is not to be ignored because we focus
on the mother's letters here. (In fact, other data lead us to believe communication similar to that we exemplify and analyze here
is exhibited by all the members of such a family.) We do have and
will use some information on the context of most material presented
here. And problems of selection of data are always with us; one
can only choose and say how it was done.

CASE A
Let us first see how letters from his own mother and from other
mothers are described by A, a patient who had been hospitalized
for several years. He had improved with hospitalization and psychotherapy to a point where he appeared to function fairly well so
long as his contacts with people were rather carefully controlled
and limited to minimize emotional involvement. In this context,
the therapist raised the question of the patient's writing to his
mother, with whom he had not communicated for four years--that
is, just prior to his breakdown. This exchange followed:

P.: I don't know, I get all fucked up.- -And I don't wanna have
anything to do with my mother, because I'll just get all fucked up.

T.: Um-hm.

P.: I mean, I start writin' to my mother--

(A brief interchange occurred on the question whether, if communication were established, mother might disturb the therapist-patient relationship. The patient denied this could happen, and plunged on.)

P.: She has--blanket letters that she writes, you know--

T.: Um.

P.: I can--I could write you a letter that my mother would write me, and then I'd write my mother and you--you'd compare the two. They start off fine--you know, the letters-- and then, suddenly, they--the--the--context changes--and--troubles, you know--what a hard time she's havin'--and then an inkling about money, and then ba-ba-boom--and toward the end of the--end of the letter she's getting "Well, why don't you do something about it?" and--"You're a big boy now" and all this other jive and--then toward the end it's--it's getting real sweet again and--

T.: That's it.

P.: For years it's the kind of letters I got.

T. (Overlapping): She reverses a couple of times.

P.: Yeah--And do you know--that--that a lot of people in these hospitals get letters like I do?--Do you know that?--Because I've listened to other guys--and other guys have taken me into their confidence--an' this is--this is the way their--their mothers write. They're in Korea, you know--foxhole--and they get a letter--they open it--Jesus Christ, it starts out just like that--

T. (Overlapping): They get a letter--

P.: What a hard time--

T. (Overlapping): --which says what a hard time she's having--

P.: Yeah--she's having--here's this poor son of a bitch--

T.: Only she ends up "Now don't worry about me."

P.: Um--"I'll manage."

The essence of this description of mothers' letters may be summarized to facilitate comparison with other data: 1) A typical letter starts off fine, with some sort of contact established. 2) Mother then shifts to an emphasis on how she has troubles. 3) She states or implies that her troubles are somehow the patient's fault, he is to blame for them, or he should be responsible for fixing them. 4) But then she blocks off effective contact and response by saying "don't worry." Also the patient emphasizes that such letters have a powerful emotional effect, upsetting and confusing him. And he claims that such letters are typical, that other patients' mothers write similar letters to them.

Our research group's theory of schizophrenia (2, 7, 10) centers on the influences exerted on human behavior by exposure to two or more messages of different level or logical type which are related but incongruent. We see such patterns of messages as etiologically influential for various types of deviant or disturbed behavior. [3] In particular, we have focused on the communication pattern which we have labeled a double bind. We see experience of this pattern as a necessary etiological condition for schizophrenia although we do not claim this alone is sufficient. The pattern may be characterized in a number of ways according to the descriptive level and emphasis chosen. At the formal level of message structure, the double bind is seen "as a situation 1) in which a person is faced with contradictory messages, 2) which are not readily visible as such because of concealment or denial, or because the messages are on different levels, and 3) in which he can neither escape, nor notice and effectively comment on the contradictions" (11). More strictly--in spite of any instances of looser wording even in this paper--we are concerned with incongruent rather than contradictory opposing messages. Simple contradictions can occur only between two directly opposite messages at the same level; this is probably rather rare, and not of major psychological importance.

The same communicational pattern, considered at the interpersonal level of mother-child interaction, appears in the form of mother approaching child when there is withdrawal from her or distance between them but then withdrawing as there is response and less distance, and so on recurrently (2, p. 257).

This picture of alternating come-but-go or affection- but-hostility messages from mother to child seems very similar to the patient's description of the abrupt alternations in his mother's letters. [4] And his description, though less explicit on this, also fits the requirement that the existence of such incongruence of messages be difficult to note and deal with effectively. The very abruptness of the shifts is disorienting, and the timing makes this worse--while appropriate response to one part of the communica-

---

[3]Some related patterns of incongruent messages appear important for more benign situations such as humor, play and psychotherapy (1, 6).

[4]Alternation would seem the most likely means for incongruent messages in writing. In speech, simultaneous yet incongruent messages, via voice versus tone or gesture, are more easily possible.

tion is developing, a reversal occurs. For example, the hostile remarks described are framed within the "love and benevolence" context established by the positive opening and closing remarks. These, as it were, set the patient up initially, lowering his guard, and block him from countering at the close.

But to what extent is this agreement of our theories and this patient's statement to be relied upon? Schizophrenics are often described as either incoherent or unreliable in what they say; also, since the therapist was not passive but agreeing and even making suggestions, there is a question of how much he may have led the patient into making this sort of statement. Fortunately, these questions can be investigated to some degree by examining next a sample of data quite free from these objectionable uncertainties.

CASE B

This sample consists of an actual letter to a hospitalized schizophrenic patient from her mother. Although there is a selective factor here--the letter was shown the director of our research project as an example following a talk on our double-bind theory--our ideas had no influence on the composition of this letter, as there was no prior contact with any of the parties involved. The letter reads:

Dear Janet [5)]

Just a few lines again

I talked to your Dad [6)] on the phone and he said you dident answer his letter. You better write to him.

I want to have you visit me one of these days & maybe you can visit him too.

And by the way you havent written to me. (You did call me).

[5)]Identifying data have been altered or omitted in this and subsequent letters; otherwise the copy is as exact as possible.

We are indebted for this letter to Dr. Lawrence Appleby, director of the research project "An Evaluation of Treatment Methods for Schizophrenia," supported by Project Grant OM-116 from the National Institute of Mental Health, U.S. Public Health Service.

[6)]The patient's parents are divorced, and the father remarried. The parents make a point of visiting Janet in the hospital separately.

And you know Janet I don't like to even think of Clem[7] it seems to remind me of trouble. Id rather just not think of him.

And dont you let the cigarette habit get stronger than you are.

Sometimes these habits have a way of doing that.

When I get a chance Ill get you a Carton.

But too much smoking is bad business.

I want so much too have you visit me as soon as possible, so be good and write to me.

Your Dad said you dident answer his letter so maybe you ought to, but dont tell him I told you.

Well I better close now. Hope I can visit you soon.

Lots & Lots of Love.

Mother

At first glance this may seem a rather trivial, empty and unimportant letter. Precisely because of this appearance, however, this letter is appropriate in pointing out the influential aspect of communication, and the subtlety of influence observable in some communications of mothers of schizophrenics.

Communication can be observed to have two always coexistent functions: 1) informative, and 2) directive. "... every message in transit has two sorts of meaning: ... a statement or report about events at a previous moment, and ... a command--a cause or stimulus for events at a later moment" (9, p. 179). In ordinary circumstances the "information" aspect of communication is given primary attention, but the directive or influential aspect of communication is of primary interest in this study, as being central to the interpersonal relationships of the communicating mothers and patients. The point relevant to the present study is the influence on a recipient organism's behavior--external and internal--that is exerted by reception of a message. In some instances such direc-

---

[7]The patient's husband, who does not bother to visit her in the hospital, and who is reported to have been sadistic to her.

tive effect may be related back to ordinary views of messages as informative. This is the case when a person is said to have heard certain facts and acted logically in accord with the information, but this special case is far too narrow to cover the whole area of influence by communication. The letters that are the subject of this article are not very informative in the usual sense but they certainly are directive, heavy with messages suited for interpersonal influence and manipulation.

Paradoxically, though, it is not a simple matter to notice and pull out for examination these directive messages. It is often difficult, and this difficulty lends effective--though false--support to those who deny any significant interpersonal etiology for schizophrenia. These problems are well exemplified in the Janet letter whose subtlety in terms of interpersonal influence, despite its apparent simplicity, may now be examined.

The letter begins with self-deprecation, "Just a few lines again," which also may 1) reflect deprecatively on the recipient as not worth more, and 2) make any strong impact it might have difficult to attribute to the communication. That is, since it is "just a few lines," if the patient should be upset on reading it one implication is that this outcome reflects something wrong with the patient rather than with the letter or its author.

Next, mother benevolently minds the patient's business in telling her to write her father, although the parents are divorced and avoid meeting. Similar influence is continued in the suggestion about possibly visiting father. Coupled to this is an expression of a wish that Janet might visit her, the mother. This looks positive, but may be difficult for the patient. In the first place, the statements about visiting father and visiting mother are closely juxtaposed and similar in phrasing, but very different fundamentally: One is a controlling suggestion concerning another person, the other expresses a wish of the writer; moreover, the people involved in the similarity are at odds with each other. This combination of similarity and difference is confusing in itself. Second, the apparent invitation to visit mother is vague and casual, an indefinite "one of these days" statement. Seen in context, with the recipient a daughter confined in a mental hospital, this casualness must to some extent convey a raising of hopes but treating them lightly, brushing the patient off again. Even this feeble overture toward contact is immediately followed by an underplayed ("and by the way") reproach ("You haven't written me"), and then another reversal ("You did call me"), with this also underplayed by being put in parentheses. The mother next reminds the patient of her own estranged husband; this appears as a gratuitous recalling of this painful topic to the daughter's mind while saying, "Id rather just not think of him."[8]

After this brief but comprehensive handling of family relation ships, the mother turns to the bad habit of smoking. She cautions her daughter, imputing a weakness or inability to take charge of her own smoking, though Janet is a grown married woman. Yet this as a personal accusation is obscured by the impersonal phrasing concretizing the "cigarette habit" and its influence. Then, having indirectly told Janet "Don't smoke so much," she promises to send a whole carton of cigarettes. And the gift offer, like the visit offer, is casual--"When I get a chance." Again, though, she disqualifies this offer by "too much smoking is bad business."

The letter then returns to the family themes. Again a completely indefinite hope about a visit home is held out, followed abruptly by an implied condition for such a visit--"so be good and write to me." The more complete message here then appears to be "I want to see you if you behave as I like." Yet this is uncertain too; the original statement is so inexplicit that nothing is even testable. There is also a further development on controlling the relationship of Janet and her father ("You ought to answer his letter" again) plus suggested conspiracy to conceal the mother's influence ("don't tell him I told you"). The letter is then terminated by unspecific, indefinite positive--"Hope I can visit you soon," and "Lots and lots of love."

This detailed recital of incongruent alternations: yes-only-no, do-only-don't, come-yet-wait--which may not be visible to the patient because of the vagueness and generality in the letter, its "played-down" nature, and its over-all framing as benevolent-- provides recurrent exemplification of messages fitting our double-bind concept.

This letter may also be viewed in broader outline, from several angles. First, how does it compare with patient A's description of mothers' letters? 1) This letter starts out neutrally rather than "fine." 2) Then follow several references to mother's troubles-- the divorced husband and the father-daughter relationship, daughter's not writing mother; the unpleasantness of thoughts of Clem;

---

[8]Perhaps this serves the function of getting rid of Clem from mother's mind, however, somewhat after the fashion classically described by Mark Twain in the tale "Punch, Brothers, Punch."

and the dangers of Janet's smoking. 3) All of these, though mentioned rather ambiguously, are connected with the patient in actuality, and the mother's remarks have some imputation of responsibility or blame to the daughter. 4) This mother does not then say "Don't worry about me" explicitly; nevertheless, each difficulty seems to be closed off as a subject and possible sympathetic response to it blocked, by means of another statement in which the mother reverses what has just been said or implied, or indicates "Well, I've washed my hands of that completely." And the closing offer of love and the hope of a visit completes the overall frame of benevolent interest. In sum, this letter fits with patient A's description well, but differs in that it appears less clearcut and much milder. This difference in intensity may be more apparent than real, as considered below in discussing the subtlety of communication in this letter.

The question of informative vs. directive communication in this letter now needs only brief further mention. It is obvious that the information in this letter is minimal, especially since much of what little seems to be informative statement is not such. That is, on closer examination the mother is telling the patient what Janet already knows--e.g., that Janet has not written to her, repeating what she has already said, or issuing vague cliches. Nearly every line, however, directly or indirectly tells the patient what to do, or indicates some way the patient should conceive of certain circumstances and feel in relation to them. We have no direct information on Janet's reaction to the influential messages in this letter; but from other cases where we have information on both the communication and reactions to it, including Cases C and D of this paper, we would expect these messages to be rather powerful in producing disturbance and confusion. The fact that the directive messages recurrently are reversed and contradicted does not reduce the amount of influence being communicated; influence is cumulative without regard to the plus or minus sign of its direction. Alternation of direction only tends to cancel out the possibilities for effective response to the influence, leaving stimulation but inhibition.

Subtlety is perhaps best shown by considering this letter's appearance on detailed rather than ordinary examination. On its face, the letter is simple to the point of crudity in wording, grammar, style and content. Yet more closely observed it has disclosed recurrent "double-bind" message patterns. Further, although this letter seems to convey little information its content deals almost exclusively with psychologically basic topics: relationships of the patient with family members, communication or the lack of it, control of behavior, and the patient's strength or weakness, goodness or badness. The apparent simplicity of this letter may itself be one basic factor in the subtlety of its influence: How could such a brief, simple, awkward letter amount to much? We have seen such a defense actually used by mothers whose communication was questioned as adversely influential. In interviews with families, for example, if the schizophrenic does manage to suggest that something mother said is ambiguous, or has a double meaning, he is likely to be squelched by being told everything is quite simple and he is just imagining things. Thus a mother's communications may be very influential or controlling in subtle ways that aid in concealing this and denying it, so that he who questions the influence is apt to be put down still further.

Unfortunately, a similar defense may be raised against the present authors--the accusation that we have read more into the letter than is there. Such accusations are not easy to meet, especially since they also are often backed by a general refusal even to consider the possible existence of such subtlety in communication, so that a particular case cannot be examined on its merits. We can only hope that our presentation here, as a whole, presents enough data, analysis, and collateral information to overcome such objections.

CASE C

The next specimen is a letter received from his mother by a young man who had been hospitalized during the acute stage of a schizophrenic episode, but was recovering and had not required hospitalization for about nine months at the time of the receipt of this letter. He lived by himself, across the nation from his parents. Communication was by letter and telephone.

This is one of many similar letters that were made available to the authors during a two-year period by this patient. Selection of this specific letter was based on size, scarcity of identifying family data, completeness unto itself, and proportion of personal comment. It reads:

Dear Jack:

It was so good to talk to you. While I was listening to TV I was thinking of you and hoping you'd phone or write telling us whats new with you.

We know you are getting along fine as you sound pretty good over the phone. I guess between school, apt, and Dr. X you are kept busy.

Today, Dad went to L. with an insurance adjuster.

Hope they'll make it as Monday they had to turn back from W. due to snow drifts. We really had bad freezing weather this past weekend. I've been staying at home catching up on some housework and doing some reading.

This morning being Ash Wednesday, we went to mass etc. I would like to attend mass every morning during lent. I'll try.

Honey, you mentioned that I sounded a bit upset the previous time we spoke to you. I believe that was the time Uncle Tony was expected here for a few days visit and naturally I don't approve of his bringing his dog along. Although the dog is no trouble I still don't feel like I like dogs hair all over the rugs etc. I under stand Uncle Tony left the dog with the Enniss's as he is not allowed to have the dog at Fort C. I don't know how Uncle Butch likes the idea as he is afraid of dogs having been bitten once when he was a child.

Then of course each time I receive a letter from Grandma its the usual kind, always complaining about conditions up there and how crowded the house is. She stays in her room most of the time as Liz does the cooking now.

However, the letters don't upset me as much as they used to especially since you told me that her hold on me including the rest of us is thru her tears etc. She makes her children feel sorry for her and that they don't do right by her but that is supposed to work both ways.

Don't worry about this problem as I don't get upset over it.

I have been feeling pretty well, no aches or pains. Dad too feels O. K. He dreamt he broke out with measles, this dream was followed by another one of you teaching before Z. University students--This was last week.

Well Jack nothing else is new so I'll close with all our love.

Your Mom.

This letter too seems relatively vacuous--chatty but insignificant, but on examining even its general surface pattern, we observe the aspects described by patient A. The letter starts out "fine," with what appears on the surface to be a warm greeting. The second stage soon develops with complaints about the weather, the relatives, and troubles with Grandma. The third stage in this letter varies in content but, in effect, conforms to the pattern. The son has already exposed himself to some responsibility for his mother's troubles with her mother by offering "therapeutic" advice ("since you told me"); mother's reference reaffirms and strengthens this responsibility, and the son finds himself really involved. The final three paragraphs complete the pattern--"Don't worry," "feeling pretty well," and "all our love."

However, this surface inspection of the letter fails to do justice to its complexity and subtlety. A more detailed analysis has revealed the presence in this letter of many hidden patterns, carried out by implication, sentence structure, context, allusion, word choice, and even mistakes in spelling and grammar ("slips of the pen"). We shall concentrate next on one such pattern.

Repeatedly, throughout the letter, a specific communicational pattern is presented which creates a deceptive air of consistency, since this consistency is actually a consistency of inconsistency. The pattern so rigidly adhered to is one of statement and disqualification. 1) A positive statement is made. 2) This statement is sooner or later disqualified by some other statement--either by a preceding frame-setting statement, or a following direct negation, or an indirect disqualification implied in the accompanying material. In a few instances, the positive statement is disqualified at its birth, so to speak, by the context it evokes. There is, on close inspection, an almost total absence of unmodified positive statement.

The opening paragraph contains several instances of this general pattern, including some in the interesting form of disqualification by the addition of excessive detail. [9] The initial statement of general interest and warmth--"Dear Jack, It was so good to talk

---

[9] This type of disqualification was first suggested to us by a research colleague, Eli Sturm, who pointed out the difference between "I missed you," "I missed you last Saturday night," and "I missed you last Saturday night at 10:16 p.m." In an important relationship, such differences have more than lexical significance.

to you"--is immediately followed by further statements which convey a partial denial of the interest. "While I was listening to TV, I was thinking of you" implies that the mother's interest was more casual, or divided between him and TV. The initial warmth is additionally disqualified by blame for neglect implied in the statement that she was "hoping you'd phone or write," in view of her many previous expressions of dissatisfaction about insufficient communication. At the same time there is the implicit message that what the mother was concerned with was relief from her own anxiety, carried in the expressions "It was so good" and "hoping."

In the second paragraph, the pattern is continued. The strong "getting along fine" is scaled down immediately to "pretty good." The "know" of the first sentence is qualified by 1) "We know," and 2) the following "I guess." This qualification is accomplished both by the step down from "know" to "guess" and the contrast between "We" and "I." The writer can be positive to the degree of "know" when an ambiguous plural is used but expresses herself indefinitely when the individual pronoun is used. The downgrading goes further in "We know... as you sound pretty good over the phone"; "We know," ambiguous as it already is, is given for its support such weak evidence as three indefinites--"sound," "pretty good," and "over the phone." Moreover, "over the phone" is written against the background of the parents' frequent expressions dissatisfaction with the phone and mail as media of communication between parents and patient, so this modifies "We know" in a specifically negative way.

The mother goes on to refer to "school, apt, and Dr. X." in a way visible as similar to "fine" and then "pretty good," when these items are considered in terms of what they currently represented in the patient's life: "School" was the most successful area--in that the patient had returned to college after his acute schizophrenic episode, and he was at least passing his courses, although the college work was quite difficult owing to his difficulties with anxiety and defective concentration. The "apt" (apartment) had a more oppressive connotation; it was the scene of the patient's most painful loneliness--the isolated rented rooms that were both the patient's defense against outside entanglements and the physical embodiment of the lonely prison in which he was emotionally confined.

Further, the parents--mother and father--had, about a month before, spent two weeks with the patient at his "apt," and the visit had been a stormy one. The "apt" then has the connotations of these storms and whatever guilt the patient may still have felt for his rebellious behavior. The guilt is further emphasized by the next reference--to the doctor, who had been conceived of by the parents as the promoter of these rebellious attitudes. The reference to the doctor also has its own special significance in that it served as a reminder of the patient's illness--his misery and humiliation, the many painful symptoms attendant upon the schizophrenic episode. School, apartment, and Dr. X, then, though presented by the mother as if positive, all have negative connotations for the son.

Subsequent paragraphs follow this general pattern. However, the pattern of disqualification is also carried through at a more macroscopic level, as two examples will indicate:

"Honey, you mentioned that I sounded a bit upset the previous time we spoke to you," etc. "Honey" is thoroughly stripped of positive connotation, a common aftermath of the use of terms of endearment in these letters, by the five-paragraph barrage that follows it. The nature of this sequence is related to the patient's having put his finger, several days previously, on symptomatic behavior in his parents. In a letter written two days prior to the mother's letter, the father wrote, "When I wrote that letter (a confused, incoherent, repetitious letter about cars and their prices-- in contrast to father's usual overly cheerful, well-organized letters) the only thing that was on my mind was the contemplated visit of Uncle Tony and his boxer dog--the thought of the visit affects me. I do not show it on the surface but unconsciously or subconsciously it works on me. These visits are getting to work on mother also. I guess that is what you read between the lines of my letter. Another thing that has been bothering me lately is my school work (teaching)."

Thus, Patient C has commented on father's disorganization in the prior letter, and also commented that mother "sounded a bit upset" on the phone. The five paragraphs following her acknowledgment of this message are largely a defensive denial or disqualification of C's remarks on their symptoms of emotional stress. (There is actually some external evidence that marital strife--soon followed by an uneasy truce--was responsible for their symptoms of stress.) This defensive and involved denial carries the implications that "Honey" was quite nasty commenting on his parents' behavior, and anyway nothing important ever happened; yet nothing is clarified nor is he really told to mind his own business.

A second example of this macroscopic disqualification starts in the next paragraph. "Then of course each time I receive a letter from Grandma" is the opening of a four-paragraph sequence in which, ignoring the secondary negations and denials within paragraphs, we can observe a series of main statements with each a modification, a scaling down, of the previous one: 1) Grandma's letters are usually complaining and (implied) unpleasant. 2) However, these letters don't upset mother "as much as they used to." 3) But then, she doesn't "get upset over it" at all. 4) Finally, "I have been feeling pretty well." The movement, in four paragraphs, is from a state of unpleasantness to a claimed state of well-being.

Add to this macroscopic graduated disqualification the subnegations of each step in the sequence and an extremely complex self-negating and negating-the-negation sort of structure emerges. We can examine a brief passage to clarify this idea.

Take the last installment, "I have been feeling pretty well, no aches or pains." "Pretty well" can have two meanings. One meaning, a positive one, conveys that the individual is feeling better than usual. This meaning could be the one intended consciously by the mother. As such, it plays its part in the negation sequence of the four paragraphs. But, in the absence of a direct statement from the mother about the intended meaning of the passage, and in association with the many other instances of negation, a less affirmative meaning must also be considered. "Pretty well" then becomes "not so well" or "fair shape, but not really good." With this meaning in mind, we have a wellness which is a negation of the disturbance originally stimulating the whole sequence, but the negating wellness is itself modified by "pretty"; even the disqualification is disqualified--in part.

Furthermore, "no aches or pains" seems to shift the whole emphasis on emotional states to physical states. The sequence of statements has been about emotional states but the physical well-being of the writer is suddenly interjected by the reference to somatic complaints. Again, "well" as a negation of "a bit upset" is cast into doubt, in a new way. But this disqualification of "well" by "no aches or pains" is possibly promoted by even a further implication. The "no aches and pains" statement has the sound of "none right now, but they're just around the corner." And then, since one does not suffer aches and pains ordinarily unless something is definitely wrong, and a pathologic condition is usually well established before these symptoms communicate its presence, doubt is then raised in the form of the specter of an as-yet-unannounced pathology implicit in "no aches or pains."

In the conclusion of the letter, there is a macroscopic example that transcends this single letter. The final "Well Jack nothing else is new so I'll close with all our love Your Mom" is similar, if not identical, to concluding phrases in letter after letter over at least a two-year period, and perhaps longer; the conventionality effectively negates "all our love." In addition, there is the use of the son's personal name within the context of this conventionality. Ordinarily, the use of the name would bespeak warmth and a personal touch, but set in the coldness of this conventionality, what is lacking becomes even more conspicuous. Finally, there is the contrast between the name and the signature "Your Mom," which itself is half folksy, half a formal title of reference.

Out of many different possible directions, the preceding analysis, in line with our theoretical interests, was focused specifically on the pattern of disqualification of almost all statements. We believe this pattern is typical in families of schizophrenics, rather than unique to this mother or this letter;[10] however, this letter particularly exhibits "progressive disqualification," as described, and the occurrence of "incipient" or "condensed" reversals, in which a position is only half stated, and then a contrasting one is half stated. These special patterns appear as rather different from the sort of reversals occurring repeatedly but subtly in Case B above, and from the very sharp reversals to be noted in Case D below, but they do fit with the more lengthy, circumstantial, and tentative style of this mother's letter, and they do fit within the general double-bind pattern as 1) a situation in which a person is presented with incongruent communications, 2) "which are not readily visible as such because... the messages are on different levels." The double bind can be developed, as demonstrated, in a variety of different ways--by apparent contradiction, by context, by implication. The crucial point is that of the disqualifying nature of the relationship between the two messages--i.e., they are incongruent and on different levels, each modifying the other. This however, is not enough. As envisioned, the double bind depends further on the inability or failure of the victim to "escape from the field." In other words, the victim must be unable to resolve the contradiction by "mature," or objective, methods: "You are putting me in a confusing position. I am not sure what to believe."

---

[10] Communication in the families of schizophrenics is discussed more generally by Haley (7).

"Oh, come on now, this is silly." Such inability presumably depends jointly on the way the incongruence is concealed or denied, and the receiver's own habits of response.

In this case, clinical material is available to confirm that the patient was strongly affected by this kind of communication. He repeatedly referred in his therapeutic hours, in a disturbed, painful, and ineffectual way, to letters received from his mother. Among other comments stimulated by this particular letter, he stated, "She says that her relatives upset her, you see, then it bounces onto my old man and it bounces onto me and so round and round we go." This comment was uttered with irritation and moderate bitterness; the underlying mood was depression. Again, "Between her and her mother, they can get ten thousand gallons of water out of a God-damn drop of sand--now don't ask me how they do it, but they can do it--dry sand! They can sure wring the tears out. I don't know." This comment was begun with irritation and a general tone of depression. The affect swiftly evolved to a wry, humorous mood. The comment ended with an explosion of inappropriate and forced laughter.

The clinical implications of this presentation are obvious. We have examined a stimulus and have noted the response. There is evidence that the stimulus pattern and the disturbed behavior response are closely related. These letters offer us the opportunity of observing how, in certain typical varieties, double binds can be presented. To amplify, let us consider letters by another mother of a schizophrenic offspring.

CASE D

Presentation of a set of several letters from one mother has two special purposes: 1) Certain patterns of communication may be visible only in combinations of these letters, not separately. 2) Some--though necessarily a limited--direct sample of the consistency and repetitiveness of such letters may thus be given.

Patient D was a young man who had suddenly developed a schizophrenic illness several years before the time of these letters, shortly after the sudden and unexpected death of his father. His clinical course had been stormy, including three hospitalizations, much psychotherapy, electroshock therapy, insulin shock therapy; at one point even lobotomy was advised. By the time of these letters, though, he had been improving gradually but continuously for some time in outpatient psychotherapy and was very concerned about increasing his external responsibilities, as by going to college or getting a job. He had a few friends, and was living in his own quarters in a town about 50 miles distant from his mother; they had seen each other only two or three times during the previous two years. However, he was largely dependent for financial support on the weekly sums his mother sent him along with her letters, which constituted a large part of her own earnings; she was continuing to work although she had remarried about a year prior to the time of these letters.

Dearest Freddie--

Almost forgot today is Thursday--I hope you are feeling O.K.-- I note on the Dr. bill that you saw him two days in a row--& am wondering if you are unusually worried or upset about something. I can't understand your being concerned in the least about taking an exam--You could pass it with your eyes shut. Honey--if I could pass an exam after all these years--& without your mental capacity--then it is silly for you to even give it a thought. Honey-- please don't be upset about school-- You are just trying it--If it doesn't work out--so you tried--

I failed at a number of jobs but kept trying because I _had_ to work--Many times I felt that I couldn't take it--lying awake at night dreading & fearing the next day--because I was scared stiff to go to work--

About your living arrangement--I don't think you can find anything cheaper--it is just a matter of saving the train fare--

How does Dr. X feel about your going to school?

We saw "At the Grand" last nite & enjoyed it--Paul Muni is wonderful--Do you eat out still--every nite? What is your phone number? Please send it to me--Honey, shall I send you some cookies? Do you have any refrigerator space? Write soon & answer my questions--

Loads of love--

Mother--

The letter begins with the superlative affectionate term of address "Dearest." In context, however, this term too is ambiguous, since this mother invariably uses it, even in the occasional letters in which she is overtly and unmistakably angry at her son.

The opening sentence states that she almost forgot it was Thursday. Since Thursday is the usual day of sending her son the money on which he lives, this emphasis suggests that the financial tie is a primary factor in their relationship, in contrast to "Dearest." Yet she "almost forgot." Is the message that she is not really focused on the financial side of the relationship--although later and in other letters there are references to the importance of the son's being careful in his spending, requests that he should get a job, and remarks on how hard she works for this money? Or does it mean that she could forget sending the money in spite of its realistic importance to him? Still further, if he were more financially independent, would she write to him at all? This is important since, although the receipt of letters is often disturbing to the patients, clinical experience indicates that they are also very much concerned about losing contact with mother.

Next she hopes that he is feeling O. K. --but makes it evident that she doubts this. She is concerned about the doctor's bill, but in other letters insists that he continue his treatment and make the most of it, she will manage to pay the bills somehow. Further, her remarks suggest--she is very aware of the dates on the bill although so uncertain of the day of the week--that she checks and evaluates differently concerning him than concerning herself. This difference also is reflected in her next choice of words; she "wonders" if he "worries" rather than saying that she herself is worrying. This wording emphasizes any worrying he may do, while leaving him more alone with it, by placing herself in a different and superior position of "benevolent" concern, rather than a more similar and equal one.

She then states the presumed cause of his presumed worrying-- a coming examination--and labels any concern over this as illegitimate and inexcusable: something "silly" that she "can't understand." Why? Because she is sure of success for him, knows his capability. This statement, however, defines his position as one where he can't win; there are two apparent alternatives, both not good. [11] 1) If he succeeds, it is really no accomplishment, since "You could do it with your eyes shut." 2) If, however, he should somehow fail, her emphasis on ability and ease makes that failure worse. In addition, the mother draws a picture of herself complementary to that for the son: She is much worse off than he

---

[11]See also discussion of the "illusion of alternatives" by Weakland and Jackson (11).

is, older, out of practice, less smart--yet she could pass an examination. This puts her in a "can't-lose" position--failure would be understandable and success real accomplishment--which further emphasizes his "can't-win" situation, while he is influenced both to sympathize with her condition and to look up to her example of success!

Then comes a sudden reversal of this entire picture. There is now a prediction of possible failure, and a statement that it doesn't matter--or maybe doesn't: "You are just trying it--If it doesn't work out--so you tried."

Only this still is not the end of it. In the next paragraph she writes of how she herself struggled and worried. If this account of her difficulties had appeared earlier, in close relation to statements about the son's having similar difficulties, it could seem more a positive message in their relationship, with a possibility for these words to indicate mother-son identification and support, in spite of her tone of rivalry, an outdoing even in difficulties. But it comes after she has criticized him for worrying, and has indicated he certainly should never fail--but perhaps is about to do so. In this context a message referring to a similarity is used in a way that sharpens the picture of oppositeness and differentiation between them: she faced greater obstacles with less help and resources than he, and yet she succeeded; this dual message also suggests again that he should be sorry for her yet look up to her. In addition, since she succeeded because she had to work, while he is supported by her, the implication again is that he will fail. Somehow it is made to sound as if this will occur in spite of her benevolence, although her own remarks about the virtues of necessity directly suggest that the son might fail because of such help.

The letter then shifts abruptly to a new topic and level of discourse, practical arrangements about going to school. These few sentences cannot be examined in detail without considerable reference to preceding correspondence. They deal with the matter of mother's advising her son where to live both "nicely" and economically, a hot topic involving her general concern to inquire into, direct, and supervise her son's behavior closely, though indirectly or covertly.

The inquiry about the therapist's views on the son's going to school is straightforward on its face, but it appears only after mother has herself delivered a set of positive and final--though variable and contradictory--pronouncements on this subject. Thus

this inquiry--and any importance of the therapist--is largely disqualified by presentation as an afterthought, although it still throws
into question the indication of all the opening remarks that mother
knows what's what as helpful authority for her son on his school
problems. Now she asks, "What does the doctor think?"

The final paragraph begins with a theme common for this mother; she (and her husband) went out socially, to a public event, and
enjoyed it. Then, however, follow remarks or inquiries, such as
"Do you eat out still--every nite?" and so on, which suggest a contrasting picture of the son's circumstances, made clearer in other
letters: Her going out to dinner, the theater, concerts, is reasonable and proper, indeed a positive social and cultural value. His
eating out is wasteful expense, and an indication of his aloneness
and lack of home life, but this bad and sad state is his own fault,
for ignoring her efforts to provide maternal care and feeding despite the distance separating them. Finally he should "write
soon"--and why? To "answer my questions." "Loads of love"
is an habitual ending.

Against this background, we may consider this mother's next
letter more briefly:

Dearest Freddie--

Hope you are O.K.--The only reason I thought you were concerned about taking the test was because you wrote that you will
be glad when it is over. When does school start--? Honey, I hope
& pray that you will be happier going to school--& feeling a sense
of accomplishment & also preparing for a future--I trust that you
are ready for the concentration & routine that it will require. If
not--then you can try again later or try something else--Perhaps
you can start with a limited program--That would probably be
best--The most difficult thing is to get started.

Honey--I don't know how you are living, but, perhaps you aren't
managing very well-- It seems that even sending you more doesn't
seem to make a difference--Before, you were taking your rent out--
Now, it is paid & you still have trouble getting along. There isn't
any more I can do--Having to pay Dr. X $50 or $60 a month makes
a big (as written this looks like "beg") difference--& I am spending
my entire salary on your needs--so am doing all I can. If only you
can earn your supplementary needs at least--because $35 a week
should take care of your necessities if you are managing properly
--You would do better to eat at home more--You can buy a good

steak & with a vegetable & fruit, have a better meal than you can buy for the same price out. Honey--I would like to come down & bring you a box of groceries--& sundries--It doesn't pay to send it--How about it?

How about going out with us to something? If you'd like to, we will arrange something. Haven't heard from anyone--I talk to Joanie occasionally--

Well Honey--Good luck tomorrow--altho' you don't need it to do well in the test-- Please write soon & let me know how everything is--Take good care of yourself--Loads of love,

Mother--

Regards from Moe (the stepfather).

P.S. Will bake something real soon--to send you--Would rather bring it to you--I miss you very much--

I'm so used to typing, I can't even write decently anymore--excuse the scribbling.

Now, after the last letter devoted mainly to his anxiety over a coming examination, it appears doubtful whether he was anxious in the first place. Perhaps both mother and son have been vague or ambiguous in expression on this; this question could only be settled by examining the son's letters also. It remains striking that regardless of what the son's message is stated to be by the mother, she largely takes a converse or opposite position. The two letters together show this neatly. In the first, she sees him as anxious, and insists this is nonsense. In the second, she agrees maybe he wasn't anxious, but then indicates that perhaps he should be: She "hopes and prays" he will be happier at school, and "trusts" he will be ready--both suggesting considerable doubt and uncertainty, where before she knew how able and ready he was. Also there are suggestions of the possibility of failure, and emphasis on initial difficulties. And at the end of the letter there is a further reversal back to the theme that he is really ready and able.

The rest of the letter contains additional statements bearing on the other themes noted for the first letter, again presented in a way that involves incongruent messages and invidious comparisons between the mother and the patient.

A very brief letter written a month later, just after the son had succeeded in entering college, provides a footnote to the preceding pair:

Dearest Freddie--

We heard your ring just as we were putting the key in the door --I am so thrilled--& wish you all the very best--Just get your school work & don't worry about anything else--Here is your chance, Honey & I know you will do well--You have what it takes --I'm very proud of you--

Loads of love--
Mother

Moe is also happy for you & wishes you luck

P.P.S. If if doesn't work out--& youre' not ready--don't worry--at least you tried.

Once more, there is a positive initial statement or overstatement--and then an undercutting reversal which appears almost an overt request that he fail. It is strikingly reminiscent of the statement of a schizophrenic patient of Bateson's on his mother's attitude toward his father's ambitions: "She was right there with him, encouraging him and encouraging him, and ready to help him quit at any moment."

Thus these three letters again present a pervasive pattern of disqualifying reversals; recurrently one statement, which alone may appear definite, is followed by a related statement of almost opposite meaning or influence. Also re-reversal may follow, apparently without limit. Details of content, specificity, length, and timing may vary, but the basic pattern is ubiquitous. Furthermore, though these reversals may seem rather blatant on analysis, again they might not easily be noticed and handled. The actual recipient of the letters was dependent on the mother both financially and emotionally, and thus in a poor position to be objectively observant and critical, and this is reinforced by the mother's repeated assertions of her benevolence and sacrifice. Also, each half of a conflicting pair of messages is commonly presented in such a sugar-coated form as to ensure its separate and uncritical acceptance: Demands for success are given together with strong compliments on ability, then suggestions of failure with prefabricated plausible excuses.

Another recurrent pattern of disqualification of messages consists in abrupt changes of subject and style (from another angle, changes of context)--e.g., from the hot issue about education to apparently casual remarks on daily activities. These shifts disqualify by seeming to drop a matter, yet leaving it hanging; instead of a reversal of direction, there is an unsignaled left turn. Abruptness plus casualness makes the occurrence and influence of these shifts also difficult to notice and handle. Both of these broad patterns thus fit in with the preceding cases and with our basic concept of the double bind. [12)]

Some clinical information again is available to support our prediction that such communication would have certain disturbing and confusing influences. During a three-year period of continuous contact with this patient, there was not one instance of beneficial effect from receiving a letter from the mother. On several occasions, his reactions to the letters were so intense--of a paranoid or a depressive nature--that extra therapy sessions were necessary. More specifically, after receiving the first of these letters, patient D was hyperactive, obsessed with themes of violence and destruction, preoccupied with his "homosexuality" and how he was different from others, and interested, in a disturbed way, in hypnosis and influence. The three letters presented here are part of a sequence of letters about the patient's college plans that was particularly disturbing. The patient was alternately preoccupied with the necessity of determining what his mother wanted him to do about college and experiencing acute rage at her. Both of these states hampered applying himself to studies and he withdrew from college within two weeks after having finally started.

[12)]It has been noted earlier that these letters also exhibit important ambiguities, as with "almost forgot it was Thursday" in this case. As analyzed in terms of probable implications, though from the nature of the case these cannot be fully proven, this ambiguous passage also involves conflicting messages, or latent incongruencies, highly concealed by the brief and fragmentary nature of the explicit message. Thus there appears to be a significant similarity between the overt double-bind pattern and at least a certain type of ambiguous communication.

In these Case D letters especially, an opportunity to observe relatively directly just what the mother communicates about the mother-child relationship is provided by some messages that make explicit or implicit comparisons between them. Two examples have already been discussed: The mother's remarks on worry and struggle in relation to success or failure, and on her social life versus the son's social life. A third such comparison is most clear in many letters not included here. The mother criticizes the son for not writing her enough and claims that his brevity must be designed to shut her out from his life. But, judging from dates and internal evidence, her own letters are no more frequent than his; also, she herself acknowledges that they are very brief but explains this away in terms of her busy schedule of activity, especially her job. This, in the context of her working to support the son, puts the onus on him again, and more; it's really because of him, and even for him, that her letters are hurried and brief.

In each of these instances the mother's comparisons, at the level of evaluation, state that they are very different, with herself fundamentally in the right and the son in the wrong, though the mother may magnanimously allow and excuse his wrongness or failure. When the descriptive content of statements is closely viewed, though, their stated behavior appears as very similar. This incongruence is marked indeed, while at the same time it is quite difficult to see clearly--some comparisons are explicit and others implicit--statements about similar behavior are spatially separated, and so on. Thus the double-bind pattern of obscured incongruence of related messages at different levels is very strongly present in communication directly about the mother-son relationship. Seeing this pattern provides one basis for understanding not only the difficulties and unhappiness of the participants in such a relationship, but also its duration, the commonly noted yet important fact that schizophrenics and their mothers have great trouble really getting together or getting apart, even over a lifetime. Relatedness and getting together are blocked when any similarities in behavior or outlook are denied by statements conveying "You're different" and "You're wrong." Personal identity and getting apart are blocked when individual differences in behavior or standards are denied by statements emphasizing similarity or claiming "Whatever you do is all right with me."

SUMMARY AND CONCLUSIONS

We have analyzed examples of letters by three mothers to their schizophrenic offspring. The intensity of this particular examination makes it important to reemphasize two points: 1) We do not see the mother of the patient alone as wittingly or unwittingly "the cause" of his behavior. We do believe that schizophrenia has its etiology mainly in family interaction, in which the father, the eventual patient, and the mother all play a large part. We have here studied letters of mothers because we think them not unique, but significant, and because they were available. Indeed, this availability may have resulted from the mothers' being the ones most concerned about the patient--not just because they are "overprotective" or managing, but equally because the fathers are "weak" and any siblings endeavor to avoid or escape the family difficulties. 2) Given these letters for study, they could have been considered from many points of view, some less apparently cold and critical. Thus the letters could be read for what they express about the writers, with the variability and inconsistency in the letters seen as reflecting the anxiety and uncertainty of these mothers as they try hard to make helpful contact with their schizophrenic children.

Here, however, we have had to select, and we chose: 1) to examine the nature of these letters as observable communication, while curbing inferences about the writers' personalities and motivations; 2) to consider the effects of such communication on its receivers.

Our detailed examination of these letters has disclosed that almost no statement ever is allowed to stand, clearly and unambiguously. Rather, another message disqualifying it, in any of a variety of ways, occurs. Further, this alteration, and the difference between the messages, is not itself made clear or explicit, as it would be by such messages as "I changed my mind on that" or a statement of different context. Instead, the differing statement is given as if it were a continuation along the same line, so that each is cast in question by the other, while the incongruence between them is ignored and obscured. In terms of formal patterns of communication, this amounts to the existence of a pervasive pattern of concealed incongruence between closely related messages.

In terms of influence, a corresponding characteristic pattern exists: First there is a message stimulating the recipient to make some particular response, often amounting to a demand for a certain action or feeling (or, negatively, a prohibition). Second, at once or after some delay insufficient to complete the response, there is another message which calls for an opposing or incompatible response. And there is denial or concealment of the exertion of influence. All this occurs at a variety of message and behavioral levels. It seems reasonable to expect paralysis or frantic activity, plus general confusion or suspicion, in response to such a pervasive and general pattern of concealed strong but incompatible influence. [13] This expectation has had confirmation both from direct observation of patients' reactions to these letters in two cases, and from patient A's statements about the reactions of himself and other schizophrenic patients. Also A's statements about the nature of such letters agree with the direct data of actual letters.

Finally, we may note again that both the major pattern of communication discerned in these letters and its effects on their recipients agree closely in main outline with our research group's original and prior concept of the double bind as a communicational pattern and our hypothesis of its relationship to schizophrenia and its etiology. While these communications by the mothers of patients represent only a segment of the information relevant and necessary for any comprehensive consideration of schizophrenia and its etiology, within this limitation we have pointed out some specific connections between data and theory.

REFERENCES

1. Bateson, G. A theory of play and fantasy. Psychiat. Res. Rep., 2:39-51, 1955.
2. Bateson, G., Jackson, D. D., Haley, J. and Weakland, J. H. Toward a theory of schizophrenia. Behavioral Sc., 1:251-264, 1956. (See p. 31, this vol.)
3. Bowen, M., Dysinger, R. H., and Basamania, Betty. The role of the father in families with a schizophrenic patient. Am. J. Psychiatry, 115:1017-1020, 1959.
4. Fleck, S., Freedman, D. X., Cornelison, A., Lidz, T. and Terry, D. The Intrafamilial Environment of the Schizophrenic Patient: V. The Understanding of Symptomatology Through the Study of Family Interaction. Presented at American Psychiatric Association Meeting, Chicago, May 1957.
5. Fry, W. F., Jr. Disturbed behavior on hospital wards. Psychiatric Quart. Suppl., Part II, 33:1-35, 1959.
6. Haley, J. Paradoxes in play, fantasy, and psychotherapy. Psychiat. Res. Rep., 2:52-58, 1955.

---

[13]The relationship between such incongruent communication and behavioral disturbance in a different context is examined by Fry (5).

7. Haley, J. The family of the schizophrenic: a model system. J. Nerv. Ment. Dis., 129:357-374, 1959. (See p. 171, this vol.)
8. Jackson, D. D. A note on the importance of trauma in the genesis of schizophrenia. Psychiatry, 20:181-184, 1957. (See p. 23, this vol.)
9. Ruesch, J. and Bateson, G. Communication: The Social Matrix of Psychiatry, Norton, New York, 1951.
10. Weakland, J. H. The "double bind" hypothesis of schizophrenia and three-party interaction. In The Etiology of Schizophrenia, D. D. Jackson (Ed.), Basic Books, New York, 1960.
11. Weakland, J. H. and Jackson, D. D. Patient and therapist observations on the circumstances of a schizophrenic episode. A. M. A. Arch. Neurol. Psychiat., 79:554-547, 1958. (See p. 87, this vol.)
12. Wynne, L. C., Ryckoff, I. M., Day, J. and Hirsch, S. I. Pseudo-mutuality in the family relations of schizophrenics. Psychiatry, 21:205-220, 1958.

AN INTERACTIONAL DESCRIPTION OF SCHIZOPHRENIA

Jay Haley

Despite all that is said about difficulties in interpersonal relations, psychiatric literature does not offer a systematic way of describing the interpersonal behavior of the schizophrenic so as to
differentiate that behavior from the normal. The schizophrenic's
internal processes are often described in terms of ego weakness,
primitive logic, or dissociated thinking, but his interpersonal behavior is usually presented in the form of anecdotes. This paper
will present a system for describing schizophrenic interactions
with other persons, a system that is of necessity based on a theoretical framework describing all interpersonal relationships. To
actually make a classification system of interpersonal relations
would require the herculean task of making natural history studies
of all kinds of people interacting with each other. This paper will
merely suggest an approach to such a classification system, first
discussing the problems involved in classifying interpersonal relations, then presenting and analyzing a conversation between two
schizophrenics, and finally indicating the significance of this kind
of approach.

The following conversation between two hospitalized schizophrenics, a brief excerpt from the verbatim conversation that will be reproduced at greater length later in this article, is an example of
the kind of interaction the paper attempts to classify.

Smith: Do you work at the air base? Hm?
Jones: You know what I think of work, I'm thirty-three in June,
do you mind?
Smith: June?
Jones: Thirty-three years old in June. This stuff goes out the
window after I live this, uh--leave this hospital. So I can't get my

Reprinted from PSYCHIATRY, 22, No. 4:321-332 (November 1959).
Copyright, The William Alanson White Psychiatric Foundation, Inc.
Washington, D.C.; reproduced by permission.

vocal cords back. So I lay off cigarettes. I'm a spatial condition, from outer space myself, no shit.

In this conversation no intrapsychic processes are immediately apparent. There is no dissociated thinking, autism, or withdrawal from reality. From what the men say one might conjecture the presence of such processes as dissociated thinking, but even without conjecture it should be possible to state what is present in this interpersonal behavior which differentiates these men from other men.

There are at least three possible psychiatric approaches to these data. The classical approach would determine whether or not the two young men are in contact with "reality." When one of them says he is from outer space and the other says the hospital is an air base, the classical theoretician would draw his conclusion of schizophrenia. He would analyze the data no further, because classical psychiatric theory assumes that these men are not responding to each other or to their environment but are behaving in an essentially random way because of some organic pathology.

Another approach, the intrapsychic, would center around the thought processes of the two patients. The analyst would conjecture about what the patients must have been thinking, or what kind of peculiar logic might have produced these odd associations. The intrapsychic point of view would presume that the conversation is meaningful, that it is based upon distorted thought processes, and that it contains so many associations unique to these men that it is necessary to know their life histories to understand why particular statements were made. From this point of view an analysis of the data is pointless, since insufficient information is provided by the conversation alone. The young men are "obviously" schizophrenic, and their statements are symbolic manifestations of deeply rooted fantasy ideas.

Finally, there is the interpersonal approach to these data, which emphasizes the ways in which the two men interact, or behave, with each other. This approach assumes that the two men are responding to each other rather than merely to their own thoughts, and that they respond in ways different from normal ways. What is potentially most scientific about the interpersonal approach is its emphasis upon observable data. The ways in which people interact with each other can be observed, whereas the identification of thought processes is inevitably based on conjecture. What is lacking in the interpersonal approach is a systematic descriptive system differentiating the deviant from the normal ways in which people interact with each other.

An ideal classification of interpersonal relations would indicate types of psychopathology, or differentiate people into classes, according to the presence or absence of certain readily observable sequences in their interaction with others. If such an ideal system could be developed, it would not only clarify diagnosis, currently based upon an antiquated system, but also clarify the etiology of psychopathology. If one says that a patient is withdrawn from reality, one says nothing about the processes which provoked this withdrawal. If one says that a patient interacts with people in certain deviant ways, then it is potentially possible to describe the learning situation which taught the person to behave in these ways.

ESTABLISHMENT OF AN INTERPERSONAL RELATIONSHIP

When two people meet for the first time and begin to establish a relationship, a wide range of behavior is potentially possible between them. They may exchange compliments, insults, sexual advances, statements that one is superior to the other, and so on. As the two people define their relationship with each other, they work out together what sort of communicative behavior is to take place in this relationship. From all the possible messages they select certain kinds and reach agreement that these rather than others shall be included. Their agreement on what is and what is not to take place can be called a mutual definition of the relationship. Every message they interchange either reinforces this definition or suggests a shift in it. If a young man puts his arm around a girl, he is indicating that amorous behavior is to be included in their relationship. If the girl says, "No, no," and withdraws from him, she is indicating that amorous behavior is to be excluded. The relationship they have together, whether amorous or platonic, is defined by the kind of messages they mutually agree shall be acceptable between them. This agreement is never permanently worked out but is constantly in process as one or the other proposes a new sort of message or as the environmental situation changes and provokes change in their behavior.

If human communication took place at only one level, the working out, or defining, of a relationship would be a simple matter of the presence or absence of messages. In that case there would probably be no difficulties in interpersonal relationships. However, human beings not only communicate, but they also communicate about that communication. They not only say something, but they also qualify or label what they say. In the example above, the young lady says, "No, no," and also withdraws from the young man. Her physical withdrawal qualifies, and is qualified by, her verbal statement. Since the qualification affirms her message, there is no particular difficulty. She is making it clear that amorous behavior does not belong in their relationship. But suppose she had said, "No, no," and moved closer to the young man. By snuggling up to him she would have qualified incongruently, or denied, her statement. When a message is qualified incongruently, then a relationship becomes more complex than when a message is simply present or absent. A classification of human behavior must take into account at least two levels of communication. To describe interpersonal behavior one must deal not only with communicative behavior but the qualifications of that behavior by the participants.

Any communicative behavior interchanged between two people does not exist separately from other behavior which accompanies and comments upon it. If one person says, "I'm glad to see you," his tone of voice qualifies his statement and is qualified in turn by it and by other qualifying messages that might also be present. Communication between people consists of 1) the context in which it takes place, 2) verbal messages, 3) vocal and linguistic patterns, and 4) bodily movement. As people communicate, their relationship is defined as much by the qualifications of their messages as by the presence or absence of messages. A person may make a criticism with a smile or a frown. The smile or frown as much as the criticism defines the relationship. An employee may tell his boss what to do, thus defining their relationship as one between equals, but he may qualify his statement with a self-effacing gesture or a weak tone of voice and thereby indicate that it is a relationship between unequals. If people always qualified what they said in a congruent way, relationships would be defined clearly and simply, even though two levels of communication were functioning. However, when a statement indicating one sort of relationship is qualified by a contradictory communication, difficulties in interpersonal relations become inevitable.

It is important to emphasize that one cannot not qualify a message. A person must speak a verbal message in a particular tone of voice, and if he says nothing, that, too, is qualified by the posture he presents and the context in which his muteness appears. Although the meanings of some qualifying messages are obvious, as when one pounds one's fists on the table when making a statement, subtle qualifications are always present. For example, the slightest upward inflection on a word may define a statement as a question rather than an assertion. A slight smile may classify a statement as ironical rather than serious. A minute body movement backwards qualifies an affectionate statement and indicates that it is made with some reservations. The absence of a message may also qualify another message. For example, if a person is silent when he is expected to speak, the silence becomes a qualifying message, and if a man neglects to kiss his wife good-bye when she expects it, the absence of this movement qualifies his other messages as much as, if not more than, the presence of it.

People tend to judge whether others are being sincere or deceitful, whether they are serious or joking, and so on, by whether they affirm what they say by congruent qualifications. And when one person responds to another with his own definition of the relationship between them, this response is to all levels of messages.

CONTROL IN A RELATIONSHIP

When one person communicates a message to another, he is maneuvering to define the relationship. The other person is thereby posed the problem of accepting or rejecting the relationship offered. He can let the message stand, thereby accepting the other person's definition, or counter with a maneuver defining it differently. He may also accept the other person's maneuver but qualify his acceptance with a message indicating that he is letting the other person get by with the maneuver.

For example, if a young man spontaneously puts his arm around a young lady, she must either accept this message, thereby letting him define the relationship, or oppose it, thereby defining the relationship herself. Or she might have controlled the definition by inviting this behavior. She may also accept it with the qualification that she is letting him put his arm around her. By labeling his message as one permitted by her, she is maintaining control of the relationship.

Any two people are posed these mutual problems: What messages, or what kinds of behavior, are to take place in this relationship? And who is to control what is to take place in the relationship and thereby control the definition of the relationship? It is hypothesized here that the nature of human communications requires people to deal with these problems, and interpersonal relations can be classified in terms of the different ways in which they do deal with them.

It must be emphasized that no one can avoid being involved in a struggle over the definition of his relationship with someone else. Everyone is constantly involved in defining his relationship or countering the other person's definition. If a person speaks, he is inevitably indicating what sort of relationship he has with the other person. By whatever he says, he is indicating, "This is the sort of relationship where this is said." If a person remains mute, he is also inevitably defining a relationship because by not speaking he is circumscribing the other person's behavior. If a person wishes to avoid defining his relationship with another and therefore talks only about the weather, he is indicating that their communication should be neutral, and this defines the relationship.

A basic rule of communications theory proposed by Bateson[1] maintains that it is difficult for a person to avoid defining, or taking control of the definition of, his relationship with another. According to this rule all messages not only report but also influence or command. A statement such as, "I feel bad today," is not merely a description of the internal state of the speaker. It also expresses something like, "Do something about this," or "Think of me as a person who feels bad." Even if one remains silent, trying not to influence another person, the silence becomes an influencing factor in the interchange. It is impossible for a person to hand over to another the entire initiative regarding what behavior is to be allowed in the relationship. If he tries to do this, he is controlling the relationship by indicating that it is one in which the other person is to determine what behavior is to take place. For example, a patient may say to a therapist, "I can't decide anything for myself; I want you to tell me what to do." By saying this, he seems to be telling the therapist to control the relationship by directing the behavior in it. But when the patient requests that the therapist tell him what to do, he is telling the therapist what to do. This paradox can arise because two levels are always being communicated--for example: 1) "I am reporting that I need to be told what to do," and 2) "Obey my command to tell me what to do." Whenever a person tries to avoid controlling the definition of a relationship, at a different level he is defining the relationship as one in which he is not in control. A person who acts helpless controls the behavior in a relationship just as effectively as another who acts authoritarian and insists on a specific behavior. Helplessness will influence the other person's behavior as much as, if not more than, direct authoritarian demands. If one acts helpless, he may

_____

[1]Gregory Bateson and Jurgen Ruesch, Communication, the Social Matrix of Psychiatry, p. 179, Norton, New York, 1951.

in one sense be controlled by the person caring for him, but by acting helpless he defines the relationship as one in which he is taken care of.

It should be emphasized here that "control" does not mean that one takes control of another person as one would a robot. The emphasis here is not on a struggle to control another person's specific behavior but rather on a struggle to control what sort of behavior is to take place in the relationship and therefore to define the relationship. Any two people must inevitably work out what sort of relationship they have, not necessarily prescribing behavior, but at least circumscribing what behavior is to take place.

AVOIDING CONTROL IN A RELATIONSHIP
I have said that it is difficult for anyone to avoid working out what sort of relationship he has with another person. However, there is one way in which a person can avoid indicating what is to take place in a relationship, and thereby avoid defining it. He can negate what he says. Even though he will be defining the relationship by whatever he communicates, he can invalidate this definition by using qualifications that deny his communications.

The fact that people communicate on at least two levels makes it possible to indicate one relationship, and simultaneously deny it. For example, a man may say, "I think you should do that, but it's not my place to tell you so." In this way he defines the relationship as one in which he tells the other person what to do, but simultaneously denies that he is defining the relationship in this way. This is what is sometimes meant when a person is described as not being self-assertive. One man might respond to his wife's request to do the dishes by saying, "No, I won't," and sitting down with his newspaper. He has asserted himself in the sense that he has defined his relationship with his wife as one in which he is not to be told what to do. Another man might respond to a similar demand by saying, "I would like to do the dishes, but I can't. I have a headache." He also refuses to do the dishes, but by qualifying his message in an incongruent way. He indicates that he is not defining the relationship by this refusal. After all, it was the headache which prevented the dishwashing, not him. In the same way, if a man strikes his wife only when drunk, the act of striking her is qualified by the implication that he isn't responsible; the effect of the liquor is. By qualifying his messages with implications that he isn't responsible for his behavior, a person can avoid defining his relationship with another. These incongruent qualifying messages may be verbal, such as, "I didn't mean to do it," or they may be conveyed by a weak voice or a hesitant body movement. Even the context may negate a maneuver to define a relationship-- for example, when one boy invites another to fight in church where a fight is not possible.

To clarify the ways in which a person might avoid defining his relationship with another, suppose that some hypothetical person decided to entirely follow through with such an avoidance. Since anything he said or did not say would define his relationship, he would need to qualify with a negation or a denial whatever he said or did not say. To illustrate the ways in which he could deny his messages, the formal characteristics of any message from one person to another can be broken down into these four elements:

(1) I
(2) am saying something
(3) to you
(4) in this situation

A person can avoid defining his relationship by negating any or all of these four elements. He can 1) deny that he communicated something, 2) deny that something was communicated, 3) deny that it was communicated to the other person, or 4) deny the context in which it was communicated.

The rich variety of ways in which a person can avoid defining a relationship can be summarized briefly.

(1) To deny that he is communicating a message, a person may label himself as someone else. For example, he may introduce himself with an alias. Or he may indicate that he personally is not speaking, but his status position is, so that what he says is labeled as coming from the boss or the professor, for example. He may indicate that he is only an instrument transmitting the message; he was told to say what he did, or God was speaking through him, and therefore he is not the one who is defining the relationship.

A person may also deny that he is communicating by labeling what he says as effected by some force outside himself. He may indicate that he is not really talking, because he is upset or deranged by liquor, or insanity, or drugs.

He may also label his messages as being the result of 'involuntary' processes within himself, so that he isn't really the one communicating. He may say, "You aren't upsetting me; it's something I ate," and deny that his sick expression is a message from him about the relationship. He may even vomit or urinate and indicate that these things are organically caused and not messages from him which should be taken as comments on a relationship.

(2) The simplest way in which a person can deny that he said something is to manifest amnesia. By saying, "I don't remember doing that," he is qualifying an activity with a statement negating it. He may also insist that what he says is being misunderstood, and that therefore the other person's interpretations do not coincide with what he really said.

Another way to deny that something is said is to immediately qualify a statement with one which contradicts it. This negates everything said as irrelevant nonsense that is therefore not a comment on the relationship. Or a person may make up a language, simultaneously communicating and negating that communication by the very fact that the language cannot be understood by the other person. In another variant, a person can indicate that his words are not means of communication but things in themselves. He may make a statement while discussing the spelling of the words in the statement, and so indicate that he has not communicated a message but has merely listed letters of words.

(3) To deny that what he says is addressed to the other person, a person may simply indicate that he is talking to himself. He may also label the other person as someone else. For example, he can avoid talking to the other person by talking to the person's status position rather than to him personally. One can be sarcastic with a salesman at the door without defining one's relationship with that person, if the comments are about salesmen in general.

Or, if a person wishes to go to an extreme, he can say that the friend he is talking to is not really a friend but is secretly a policeman. Everything he says is then labeled as a statement to a policeman and therefore cannot define his relationship with his friend.

(4) To deny that what he says is said in this situation, a person can label his statements as referring to some other time or place. He can say, "I used to be treated badly and I'll probably be treated badly in the future," and these temporal qualifications deny his implication that he is treated badly at the present moment. Similarly, he can say, "A person I used to know did such and such," and by

making it a past relationship he denies that his statement is a comment on the present relationship.

To negate a situational statement about his relationship most effectively, he can qualify it with the statement that the place is some other place. He may label a psychiatrist's office as a prison and thereby deny that his statements are about his relationship with the psychiatrist.

In summary, these are ways of avoiding a definition of the relationship. When everything a person says to another person defines the relationship with that person, he can avoid indicating what sort of relationship he is in only by denying that he is speaking, denying that anything is said, denying that it is said to the other person, or denying that the interchange is occurring in this place at this time.

INTERPERSONAL RELATIONSHIPS IN SCHIZOPHRENICS

It seems apparent that the list of ways to avoid defining a relationship is a list of schizophrenic symptoms. A psychiatrist makes a classical diagnosis of schizophrenia when he observes the most obvious manifestation of schizophrenia, an incongruity between what the patient communicates and the messages which qualify that communication. His movements negate or deny what he says, and his words negate or deny the context in which he speaks. The incongruities may be crude and obvious, like the remark, "My head was bashed in last night," made by a patient whose head is in good shape; or they may be subtle, like a slight smile or odd tone of voice. If the patient denies that he is speaking, either by referring to himself in the third person or calling himself by another name, the psychiatrist notes that he is suffering from a loss of identity. If the person indicates that "voices" are saying these things, he is described as hallucinating. If the patient denies that his message is a message, perhaps by busily spelling out his words, the psychiatrist considers this a manifestation of dissociated thinking. When the patient denies that his message is addressed to the other person, the psychiatrist considers him delusional. If the patient denies his presence in the hospital by saying that he is in a castle or a prison, the psychiatrist notes that he is withdrawn from reality. When the patient makes a statement in an incongruent tone of voice, he is manifesting inappropriate affect. If he responds to the psychiatrist's behavior with messages which qualify that behavior incongruently, he is autistic. [2]

---

[2] This description deals with the behavior of the schizophrenic and not with his subjective experiences, which, of course, may be terrifying.

The classic psychiatric symptoms of schizophrenia can be described interactionally as indicating a pathology centering around a disjunction between the person's messages and the qualifications of those messages. When a person manifests such a disjunction so that what he says is systematically negated by the ways he qualifies what he says, he is avoiding defining his relationship with other people. The various and seemingly unconnected and bizarre symptoms of schizophrenia can be seen to have a central and rather simple nucleus. If one is determined to avoid defining his relationship, or avoid indicating what sort of behavior is to take place in a relationship, he can do so only by behaving in those ways which are describable as symptoms of schizophrenia.

It was suggested earlier that nonschizophrenics may at times also avoid defining their relationships with others. Someone may deny he is doing something by qualifying his activity with the statement that a somatic influence or liquor is doing it and not him. These are patterns of other psychopathologies, and partial ways of avoiding defining a particular relationship at a particular time. At best they tend to be temporary, since headaches ease up and liquor wears off. If a person is more determined to avoid defining his relationship with anyone at any time, and if anything he says or does defines his relationship, then he must behave like a schizophrenic and fully and completely deny what he is saying or doing in his interaction with others. Different types of schizophrenics could be classified in terms of different patterns, and some of their patterns are observable in normal people. The differences from the normal lie in the consistency of the schizophrenic's behavior and the extremes to which he goes. He will not only deny that he is saying something, but he will also deny it in such a way that his denial is denied. He does not merely use a name other than his own, he uses one which is clearly not his, such as Stalin, or in some other way negates his denial. Whereas more normal people will congruently negate something they say, the schizophrenic manifests incongruence even at this level.

To illustrate schizophrenic behavior let me cite a common occurrence. When a normal person takes out a cigarette and does not have a match he usually says to another person present, "May I have a light?" When he does this, he is qualifying a message concerning his unlighted cigarette with a congruent message about the need for a match, and he is defining his relationship with the other person by asking for a light. He is indicating, "This is the sort of relationship where I may request something." Under the same circumstances, a schizophrenic may take out a cigarette, look in his pockets for a match, and then hold the cigarette up in the air and stare at it silently. The person with the schizophrenic is faced with a rather peculiar sequence of communication. He is being appealed to for a match, and yet he is not. By merely staring at the cigarette, the schizophrenic is qualifying his message about an unlighted cigarette with an incongruent message. He is indicating that it is something to be stared at, not something to be lit. If he held up the cigarette as if it should be lit, he would be implicitly asking for a light and thereby defining his relationship with the other person. He can avoid indicating what sort of behavior is to take place, and therefore what sort of relationship he is in, only by looking at the cigarette in a detached way. A more obvious example is the behavior of a schizophrenic in a room with a stranger. He may not speak to the stranger, but since not speaking to him indicates what sort of relationship it is, the schizophrenic is likely to appear excessively preoccupied with something in the room, or with his thoughts. In this way he denies that he is defining his relationship with the other person by the way in which he qualifies his behavior.

By qualifying his messages to other people incongruently, the schizophrenic avoids indicating what behavior is to take place in his relationships and thereby avoids defining his relationships. The current trend in psychotherapy for schizophrenics takes into account this interpersonal behavior. The experienced therapist tends to take the schizophrenic's statements as statements about the relationship, and to ignore the denials of this. If the patient begins to talk in an odd language, such a therapist is less likely to interpret the symbolic content of that language and more likely to say something like, "I wonder why you're trying to confuse me," or, "Why do you speak to me in this way?"

ANALYSIS OF A SCHIZOPHRENIC CONVERSATION

To illustrate how the foregoing description of interpersonal relationships applies to schizophrenics, a recorded conversation between two young men will be presented here and subsequently analyzed. The numbers in brackets will be used in the analysis following the conversation to identify the passages analyzed. This conversation between two hospitalized schizophrenics took place when the men were left alone in adjoining offices where they could see each other through a connecting door. The men were presumably talking together for the first time, although they may have seen each other previously when entering the same building.

Jones (1): (Laughs loudly, then pauses.) I'm McDougal, myself. (This actually is not his name.)

Smith (2): What do you do for a living, little fellow? Work on a ranch or something?

Jones (3): No, I'm a civilian seaman. Supposed to be high mucka-muck society.

Smith (4): A singing recording machine, huh? I guess a recording machine sings sometimes. If they're adjusted right. Mm-hm. I thought that was it. My towel, mm-hm. We'll be going back to sea in about--eight or nine months though. Soon as we get our--destroyed parts repaired. (Pause.)

Jones (5): I've got lovesickness, secret love.

Smith (6): Secret love, huh? (Laughs.)

Jones: Yeah.

Smith (7): I ain't got any secret love.

Jones (8): I fell in love, but I don't feed any woo--that sits over--looks something like me--walking around over there.

Smith (9): My, oh, my only one, my only love is the shark. Keep out of the way of him.

Jones (10): Don't they know I have a life to live? (Long pause.)

Smith (11): Do you work at the air base? Hm?

Jones (12): You know what I think of work, I'm thirty-three in June, do you mind?

Smith (13): June?

Jones (14): Thirty-three years old in June. This stuff goes out the window after I live this, uh--leave this hospital. So I can't get my vocal cords back. So I lay off cigarettes. I'm a spatial condition, from outer space myself, no shit.

Smith (15): (Laughs.) I'm a real space ship from across.

Jones (16): A lot of people talk, uh--that way, like crazy, but Believe It or Not by Ripley, take it or leave it--alone--it's in the Examiner, it's in the comic section, Believe It or Not by Ripley, Robert E. Ripley, Believe It or Not, but we don't have to believe anything, unless I feel like it. (Pause.) Every little rosette--too much alone. (Pause.)

Smith (17): Yeah, it could be possible. (Phrase inaudible because of airplane noise.)

Jones: I'm a civilian seaman.

Smith (18): Could be possible. (Sighs.) I take my bath in the ocean.

Jones (19): Bathing stinks. You know why? Cause you can't quit when you feel like it. You're in the service.

Smith: I can quit whenever I feel like quitting. I can get out when I feel like getting out.

Jones: (Talking at the same time.) Take me, I'm a civilian, I can quit.

Smith: Civilian?

Jones: Go my--my way.

Smith (20): I guess we have, in port, civilian. (Long pause.)

Jones (21): What do they want with us?

Smith: Hm?

Jones (22): What do they want with you and me?

Smith (23): What do they want with you and me? How do I know what they want with you? I know what they want with me. I broke the law, so I have to pay for it. (Silence.)

As Smith and Jones communicate and thereby inevitably maneuver to define their relationship, they obviously and consistently qualify their statements with negations. On the recording from which this transcript was taken, the qualifying inflections of voice make the incongruencies even more apparent.

The following brief examination of the verbal aspects of the conversation will indicate the ways that each of the two schizophrenics denies that he is defining a relationship: denial that he is communicating, denial that something is communicated, denial that it is communicated to the other person, or denial of the context in which it is communicated.

Jones (1). The conversation begins when Jones gives a peculiarly loud and abrupt laugh followed by a pause. He then introduces himself in a friendly manner, but uses an alias, negating his move toward intimacy by the qualifying statement that he, Jones, is not making such a move.

Smith (2). Smith replies with a friendly inquiry about the other person, but calls him a little fellow, qualifying his overture with an unfriendly comment on the other's size. (Jones is actually a little fellow who indicates that he is not too happy about this by speaking in an artificially deep bass voice.) Smith also poses the friendly question of whether Jones works "on a ranch or something," when it is obvious that Jones is a patient in a mental hospital and incapable of making a living; thus he denies that he is replying to Jones, a hospital patient.

Jones (3). Jones denies that he is a patient by calling himself a civilian seaman, and then denies this by qualifying it with a statement that he is supposed to be high mucka-muck society. He has set up a situation in which no matter what he, Jones, says, it cannot be about his relationship with Smith because he isn't speaking.

Smith (4). Smith mentions the recording machine (which is in the room but out of Jones' sight) and says that a recording ma-

chine can "sing," or inform. But this friendly warning, which
would define their relationship as a sharing one, is qualified by a
negation of it: he muses about the recording machine as if he were
talking to himself and not the other person. He also denies that he
is giving a warning by qualifying his statement with a quite incongruent one mentioning a towel. He next makes a possible statement about their relationship by saying, "We'll be going back to
sea," but since they aren't seamen the statement negates itself.

Jones (5). After a pause, Jones says he has lovesickness, a
secret love. This is perhaps a comment on Smith's sharing statement about being seamen, yet he denies, or leaves ambiguous, the
possibility that he is talking about Smith.

Smith (6 and 7). Smith apparently accepts this as a possible
statement about their relationship since he laughs uncomfortably
and says he doesn't have a secret love.

Jones (8). Jones then points out that he isn't talking about himself or Smith but about someone who looks like himself walking
around over there. Since no one is walking around over there he
qualifies his previous statement about love with a denial that he
or Smith was the one talked about.

Smith (9). Smith points out that his love is the shark and it's
best to keep out of the way of him. He denies that he is defining
his relationship with Jones by making it himself and a shark that
is talked about.

Jones (10). Jones subsides with a statement about being picked
on or rejected, but he denies that he is referring to Smith by saying, "Don't they know I have a life to live?"

Smith (11). After another pause, Smith makes a friendly overture but negates it as a statement about their relationship with an
incongruence about the place. He calls the hospital an air base.

Jones (12). Jones replies rather aggressively with a statement
about his age, thereby denying his patient status by making his age
the reason for his inability to work--as if he were saying, "It's
not me, it's my age." However, he counters this denial by a
statement contradicting it when he states his age as thirty-three.
If he had said, "I am eighty-six," he would have been congruently

stating age as a reason for not working. Thus he even denies his denial. [3)]

Smith (13). Smith chooses from his statement the least relevant part, the fact that in June the man will be thirty-three. How different such a reply is from a possible one qualifying Jones' statement, "Do you mind?" Rather than acknowledge "Do you mind?" as a statement about what sort of behavior is to take place in the relationship, and perhaps apologize for bringing up work, Smith comments on the month of June. In this way he denies that Jones' "Do you mind?" is a statement defining the relationship.

Jones (14). Jones makes a congruent statement about the context, saying it is a hospital, but qualifies this with the statement that all he needs to do is give up cigarettes. He promptly negates this statement that implies there is nothing really wrong with him by saying he is a spatial condition from outer space.

Smith (15). Smith joins him in this with a laugh and says he is also a space ship. Although they are mutually defining their relationship, they are negating this definition by the statement that they are not two persons sharing something but two creatures from outer space. This turns their statements about the relationship into statements about a fictional relationship.

Jones (16). Jones again qualifies the context congruently by mentioning talking "like crazy," but he immediately qualifies this with a series of statements incongruent with it and with each other as he talks about Ripley, and the comic section, and ends up saying "too much alone."

Smith (17 and 18). Smith responds to these statements by talking to himself and not the other person.

Jones (19). When Smith mentions bathing, Jones joins his monologue and once again makes a comment that has implications about

---

[3)] The incongruence of this third level of schizophrenic communication is one of the basic differences between the schizophrenic and the normal, as was mentioned earlier. Almost every statement in this recording consists not only of denials but of negations of those denials. When Jones introduces himself as "McDougal," he does so in a tone of voice which seems to indicate his name isn't really McDougal. An examination of this third level probably requires kinesic and linguistic analysis and is merely mentioned here.

sharing their situation. This is negated by his qualifying it with a statement that they are in the service.

Smith (20). Smith joins him in a denial that this is a hospital by calling the place a port.

Jones (21 and 22). After a pause, Jones makes a direct, congruent statement defining their relationship, "What do they want with us?," and he even repeats this when it is queried by Smith. This statement and the way it is qualified are congruent and in this sense it is a sane statement. He maneuvers to define the relationship without denying that he is doing so.

Smith (23). Smith rejects this maneuver. He first says, "How do I know what they want with you? I know what they want with me." This statement is congruent with what Jones has said and defines his relationship with Jones even though he is rejecting Jones. In this sense it is a sane reply. However, Smith then qualifies his congruent statement with a thorough negation of it. By saying, "I broke the law, so I have to pay for it," he denies the place is a hospital, denies that he is talking about himself, since he hasn't broken the law, and denies that he and Jones are patients by making the place a prison. With one message he avoids defining his relationship with Jones and discards the attempt of Jones to work toward a mutual definition of their relationship. This denial ends the conversation and the relationship.

This brief analysis deals with only half the interaction between Smith and Jones. The ways in which they interpret, or respond to, the other person's statements have not been completely discussed. However, it seems apparent that they qualify each other's statements with messages which deny they are from that person, deny they are messages, deny they are addressed to the receiver, and deny the context in which they take place. The schizophrenic not only avoids defining his relationship with another person, he also can be exasperatingly skillful at preventing another person from defining his relationship with him. It is such responses which give one the feeling of not being able to "reach" a schizophrenic.

What makes it "obvious" that these two men behave differently from other men is the extreme incongruence between what they say and the ways they qualify what they say. Two normal men meeting for the first time would presumably introduce themselves and make some inquiry into each other's background as a way of seeking out some common interest. If the context was at all appropriate, they would work toward defining their relationship more clearly with each other. Should one say something that seemed out of place, the other would probably query it. They would not only be able to qualify what they said congruently, but they would be able to talk about their communications to clarify their understanding and therefore the relationship. Disagreements would tend to reach a resolution. However, when one of the participants in a conversation is determined to deny that what he says has anything to do with the relationship being worked out, then inevitably the conversation will have the disjunctive quality of schizophrenia.

If one should ascribe any goal or purpose to human relations, it would appear to be a highly abstract one. The wife who maneuvers to get her husband to do the dishes does not merely have as her goal his acquiescence in this act. Her larger goal seems to be related to an attempt to work out a definition of what sort of relationship they have with each other. Whereas more normal people work toward a mutual definition of a relationship and maneuver each other toward that end, the schizophrenic seems rather to desperately avoid that goal and work toward the avoidance of any definition of his relationship with another person.

THE SIGNIFICANCE OF THE ANALYSIS OF INTERPERSONAL RELATIONSHIPS

When schizophrenia is described as a disjunction between several levels of messages, questions can be posed about what sort of learning situation would induce such behavior. If one says the schizophrenic is withdrawn from reality or has delusions, such a description does not give any clues as to the etiology of the psychopathology. However, if one says the schizophrenic avoids defining his relationship with anyone by qualifying his statements incongruently, one can speculate about the kind of family interaction which encouraged this behavior. Not only can one speculate, but one can also observe the patient interacting with his family, to see if an interactional origin is apparent.

Preliminary investigations of schizophrenic patients interacting with their families suggest that the patient's way of qualifying his statements incongruently is a habitual response to incongruent messages from his parents. As an illustration, suppose that a mother said to her child, "Come and sit on my lap." Suppose also that she made this request in a tone of voice which indicated she wished the child would keep away from her. The child would be faced with the message, "Come near me," qualified incongruently by the message, "Get away from me." The child could not satisfy these incongruent demands by any congruent response. If he came near her, she would become uncomfortable because she had indicated by her tone of voice that he should keep away. If he kept away, she would become uncomfortable because after all she was inviting him to her. The only way the child could meet these incongruent demands would be to respond in an incongruent way; he would have to come near her and qualify that behavior with a statement that he was not coming near her. He might, for example, come toward her and sit on her lap while saying, "Oh, what a pretty button on your dress." In this way he would sit on her lap, but he would qualify this behavior with a statement that he was only coming to look at the button. Because human beings can communicate two levels of message, the child can come to his mother while simultaneously denying that he is coming to her--after all, it was the button he came to be near.

By saying, "Come sit on my lap," in a tone of voice which indicates, "Keep away from me," the mother is avoiding defining her relationship with the child. More than that, she is making it impossible for the child to define his relationship with her. He cannot define the relationship as one of closeness nor can he define it as one of distance if he is to satisfy her incongruent demands. He can only manifest incongruent messages himself and thereby avoid defining his relationship with her.

It seems possible that incongruent messages from a mother could impose on her child a response which avoids defining his relationship with her. It also seems possible that should the child define his relationship with her by communicating congruent messages, she could respond in an incongruent way and thereby compel him to avoid defining his relationship with her. In theory at least, it seems conceivable that a systematic incongruence between levels of messages could be manifested by someone if the communicative behavior within his family enforced such incongruence. [4] This would be particularly so if the child was largely confined to one relationship so that he did not learn to experience other kinds of behavior with other people. It is "socially acceptable" for a child to respond to his mother's incongruent request to sit on her lap by coming to her and saying, "Oh what a pretty button." Yet

---

[4]Parental behavior consisting of incongruent messages has been defined elsewhere as a "double bind" situation. See Gregory Bateson, Don D. Jackson, Jay Haley, and John Weakland, "Toward a Theory of Schizophrenia, "Behavioral Science, 1:251-264, 1956. (See p. 31, this vol.)

this behavior is formally the same as that of the schizophrenic who becomes frightened and enters his doctor's office asking if this is Grand Central Station. He behaves as if he is seeking reassurance and simultaneously qualifies that behavior by a denial of it. The difference lies in the fact that his denial itself is qualified incongruently--he negates the denial by making it clearly fantastic.

A logical hypothesis about the origin of schizophrenic behavior, when the behavior is seen in communications terms, would involve the family interaction of the patient.[5] If a child learned to relate to people in a relationship with parents who constantly induced him to respond to incongruent messages, he might learn to work out his relationships with all people in those terms. It would seem to follow that the control of the definition of relationships would be a central problem in the origin of schizophrenia.

---

[5] For a fuller discussion of the family of the schizophrenic see Jay Haley, "The Family of the Schizophrenic; a Model System," J. of Nervous and Mental Disease, 129:357-374, 1959. (See p. 171, this vol.)

THE FAMILY OF THE SCHIZOPHRENIC: A MODEL SYSTEM

Jay Haley

This paper will attempt to show that schizophrenic behavior serves a function within a particular kind of family organization. The emphasis in this description will be on the interactive behavior of the schizophrenic and his parents rather than on their ideas, beliefs, attitudes, or psychodynamic conflicts. This work is largely based on an examination of a small sample of families participating in therapeutic sessions where parents and schizophrenic child, as well as siblings, are seen together and recorded. An excerpt from a recording of a family session will be presented and analyzed in terms of the observable behavior of family members, to illustrate the hypothesis that the family of the schizophrenic is a special kind of system which can be differentiated from other family systems.

The hypothesis that schizophrenia is of family origin has led to a number of investigations of schizophrenic patients and their parents. These studies include both impressions of family members and attempts at statistical measurement of individual traits of parents or the conflict between them. Typically the mother of the schizophrenic is described as dominating, overprotective, manipulative of the child and father, and also overtly rejecting (18). The father is usually described as weak and passive, holding aloof from the patient (15, 17), and occasionally overtly rejecting and cruel (8). Many investigators mention a certain percentage of fathers or mothers who appear "normal."

Besides reporting descriptions of the individuals in the family, investigators report on the relationship between the parents on the assumption that conflict between father and mother could be rela-

Reprinted from the JOURNAL OF NERVOUS AND MENTAL DISEASE, 129:357-74, 1959. Copyright   by the Williams and Wilkins Company, Baltimore; reproduced by permission.

ted to disturbance in the child. Lidz and Lidz (13) reported in 1949 that 20 of 35 schizophrenic patients had parents who were clearly incompatible. Tietze (20) reported in the same year that 13 of 25 mothers of schizophrenic patients reported unhappy marriages and nine marriages which were described as "perfect" were found by the investigator to be otherwise. In 1950 Gerard and Siegal (7) found strife between 87 per cent of the parents of 71 male schizophrenic patients in contrast to 13 per cent found in the controls. In the same year Reichard and Tillman (17) noted the unhappy marriages of parents of schizophrenics. Frazee (8) in 1953 reported that 14 of 23 parents were in severe conflict with each other and none had only moderate conflict in contrast to 13 control parents who had only moderate conflict. Lidz (16) reported in 1957 that all of 14 families of schizophrenic patients contained marital relationships which were seriously disturbed. Bowen (6) describes the parents in this type of family as experiencing "emotional divorce." Wynne uses the term "pseudo mutuality" to describe the difficulties family members have with each other (23).

These studies provide strong evidence for conflict between the parents of schizophrenics, but do not clarify what strife between parents has to do with schizophrenia in a child. After all, there is conflict between parents who do not have schizophrenic children. Similarly, to show that the mothers of schizophrenic patients are dominating and overprotective and the fathers weak and passive does not clarify how schizophrenia is appropriate in families with such parents. Psychiatric terminology seems particularly unsuited to this problem. The language of psychiatry either describes the processes within an individual, such as his needs, fantasies, anxieties, and so on, or provides static descriptions of two individuals in dominant-submissive or rejecting or dependent relationships. When schizophrenia is described in the traditional psychiatric way, and when other family members are seen with the biased emphasis upon the process in the individual, it is difficult to relate schizophrenia to a family.

Currently most groups investigating schizophrenia and the family are recognizing that the total family unit is pathogenic, and there are attempts to develop a language which will describe the interaction of three or more people. A transition would seem to have taken place in the study of schizophrenia; from the early idea that the difficulty in these families was caused by the schizophrenic member, to the idea that they contained a pathogenic mother, to the discovery that the father was inadequate, to the current emphasis upon all three family members involved in a pathological system of interaction. Although it would seem impossible at this time to provide a satisfactory language for describing the complex interaction of three or more people, this paper will suggest a rudimentary approach to such a descriptive system. An essential requirement of any such description is that it show the adaptive function of schizophrenic behavior within the family system.

The present paper is a product of the current research conducted by the Bateson project. Historically this project began as a general investigation of the nature of communication and began to focus on the communication of the schizophrenics in 1953. The observation that the schizophrenic consistently mislabels his communication led Bateson to deduce that he must have been raised in a learning situation where he was faced with conflicting levels of message. From this came the "double bind" hypothesis (5) which was put together with Jackson's emphasis on schizophrenia serving a homeostatic function in the family (12). The research project then brought together the families of schizophrenics to observe the actual behavior in the family. Basically the double bind hypothesis was a statement about two-person interaction and it has been extended to areas outside of schizophrenia (9, 11). When the family was seen as an interactive unit, there was an attempt to extend the double bind concept to a three person system (21). Currently the project is attempting to devise a theoretical system for describing the family as a unit and this attempt had led to several papers (2, 3, 4) including this one.

The importance of describing a total system rather than elements within it may explain some of the inconsistencies in the description of individuals in the family and conflict between them. For example, it is possible that a mother could show rejecting traits when her child is ill and dependent upon her, and overprotective traits when he begins to recover and attempt to achieve independence from her. Similarly, parents may not show discord when their child is psychotic and they are drawn together by this burden, but conflict could appear should the child behave more assertively and so threaten to leave them. Alanen (1) studied mothers of schizophrenic patients and found many of them within the limits of the "normal" on the basis of Rorschach tests and individual interview. He mentions, almost in passing, "Some of the cases in which the mother of a schizophrenic patient had been relatively healthy belong to those in which the father was seriously disturbed. The wives of all fathers who had developed chronic psychosis belong, for example, to this category." If the 'normality' or the pathology of a family member depends upon the influence of the behavior of other family members at that time, only a study of the total family system will show consistent findings.

The focus of a family study should be on the total family and on the interaction of parents and children with each other rather than on the interaction of family members with interviewers or testers. What a family member reports to an investigator about his relationship with another family member is only hearsay evidence of what actually takes place. To study the system of interaction in the family of the schizophrenic it is necessary to bring family members together over a period of time and directly observe them relating to one another. Inevitably the fact of observing the family introduces a bias into the data for they may behave differently when observed than when not observed. It would seem to be impossible to leave the observer out of this sort of study, and the problem is to include him in the situation in such a way as to maximize the information he can gain. The most appropriate type of observation would seem to be in a therapeutic context. There is serious doubt as to whether this type of family can be brought together without therapeutic support. If the parents are merely asked to be observed interacting with their schizophrenic child, the question is automatically raised whether they have something to do with the illness of the child; accordingly guilts and defenses are aroused and must be dealt with in the situation. Long term observation of the family is also necessary since they may give one impression in a single interview and quite another when they have talked together many times and pretenses are dropping. The presence of a therapist is necessary as sensitive areas in the relationships are touched upon when family members get more intensively involved with one another. Long-term observation also provides an opportunity to verify hypotheses and make predictions as family patterns are observed occurring again and again. Finally, the introduction of a therapist makes possible the observation of a family responding to planned intervention. As ideas are presented to the family, or as therapeutic change is threatened, the family can be observed maintaining their system under stress.

Although the expense of regular filming of therapy sessions is prohibitive, the occasional use of film and the constant use of tape recordings provides data which may be studied at leisure.

AN ILLUSTRATION OF FAMILY BEHAVIOR

Since few investigators have the opportunity to observe a schizophrenic and his parents interacting with one another, an illustration is offered here. The following excerpt is transcribed verbatim from a recording of an interview where a patient and his parents were seen weekly as an adjunct to his individual therapy, because of his previous inability to see his parents for even a few minutes without an anxiety attack. The patient, a thirty nine year old man, suffered a breakdown in the army and was diagnosed as a schizophrenic. After discharge he returned home and remained with his parents for the following ten years. There were several abortive attempts to leave home and go to work. He was employed for little more than a year during those ten years and was supported by his parents during his temporary absences from home. When he entered the hospital, at the insistence of his parents, he was hallucinating, behaving in a compulsive way, exhibiting bizarre mannerisms, and complaining of anxiety and helplessness.

Earlier in the interview the patient had been saying he felt he was afraid of his mother, and finally she brought out a Mother's Day Card she had just received from him. It was a commercial card with the printed inscription, "For someone who has been like a mother to me." The patient said he could see nothing wrong with the card nor understand why his mother was disturbed about receiving it.

Patient:	Uh, read the outside again.
Mother:	All right, the outside ways, "On Mother's Day, with best wishes"--everything is very fine, it's wonderful, but it's for someone else, not for your mother, you see? "For someone who's been like a mother to me."
Father:	In other words, this card made mother think. So mother asked me...
Mother:	(interrupting) When you...
Father:	(continuing) what I think about it. So I said, "Well, I don't think Simon--meant that way, maybe he...
Patient:	(interrupting) Well, I mean you can interpret it, uh-- uh, you've been like a mother is uh supposed to be.
Father:	No, no.
Patient:	(continuing) a good--a real good mother.
Therapist:	Why don't you like the idea that he might have deliberately sent that?
Father:	Deliberately? Well...
Mother:	(overlapping and interrupting) Well, that's what I...
Father:	(continuing) well, he says he didn't, he agrees...
Mother:	(continuing) Well, I mean I believe our son would have...

Father:	(overlapping and continuing) that he couldn't get another card.
Patient:	(interrupting) Well, I meant to sting you just a tiny bit by that outside phrase.
Mother:	(overlapping) You see I'm a little bit of a psychiatrist too, Simon, I happen to be--(laughing) So I felt so--when you talked to (the therapist) I brought along that card--I wanted to know what's behind your head. And I wanted to know--or you made it on purposely to hurt me--Well, if you did, I--I...
Patient:	(interrupting) Not entirely, not entire...
Mother:	(interrupting and overlapping) I'll take all--Simon, believe me, I'll take all the hurt in the world if it will help you--you see what I mean?
Therapist:	How can you...
Mother:	(continuing) Because I never meant to hurt you--Huh?
Therapist:	How can you hurt anybody who is perfectly willing to be hurt? (short pause)
Father:	What's that?
Mother:	I uh--a mother sacrifices--if you would be--maybe a mother you would know too. Because a mother is just a martyr, she's sacrificing--like even with Jesus with his mother--she sacrificed too. So that's the way it goes on, a mother takes over anything what she can help...
Therapist:	(interrupting) What mother?
Mother:	(continuing) her children.
Patient:	(interrupting and overlapping) Well, uh, I'll tell you Ma--listen, Ma, I didn't mean to--to sting you exactly that outside part there.
Therapist:	Well, you said so.
Patient:	Oh, all right, but it--it wasn't that exactly. No, I'm not giving ground--uh--it's hard to explain this thing. Uh--uh--What was I going to say. Now I forgot what I was going to say. (short pause) I mean I felt that this--this is what I mean, uh--that I felt that you could have been a better mother to me than you were. See there were things.
Mother:	Uh...
Father:	Well you said...
Patient:	(interrupting) You could have been better than you were. So that's why--that's what I felt--it was, uh--uh, was all right to send it that way.
Mother:	Well, if you meant it that way that's perf--that's what I wanted to know--and that's all I care--you see. But

I still say, Simon, that if you would take your father
and mother just like they're plain people--you just
came here and you went through life like anybody else
went through--and--and don't keep on picking on them
and picking them to pieces--but just leave them alone--
and go along with them the way they are--and don't
change them--you'll be able to get along with everybody, I assure you.

Patient: (interrupting) I mean after all a card is a card--why
I d--it seems to me kind of silly (anguish in his voice
and near weeping) to bring that thing in here--they
have sold them at the canteen, Ma...

Therapist: Are you anxious now...

Patient: Why...

Therapist: Are you anxious now because she said...

Patient: I shouldn't be blamed for a thing like that, it's so
small...

Mother: (overlapping) I'm not blaming you.

Patient: (continuing) I don't even remember exactly what the
thing was.

Mother: (overlapping) Well, that's all I wanted to know
(laughs)

Patient: (continuing) I didn't want to--to--to--to blame you or
nothing.

Therapist: Will you slow down a minute. Are you anxious now
because she said she didn't like to be picked on? And
you've sort of been picking on her today. Is that what's
making you so--upset?

Patient: No, it's now what's making me upset. That they s--
after all, mother's got to realize that those people--
the people that sell the cards--they sell them and
people buy them--the wording isn't exactly right--I've
stood for half an hour in a store sometimes picking--
picking out a card to send mother or to send to one of
the family where I wanted to get the wordings just so--
and the picture on the thing just so. I was just too particular, that was before I took sick...

Therapist: I think you did that this time too--

Patient: (continuing) And came back to the hospital. No I
wasn't--I bought that thing in five minutes. There was
only a choice of four cards--but of course that helped.
But I--I--I--uh, I--I do have--I've changed now with
those cards, I'm not as particular as I used to be. I
mean uh--peop--they sell those cards and, uh--I don't
think that they--they got--they don't mean anything by

the words. Uh, --they're sold for people to buy, they're
sold for people to buy.

Therapist: (overlapping) The person who sends them ought to
mean something by the words.

Patient: No, but I...

Therapist: And you seem to be denying that you sent...

Patient: No, I think that can be interpreted in different ways.

Therapist: Sure, it's pretty safe, but not quite safe enough apparently.

Patient: Is that the way you feel too?

Therapist: I feel you tried to say something indirectly so you'd be
protected.

Patient: (interrupting) No, I wasn't, I just felt that--that--
that thing.

Therapist: Now you're...

Patient: (continuing) was--was--all right I'm changing a little
bit. Uh, --that that mother was a good enough mother.
It says "For someone that's been like a mother to me."

Father: A _real_ mother.

Patient: Yeah, a _real_ mother--so that's all.[1]

Despite its brevity, this excerpt illustrates a typical kind of
interaction in this type of family. From the point of view of psychiatric diagnosis, the patient manifests such symptoms as:
1) blocking and forgetting what he was going to say, 2) showing
concretistic thinking when he says "a card is a card," 3) implying
that someone else caused the difficulty ("They sell them in the canteen" and later in the interview implying in a rather paranoid way
that it was the fault of a post office clerk for mailing it) and 4)
claiming amnesia ("I don't even remember what the thing was").
Although less dramatic than symptoms manifested by the full-
blown psychotic patient, his behavior could be said to be schizophrenic.

Another family could have responded in this situation rather
differently. Should a child in another family send his mother such
a card, she might respond to it in any of a variety of ways. And
whatever way chosen, her husband and child would also have a
range of possible ways to respond to her. This particular family
selects these ways, and a description of this family must 1) de-

---

[1] This excerpt is not offered as an example of family therapy
but rather as an example of family behavior. The parents in this
case were not considered to be patients and the family as a unit
was not officially undergoing treatment.

scribe the formal patterns in this type of interaction in such a way
as to 2) differentiate the patterns from other possible ones, or
those in other families.

POSSIBILITIES OF A THREE-PERSON SYSTEM

One way to describe a particular family is to present its type of
interaction against the background of the potential ways a mother,
father, and child might interact with one another. If any set of
parents and child are brought together in a room, what sort of
communicative behavior is potentially possible between them?

1. Whatever they do together can be seen as communication
between them; each will do something and each will respond. Although it seems obvious, it is particularly important to emphasize
that family members cannot avoid communicating, or responding,
to one another when they are in the same room. If one speaks to
another and he does not answer, his not-answering is a response
in a real and meaningful sense.

2. Not only must parents and child communicate with each
other, but each must communicate on at least two levels. Whatever one says and does will inevitably be qualified by the other
things he says and does, and when any piece of communication is
about, or qualifies, another piece of communication they can be
said to be of different levels. Whenever anyone speaks to another
person he must qualify what he says because he must speak in a
tone of voice, with a body movement, with other verbal statements,
and in a particular context. What he says will be qualified with an
indication of what sort of statement it is, i.e. a joking statement,
a sincere one, an unimportant one, a command, a suggestion, and
so on. A man can smile and murder as he smiles, and if his behavior is to be described both levels of communication must be included.

If a man says, "I won't stand for that any more!" in a tone of
voice which indicates anger and with a gesture of putting a stop to
it in a situation where what he says is appropriate, then his statement and qualifications can be said to be congruent, or to "affirm,"
each other. Messages and their qualifiers can also be incongruent.
If a mother makes a punishing statement while labeling what she
does as benevolent, she is disqualifying what she says, or manifesting an incongruence between her levels of message. It is important to note that she is not contradicting herself. Contradictory
statements are of the same level, such as, "I will do it," and "I
won't do it." Incongruent statements are of different levels: "I

will do it, " said in a tone of voice which indicates, "Don't take what I say seriously." Whether family members qualify their own statements incongruently or congruently, and under what circumstances they do so, can be described as they interact with one another.

3. The three people in the room must also qualify each other's statements. As they respond to one another, they are inevitably commenting upon, or classifying, each other's statements. They may affirm what each other says, or they may disqualify the other's statements by indicating that isn't the sort of thing that should be said. If mother says, "I brought you some candy, " and her son says, "You treat me like a child, " the son is disqualifying his mother's communication. If he accepts it with a statement of thanks, he is affirming her statement. A description of parents and child must include whether, and under what circumstances, they affirm or disqualify each other's behavior.

4. When three people are in a room, some sort of leadership will take form, even if only in terms of who will speak before the others do. Any one of the three may initiate something, and the other two may go along with him or attempt to take leadership themselves. In some families, father and child may consistently turn to mother for a decision, other families may label father as the final arbiter, while other parents may lean on their child for the initiation of what is to happen.

5. The three people may also form any or all of various possible alliances. It is possible for the three of them to ally against the outside world, or for one to ally with someone in the outside world against the other two, or two may ally against the third. In some families father and mother may form a coalition against the child, in others the child may ally with one of his parents against the other, and so on.

6. Finally, when something goes "wrong, " there are a variety of possible arrangements for the three people to handle blame. All three may each acknowledge blame, one may never accept blame for anything, two may consistently blame the third, and so on.

This list of some of the possibilities in a three person system is made more complex by the fact that a family member may form an alliance but indicate he isn't forming one, or may take blame but qualify his statement with an indication that he really isn't to blame.

The possible range of maneuvers is considerably increased when people are seen to communicate at multiple levels.

THE RULES IN THE FAMILY OF THE SCHIZOPHRENIC

Given a potential range of behavior between three people in a family system, it becomes possible to look at any one type of family as restricted to a certain range of that potential. No one family will interact in all possible ways: limited patterns of interaction will develop. The patterns described here are those in a particular sample and are those which occur when parents and schizophrenic child interact <u>with</u> <u>each</u> <u>other</u>. They may behave differently with other people, including psychiatric investigators or siblings of the schizophrenic child. Although siblings are included in our observation of this type of family, the description offered here is of the three person system, partly for simplification in this presentation and partly because parents and schizophrenic child form a special triadic system in the larger family unit.

THE WAYS FAMILY MEMBERS QUALIFY THEIR OWN STATEMENTS

Consistently in this type of family the individual members manifest an incongruence between what they say and how they qualify what they say. Many people do this under certain circumstances, but when these family members interact they confine themselves almost entirely to disqualifying their own statements.

In this excerpt, the mother confronts her son with the Mother's Day Card because she didn't like it, but she emphasizes what a wonderful card it is. Then she says she wants to know what was behind his head and if he sent it to hurt her, and she laughs. In a context of accusing him of hurting her, she says she wants to be hurt and is willing to take all the hurt in the world to help him. Her description of herself as a special person who will sacrifice all is qualified a few moments later by the statement that she and her husband are just plain people and her son should treat them like anybody else. This "benevolent advice" is offered in a punishing tone of voice and context. When her son says she shouldn't blame him, she qualifies her statements as not being blaming. Consistently what she communicates she qualifies in an incongruent way.

The father is only briefly in this excerpt, but while there he indicates that the son didn't mean to say what the card said, and, besides, the card said she was a real mother.

The son also manifests incongruent behavior. He sends a card to his mother on Mother's Day which indicates she is not really his mother. He further qualifies this message by indicating there was nothing wrong with it and then suggests that it says she is like a mother is supposed to be. Following this, he indicates that it means she could have been a better mother than she was. He then protests that it was silly of her to bring the card in, and qualifies this with the statement that they sell them in the canteen. Besides he doesn't remember what the thing was. After indicating that he bought the card hurriedly, he qualifies this by saying it took him five minutes to choose among four cards. He adds that one should be careful in choosing cards with exact wording, but people sell those cards and they don't mean anything by the words. Finally, he qualifies his greetings by saying that it meant she was not only a good enough mother but a real mother.

The more extreme incongruence between the son's levels of message differs from that of his mother, and this difference will be discussed later. Yet basically a similar pattern of communication is apparent. The mother does not say, "You shouldn't have sent me this card--what do you mean by it?" which is implied by her bringing the card to the session. The son doesn't say, "I sent it to you to sting you, but I'm sorry I did now." The mother is condemning him for sending her the card, but she qualifies her messages in such a way that she indicates she isn't condemning him. The son apologizes for sending the card, but he qualifies his apology in such a way that he isn't apologizing. Father indicates the son didn't mean what he said, and the card didn't say what he didn't mean anyhow. Although these incongruencies between what is said and how it is qualified are apparent in the verbal transcript, they are even more apparent when the vocal inflections on the recording are heard. Mother's tone of voice and laughter are inappropriate and thereby disqualify what she is saying, and father and son similarly do not make a flat statement which is affirmed by the ways they say it.

One can listen to many hours of recordings of conversations between parents and schizophrenic child without hearing one of them make a statement which is affirmed. Usually if one finds an exception, it proves on closer examination to fit the rules. For example, during a filmed session a family was asked to plan to do something together and the father said in a positive way that they were going to do this and do that. He fully affirmed his statements by the ways he said them. However, a few minutes later he said he was only saying these things because they should say something in front of the camera, thus disqualifying his previous statements.

HOW FAMILY MEMBERS QUALIFY EACH OTHER'S STATEMENTS

Although it is possible for family members to affirm or disqualify each other's statements, in this type of family the members consistently disqualify what each other says. In this excerpt
it is difficult to find any statement by one person affirmed by another. The son has actually disqualified his mother's whole past
maternal behavior at one stroke by sending her such a card.
When she protests, he indicates her protests are not valid. Similarly, the mother disqualifies the greeting she received from her
son and also his defenses of it. When he indicates there is nothing wrong with it, she labels this as in error. When he indicates he knew what he was doing and meant to "sting" her a bit,
she indicates this was in error. Father joins them to disqualify
both the son's message, since he didn't mean it, and his defense
of the message. No one affirms what anyone says except 1) when
the son says he doesn't remember what the card was, and his
mother says that is all she wanted to know; 2) when the father says
the card means she is a real mother, and the son agrees. Both
of these affirmations involve symptomatic behavior by the son:
amnesia and distortion of reality. From this excerpt one might
hypothesize that the family members will disqualify what each
other says except when the child is behaving in a symptomatic
way. Such a hypothesis requires more careful investigation.
Apparently even symptomatic behavior by the child is usually disqualified except in certain contexts. When the mother is under
attack, the parents may affirm psychotic behavior but not necessarily at other times.

It might be argued that the behavior in this excerpt is excep-
tional since it deals with a moment of crisis. However, analysis
of other interviews suggests that the pattern is typical. In a previous paper (5) the relationship between mother and schizophrenic
child was described as a "double bind" situation in that the mother
imposed incongruent levels of message upon the child in a situation where the child must respond to conflicting requests, could
not comment on the contradictions, and could not leave the field.
Further investigation indicates that this kind of communication
sequence is a repetitive pattern between all three family members.
Not only is each constantly faced with conflicting levels of message, but each finds his response labeled as a wrong one. (Family therapy with this type of family has its unrewarding aspects
since almost any comment by the therapist is similarly disqualified.)

Typically if one family member says something, another indicates it shouldn't have been said or wasn't said properly. If one criticizes the other, he is told that he misunderstands and should behave differently. If one compliments the other, he is told he doesn't do this often enough, or he has some ulterior purpose. Should a family member try to avoid communicating, the others will indicate this "passivity" is demanding and indicate he should initiate more. All family members may report they always feel they are in the wrong. However, they do not necessarily directly oppose each other or openly reject one another's statements. If one suggests going to a particular place, the other may not say "No," but rather he is likely to indicate, "Why must we always go where you suggest?" Or the response may be the sigh of a brave martyr who must put up with this sort of thing. Typically the family members may not object to what one another says, but to their right to say it. Often open disagreements are prevented by an atmosphere of benevolent concern and distress that the other person misunderstands. Family members may also respond in an affirmative way when their response would be appropriate only if the person had made some other statement.

It is important to emphasize that a formal pattern is being described here which may manifest itself in various ways. A mother may be overprotective and thereby disqualify what the child does as insufficient or inadequate. She may also be rejecting and similarly disqualify what he does as unacceptable. She may also withdraw when the child initiates something as a way of disqualifying his offer. Similarly, father may viciously condemn mother or child or merely be passive when they seek a positive response from him, and in both cases he is disqualifying their communication.

Although it is not uncommon for people to disqualify each other's statements, ordinarily one would expect affirmation also to occur. However, when observing these families one does not hear even affectionate or giving behavior appreciated or affirmed. If one person indicates a desire for closeness, another indicates this is done in the wrong way or at the wrong time. (However, if one suggests separation the other will also indicate this is the wrong thing to do. Typically in these families the mother regularly threatens separation but does not leave, and the father does not often threaten separation but spends a good deal of his time away from home or "leaves" by drinking heavily while staying home.) Typically family members behave as if they are involved in what might be called a compulsory relationship. For example, a mother in one family indicated with some contempt that her husband was afraid to leave her because he could not stand being alone. She suggested he was cruel to her because he was angry at being tied to her. She also rejected his affectionate overtures because she considered them only a kind of bribery to insure staying with her. She herself was unable to leave him even for a night, though he was drunk several nights a week and beat her regularly. Both felt the association was not voluntary, and so neither could accept as valid any indication from the other about wanting to be together. A compulsory relationship is also typical of the parent and schizophrenic child. Since the child is considered incapable of leaving home and associating with others, his staying at home is taken as involuntary. Therefore should he indicate a desire to be with his parents, they tend to disqualify his overtures as merely a request that they not turn him out, and he finds his affectionate gestures disqualified.

LEADERSHIP IN THE FAMILY

Since family members tend to negate their own and each other's communication, any clear leadership in the family is impossible. Typically in these families the mother tends to initiate what happens, while indicating either that she isn't, or that someone else should. The father will invite her to initiate what happens while condemning her when she does. Often they suggest the child take the lead, and then disqualify his attempts. These families tend to become incapacitated by necessary decisions because each member will avoid affirming what he does and therefore is unable to acknowledge responsibility for his actions, and each will disqualify the attempts of any other to announce a decision. Both the act of taking leadership and the refusal to take leadership by any one family member is condemned by the others. The family "just happens" to take actions in particular directions with no individual accepting the label as the one responsible for any action.

ALLIANCES

Similarly, no labeled alliances are permitted in the family. A family coalition against the outside world (represented, say, by an observer), breaks down rather rapidly. Such individuals are also unable to form an alliance of two against one. Often they may appear to have such an alliance, as they tend to speak "through" one another. For example, the mother may ask for something for her child as a way of indicating that her husband deprives her, and so appear in alliance with the child. Or when the parents begin to express anger at each other, they may turn on the child for causing their difficulties and so appear in a coalition against him. Yet should the coalition be labeled, it will break down. If the child says, "You're both against me," one or the other parent will disqualify this remark and so deny the coalition. If father should say to mother, "Let's stick together on this," she is likely to say, "I'm afraid you'll back down at the last minute," or "It isn't my fault when we don't stick together." The mother and child may appear to form a coalition against the father, but should the child say, "Father treats us badly," mother is likely to say, "He has his troubles too," even though a moment before she may have been complaining to the child about how badly they were both treated by the father. Family members behave as if an alliance between two of them is inevitably a betrayal of the third person. They seem to have difficulty functioning in a two-person relationship, and as a result the separation of any one of the three from the others is a particular threat.

What confines the members so rigidly within their system is the prohibition on intimate alliances of one member with someone outside the family. As a result, the family members are inhibited from learning to relate to people with different behavior and so are confined to their own system of interaction.

DEFENSE AGAINST BLAME

Characteristically the mothers in these families defend themselves by "transfer of blame." Such a defense follows from the mother's consistent manifestation of incongruent levels: what she does, she qualifies as not having been done or not done in that way. If the child becomes disturbed, it happens "out of the blue." If anything goes wrong, mother indicates it is the fault of someone else. In those rare instances where she does admit she did something wrong, she indicates she did it only because she was told to, or out of duty, so that it wasn't her fault. She may also indicate that something must be wrong with the other person, since he ought not to have been affected by what she did, particularly when she didn't really do it. Even when her behavior affects someone pleasantly, she must deny that it was her fault. Typically she presents herself as helplessly pushed by forces outside her control.

The fathers also follow the family rule of incongruently qualifying their messages, yet they cannot use the same denial of blame and remain with their wives. They tend to use types of defense which complement her defense, and these are of three kinds. 1) Fathers who are withdrawn and passive, accept the blame their wives put upon them, but indicate by their unresponsiveness that they are blamed falsely and do not agree with her. 2) Fathers who have temper tantrums and blame their wives, put the blame on false or exaggerated grounds so the wife can easily point out her innocence. This type of father is easily blamed since he is dominating and tyrannical, yet by going too far he indicates he is an innocent victim driven by forces outside his control. 3) Some fathers do not blame their wives but also do not blame themselves or anyone else. Such fathers make an issue of semantic difference. If asked if they or their wives are at fault, a typical reply is, "Just what do you mean by 'fault'?" By accepting no implicit definition and not defining anything themselves, they obscure everything. Any particular father may manifest these three types of defense, all of which involve both disqualification of one's own statements and a disqualification of the other person's statements.

The child tends to use two types of defense. When "sane" he may blame himself and indicate that everything wrong with the family centers in him, an attitude the parents encourage, while at the same time he gives an impression of being blamed unjustly. When "insane" he negates his own statements and those of others by denying that anything happened. Or, if it did, he wasn't there—besides it wasn't him and it happened in another place at a time when he had no control over himself. The "withdrawal from reality" maneuvers of the schizophrenic make it impossible for him to blame himself or his parents since he defines himself as not of this world.

THE "DIFFERENT" BEHAVIOR OF THE SCHIZOPHRENIC
The inability of the schizophrenic to relate to people and his general withdrawal behavior seems understandable if he was raised in a learning situation where whatever he did was disqualified and if he was not allowed to relate to other people where he could learn to behave differently. Should he be reared in a situation where each attempt he made to gain a response from someone was met with an indication that he should behave in some other way, it would be possible for an individual to learn to avoid trying to relate to people by indicating that whatever he does is not done in relationship to anyone. He would then appear "autistic." However, the peculiar distortions of communication by the schizophrenic are not sufficiently explained by this description of his learning situation. If schizophrenic behavior is adaptive to a particular type of family, it is necessary to suggest the adaptive function involved when a person behaves in a clearly psychotic way.

The recovering schizophrenic patient, and perhaps the pre-psychotic schizophrenic, will qualify what he says in a way similar to that used by his parents. His behavior could be said to be "normal" for that family. However, during a psychotic episode the schizophrenic behaves in a rather unique manner. To suggest how such behavior might serve a function in the family, it is necessary both to describe schizophrenia in terms of behavior and to suggest the conditions under which such behavior might occur. To describe schizophrenic behavior, it is necessary to translate into behavioral terms such diagnostic concepts as delusions, hallucinations, concretistic thinking, and so on.

What appears unique about schizophrenic behavior is the incongruence of all levels of communication. The patient's parents may say something and disqualify it, but they will affirm that disqualification. The schizophrenic will say something, deny saying it, but qualify his denial in an incongruent way. Schizophrenic behavior described in this way has been presented elsewhere (10), but it may be summarized briefly here.

Not only can a person manifest an incongruence between levels of total message, but also between elements of his messages. A message from one person to another can be formalized into the following statement: I (source) am communicating (message) to you (receiver) in this context.

By his body movement, vocal inflections, and verbal statements a person must affirm or disqualify each of the elements of this message. The symptoms of a schizophrenic can be summarized in terms of this schema.

1) Source. A person may indicate that he isn't really the source of a message by indicating that he is only transmitting the idea of someone else. Therefore he says something but qualifies it with a denial that he is saying it. The schizophrenic may also qualify the source of the message in this way, but he will qualify his qualifications in an incongruent way. For example, a male schizophrenic patient reported that his name was Margaret Stalin. Thus he indicated that he wasn't really speaking, but by making his denial clearly fantastic he disqualified his denial that he was speaking. Similarly a patient may say that "voices" are making the statement. In the excerpt presented, the patient denies that he is responsible for the greeting card message by saying "they sell them in the canteen," and yet this denial is by its nature self-disqualifying and so his messages become incongruent at all levels.

2) <u>Message</u>. A person may indicate in various ways that his words or action are not really a message. He may indicate, for example, that what he did was accidental if he blurts something out or if he steps on someone's foot. The schizophrenic may indicate that his statement isn't a message but merely a group of words, or he may speak in a random, or word salad, way, thus indicating that he isn't really communicating. Yet at the same time he manages to indicate some pertinent points in his word salad, thus disqualifying his denial that his message is a message. In the excerpt given above, the patient says, "a card is a card," as a way of denying the message communicated. He also says that he doesn't remember what the thing was, thus denying the message existed for him. However, both these qualifications of the message are also disqualified: the card obviously isn't merely a card, and he can hardly not remember what the thing was when he is looking at it.

3) <u>Receiver</u>. A person may deny this element in a message in various ways, for example by indicating he isn't really talking to the particular person he is addressing, but rather to that person's status. The schizophrenic patient is likely to indicate that the doctor he is talking to isn't really a doctor, but, say, an FBI agent. Thereby he not only denies talking to the physician, but by labeling the receiver in a clearly fantastic way he disqualifies his denial. Paranoid delusionary statements of this sort become "obvious" by their self-negating quality.

4) <u>Context</u>. A person may disqualify his statement by indicating that it applies to some other context than the one in which it is made. <u>Context</u> is defined broadly here as the situation in which people are communicating, including both the physical situation and the stated premises about what sort of situation it is. For example, a woman may be aggressively sexual in a public place where the context disqualifies her overtures. The typical statement that the schizophrenic is "withdrawn from reality" seems to be based to a great extent on the ways he qualifies what he says by mislabeling the context. He may say his hospital conversation is taking place in a palace, or in prison, and thereby disqualify his statements. Since his labels are clearly impossible, his disqualification is disqualified.

These multiple incongruent levels of communication differentiate the schizophrenic from his parents and from other people. If a person says something and then negates his statement we judge him by his other levels of message. When these too are incongruent so that he says something, indicates he didn't, then affirms one or the other, and then disqualifies his affirmation; there is a tendency to call such a person insane.

From the point of view offered here, schizophrenia is an intermittent type of behavior. The patient may be behaving in a schizophrenic way at one moment and in a way that is "normal" for this type of family at another moment. The important question is this: Under what circumstances does he behave in a psychotic way, defined here as qualifying incongruently all his levels of message ?

In this excerpt of a family interaction, the patient shows psychotic behavior when he is caught between a therapist pressuring him to affirm his statements and his parents pressuring him to disqualify them. From this point of view, the patient is faced with a situation where he must infringe the rules of his relationship with the therapist or infringe his family rules. His psychotic behavior can be seen as an attempt to adapt to both.[2] By behaving in a psychotic way he could 1) affirm his statement about his mother, thus following the rule in the therapeutic relationship for affirmative statements, 2) disqualify his critical statement of the mother, thus following the family rules that mother is not to be blamed in a way so that she can accept blame and all statements are to be disqualified, and 3) synthesize these two incompatible theses by indicating that the message wasn't his (it wasn't really a message, he couldn't remember it, and he didn't really send it). It can be argued that psychotic behavior is a sequence of messages which infringe a set of prohibitions but which are qualified as not infringing them. The only way an individual can achieve this is by qualifying incongruently all levels of his communication.

The need to behave in a psychotic way would seem to occur when the patient infringes a family prohibition and thereby activates himself and his parents to behave in such a way that he either returns within the previous system of rules or indicates

---

[2]An attempt to synthesize two incompatible situations by a perceptual change is suggested in Weakland and Jackson (22). Describing an incident during a psychotic breakdown, they say, "Psychotic delusions allowed him to free himself of decision making. For example, the cab driver is a hospital attendant in disguise. There is no problem in Home vs. Hospital; it has been resolved."

somehow that he is not infringing them. Should he successfully infringe the system of family rules and thereby set new rules, his parents may become "disturbed." This seems to occur rather often when the patient living at home "improves" with therapy. When improving in therapy he is not only infringing the family prohibitions against outside alliances but he may blame the mother in a reasonable way and affirm his statements or those of others. Such behavior on his part would shatter the family system unless the parents are also undergoing therapy. The omnipotent feelings of the schizophrenic patient may have some basis, since his family system is so rigid that he can create considerable repercussions by behaving differently.

A patient is faced with infringing family prohibitions when 1) two family prohibitions conflict with each other and he must respond to both, 2) when forces outside the family, or maturational forces within himself, require him to infringe them, or 3) when prohibitions special to him conflict with prohibitions applying to all family members. If he must infringe such prohibitions and at the same time not infringe them, he can only do so through psychotic behavior.

Conflicting sets of prohibitions may occur when the individual is involved with both mother and therapist, involved with a therapist and administrator in a hospital setting (19), or when some shift within his own family brings prohibitions into conflict. This latter would seem the most likely bind the patient would find himself in when living at home, and an incident is offered here to describe psychiatric behavior serving a function in the family.

A twenty one year old schizophrenic daughter arrived home from the hospital for a trial visit and her parents promptly separated. The mother asked the girl to go with her, and when she arrived at their destination, the grandmother's home, the patient telephoned her father. Her mother asked her why she turned against her by calling the father, and the daughter said she called him to say goodbye and because she had looked at him with an "odd" look when they left. A typical symptom of this patient when overtly psychotic is her perception of "odd" looks, and the problem is how such a message is adaptive to the family pattern of interaction.

The incident could be described in this way. The mother separated from father but qualified her leaving incongruently by saying it was only temporary and telling him where she was going.

The father objected to the mother's leaving, but made no attempt to restrain her or to persuade her to stay. The daughter had to respond to this situation in accord with the prohibitions set by this family system: she had to disqualify whatever she did, she had to disqualify what her mother and father did, she could not ally with either mother or father and acknowledge it, and she could not blame the mother in such a way that the mother would accept the blame.

The girl could not merely do nothing because this would mean remaining with father. However, by going with the mother she in effect formed an alliance and so infringed one of the prohibitions in the family system. The girl solved the problem by going with mother but telephoning her father, thus disqualifying her alliance with mother. However, her mother objected to the call, and the daughter said she only called him to say goodbye, thus disqualifying her alliance with father. Yet to leave it this way would mean allying with mother. She qualified her statement further by saying she called father because she gave him an "odd look" when she left him. By having an odd look, she could succeed in not siding with either parent or blaming mother. She also manifested schizophrenic behavior by qualifying incongruently all levels of message and thereby adapting to incongruent family prohibitions. Previously the girl could withdraw to her room to avoid the alliance problem, but when mother stopped staying home while saying she was going to leave, and left while saying she was not really leaving, the girl was threatened by a possible alliance whether she went with her mother or stayed at home. Her incongruent, schizophrenic behavior would seem necessary to remain within the prohibitions of the family at those times. If one is required to behave in a certain way and simultaneously required not to, he can only solve the problem by indicating that he is not behaving at all, or not with this particular person in this situation. The girl might also have solved the problem by disqualifying her identity, indicating the context was really a secret plot, indicating that what she did was what voices told her to do, or speaking in a random or word salad way. In other words, she could both meet the prohibitions in the family and infringe them only by disqualifying the source of her messages, the nature of them, the recipient, or the context, and so behave in a psychotic fashion.

It is important to emphasize that schizophrenic behavior in the family is adaptive to an intricate and complicated family organization which is presented here in crude simplicity. The network of family prohibitions confronts the individual members with

almost insoluble problems. This particular incident was later
discussed with the parents of this girl, and the mother said her
daughter could have solved the problem easily. She could have
stayed with father and told him he was wrong in the quarrel which
provoked the separation. This would seem to be the mother's
usual way of dealing with this kind of situation--she stays with
father while telling him he is wrong. However, the mother leaves
herself out of this solution by ignoring the fact that she asked her
daughter to go with her. This request was even more compli-
cated--the mother asked the daughter to go with her during a period when the mother was saying the daughter must return to the
hospital because she could not tolerate associating with her.
When the parents reunited later that week, the girl was returned
to the hospital because mother said she could not stand daughter
in the room watching her, and she could not stand daughter out of
the room thinking about her.

The approach offered here differs from the usual psychodynamic explanations. It would be possible to say that the mother's concern about leaving the daughter with the father, even when she
could not tolerate the girl's company, might center in the family's
concern about incestuous desires between father and daughter.
Such a psychodynamic hypothesis could be supported. Later in
therapy the father and daughter planned a picnic alone together
when they decided they should see more of each other without
the mother being present. The evening of the day this was arranged, the therapist received a telephone call from the disturbed
mother. She reported that she and her husband had been drinking
and arguing all evening and she reported that her husband had
told her it was natural for a father to have sexual relations with
his daughter. The husband's report was that he had not said this.
(He had said it was natural for a father to have sexual feelings
for his daughter, but this did not mean he would do anything about
it.) This crisis over suggested possible incest could be explained
by saying that the threat of closeness between father and daughter
aroused forbidden incestuous desires in them. However, it was
the mother who made an issue over the possible incest. From the
psychodynamic point of view, hints and discussions of incest
would represent unconscious conflicts. From the point of view
offered here, this type of discussion is an aspect of family stra-
tegy. To label a relationship as possibly incestuous would be
one further way of enforcing a prohibition on alliances between
father and daughter. Such a maneuver is similar to one where
the mother inhibits a relationship between father and daughter by
insisting that the father should associate more with the daughter,

thus arousing his negative behavior as well as the issue of whether he neglected the daughter. The approach offered here does not deal with supposed motivating forces within the individuals concerned, but with the formal characteristics of their behavior with each other. 3)

THE FUNCTION OF FAMILY BEHAVIOR

The difficulty for this type of family would seem to lie in the inflexibility of their family system. They often maintain the system despite the sturdy attempts of a family therapist to help them deal with each other more amicably. Apparently family members gain only discord, dissension, and a constant struggle with one another, or periods of withdrawal in a kind of truce, yet they continue so to behave. It would be possible to postulate psychodynamic causes for this type of behavior, or self-destructive drives could be sought, but an attempt is made here to develop an alternative descriptive language centering on the peculiar sensitivity of people to the fact that their behavior is governed by others.

When people respond to one another they inevitably influence how the other person is to respond to them. Whatever one says, or doesn't say, in response to another person is a determinant of the other person's behavior. For example, if one criticizes another, he is indicating that critical statements from him are permissible in the relationship. The other person cannot not respond, and whatever response he makes will govern the critical person's behavior. Whether the criticized one gets angry, or weeps helplessly, or passively accepts the criticism, he must either be accepting the rules or countering with other rules. These rules for relationships which people establish with each other are never permanently set but are in a constant process of reinforcement as the two people interact and govern each other's behavior.

---

3)Although statements in the form of family rules deal with observable behavior and are therefore verifiable, the verification depends to some extent upon the skill of the observer. Such statements are more reliably documented by placing the family in a structured experimental situation where the results depend upon whether or not the family functions under certain prohibitions. The Bateson project is now beginning a program of experiments with families similar to the small group experiments of Alex Bavelas.

Every human being depends upon other people not only for his survival but for his pleasure and pain. It is of primary importance that he learn to govern the responses of other people so they will provide him satisfaction. Yet a person can only gain satisfaction in a relationship if he permits others to cooperate in setting the rules for the relationship and so influence and govern him. The person who dares not risk such control over him would seem to provoke his own misery by attempting to avoid it. If someone has suffered a series of hurts and frustrations with people he trusted, he tends to try to become independent of people--by not getting involved with them in such a way that they can gain control over his feelings or his behavior. He may literally avoid people; he may interact with them only on his own terms, constantly making an issue of who is going to circumscribe whose behavior; or he may choose the schizophrenic way and indicate that nothing he does is done in relationship to other people. In this fashion he is not governing anyone and no one is governing him.

The family of the schizophrenic would seem to be not only establishing and following a system of rules, as other families do, but also following a prohibition on any acknowledgement that a family member is setting rules. Each refuses to concede that he is circumscribing the behavior of others, and each refuses to concede that any other family member is governing him. Since communication inevitably occurs if people live together, and since whatever one communicates inevitably governs the behavior of others, the family members must each constantly disqualify the communications of one another. Should one affirm what he does or what another does, he risks conceding that he is governed by the other with all the consequences that follow being disappointed again by an untrustworthy person. Schizophrenic behavior can be seen as both a product and a parody of this kind of family system. By labeling everything he communicates as not communicated by him to this person in this place, the schizophrenic indicates that he is not governing anyone's behavior because he is not in a relationship with anyone. This would seem to be a necessary style of behavior at times in this type of family system, and it may become habitual behavior. Yet even psychotic behavior does not free the individual from being governed or from governing others. The person who insists that he does not need anyone at all and is completely independent of them requires people to put him in a hospital and to force feed him. To live at all one must be involved with other people and so deal with the universal problem of who is going to circumscribe whose behavior. The more a person tries to avoid being governed or governing others, the more helpless he becomes and so governs others by forcing them to take care of him.

A MODEL FOR DIFFERENTIATING TYPES OF FAMILIES

What is lacking in the study of interpersonal relations is a method of describing, by way of some analogy the process which takes place when two or more people interact with one another. Although there are models for inner activity, e.g., the id-ego-superego metaphor, there is not yet a model for human inter-action. Implicit in the approach to the schizophrenic family offered here there is such a model. The essential elements of it are: 1) the proposition that human communication can be classified into levels of message, 2) the cybernetic idea of the self-corrective, governed system. If a family confines itself to re-petitive patterns within a certain range of possible behavior, then they are confined to that range by some sort of governing process. No outside governor requires the family members to behave in their habitual patterns, so this governing process must exist within the family. A third essential point is that when peo-ple respond to one another they govern, or establish rules, for each other's behavior.

To describe families, the most appropriate analogy would seem to be the self-corrective system governed by family mem-bers influencing each other's behavior and thereby establishing rules and prohibitions for that particular family system. Such a system tends to be error-activated. Should one family member break a family rule, the others become activated until he either conforms to the rule again or successfully establishes a new one.

A system of three organisms each governing the range of be-havior of the other two, and each communicating at multiple lev-els, is both a simple idea and a complex model. Yet such an approach offers a general theoretical framework within which the specific rules of any one type of family system can be classified. The rudiments of such a system are suggested here at the most general level. The family of the schizophrenic is a particularly good model for this approach because of the narrow limits of their system. Our few preliminary observations of families con-taining children without symptoms, children who are delinquent, and children with asthma, lead us to believe that the interaction in the family of the schizophrenic is unique. Members of other types of family sometimes disqualify each other's statements but only under certain circumstances. Mutual affirmation will also occur. We have observed, for example, parents of an asthmatic child finishing each other's sentences and having this approved. Should the father of a schizophrenic finish the mother's sentence, it seems inevitable that she would indicate he provided the wrong ending. In other families leadership will stabilize into a pattern accepted by family members. Certain alliances will be allowed in some types of families, notably the delinquent where the child is capable of forming labeled alliances in gangs outside the family. In the family of the schizophrenic the range of behavior is as limited and inflexible as is the behavior of the schizophrenic in contrast to other people.

The observation of this type of family system inevitably takes place after the child has manifested a schizophrenic episode. Whether the family behaved in a similar way prior to his diagnosis is unknowable. In this sense it is difficult to assert that the interaction in his family "caused" schizophrenia. There are two possibilities. 1) If the family is a self-corrective system and the child behaves intermittently in a schizophrenic way, then schizophrenic behavior is a necessary part of this family system. 2) Alternatively, schizophrenic behavior as a result of a particular family system which has been disrupted by forces outside the system, such as maturation of the child or environmental influence. The family then reorganizes a new system which includes the schizophrenic behavior as an element, and this is what we are presently examining. The evidence leads us to believe that schizophrenic behavior in the child is reinforced by the present family system.

Although psychotic behavior may serve a function in a family system, a risk is also involved. The patient may need to be separated from the family by hospitalization and so break up the system, or he may enter therapy and change and so leave the system. Typically the parents seem to welcome hospitalization only if the patient is still accessible to them, and they welcome therapy for the patient up to the point when he begins to change and infringe the rules of the family system while acknowledging that he is doing so.

REFERENCES

1. Alanen, Y. The mothers of schizophrenic patients. Acta psychiat. et neurol. scandinav., 33: Suppl. 124, 1958.
2. Bateson, G. Cultural problems posed by a study of schizophrenic process. Presented at the American Psychiatric

198

Association, Conference on Schizophrenia, Honolulu, 1958. In press.

3. Bateson, G. The group dynamics of schizophrenia. Presented at the Institute on Chronic Schizophrenia and Hospital Treatment Programs, Osawatomie State Hospital, Osawatomie, 1958, In press.,

4. Bateson, G. The new conceptual frames for behavioral research. Presented at the Sixth Annual Psychiatric Institute Conference at the New Jersey Neuro-Psychiatric Institute, Princeton, New Jersey, 1958. In press.

5. Bateson, G., Jackson, D. D., Haley, J. and Weakland, J. Toward a theory of schizophrenia. Behavioral Sc., 1:251-264, 1956. (See p. 31, this vol.)

6. Bowen, M., Dysinger, R. H. and Basaminia, B. The role of the father in families with a schizophrenic patient. Paper presented at the annual meeting of the American Psychiatric Association, May, 1958.

7. Gerard, D. L. and Siegel, J. The family background of schizophrenia. Psychiat. Quart., 24:47-73, 1950.

8. Frazee, H. E. Children who later became schizophrenic. Smith. Coll. Stud. Social Work, 123:125-149, 1953.

9. Haley, J. Control in psychoanalytic psychotherapy. Progr. Psychotherapy, 4:48-65, 1959.

10. Haley, J. An interactional description of schizophrenia. Psychiatry, to be published. (See p. 151, this vol.)

11. Haley, J. An interactional explanation of hypnosis. Am. J. Clin. Hypnosis, 1:41-57, 1958.

12. Jackson, D. D. The question of family homeostasis. Psychoanalyt Quart., 31: Suppl.; 79-90, 1957. (See p. 1, this vol.)

13. Lidz, R. W. and Lidz, T. The family environment of schizophrenic patients. Am. J. Psychiat., 106:332-345, 1949.

14. Lidz, T., Parker, B. and Cornelison, A. R. The role of the father in the family environment of the schizophrenic patient. Am. J. Psychiat., 113:126-132, 1956.

15. Lidz, T., Cornelison, A. R., Fleck, S. and Terry, D. The interactional environment of schizophrenic patients. I. The Father. Psychiatry, 20:329-342, 1957.

16. Lidz, T., Cornelison, A. R., Fleck, S. and Terry, D. The intrafamilial environment of schizophrenic patients. II. Marital schism and marital skew. Am. J. Psychiat., 114:241-248, 1957.

17. Reichard, S. and Tillman, G. Patterns of parent-child relationships in schizophrenia. Psychiatry, 13:247-257, 1950.

18. Rosen, J. N. Direct Analysis. Grune & Stratton, New York, 1951.
19. Stanton, A. H. and Schwartz, M. S. The Mental Hospital. Basic Books, New York, 1954.
20. Tietze, T. A study of the mothers of schizophrenic patients. Psychiatry, 12:55-65, 1959.
21. Weakland, J. The "double bind" hypothesis of schizophrenia and three-party interaction. In The Study of Schizophrenia. Basic Books, New York. In press.
22. Weakland, J. H. and Jackson, D. D. Patient and therapist observations on the circumstances of a schizophrenic episode. A. M. A. Arch. Neurol. & Psychiat., 79:554-574, 1958. (See p. 87, this vol.)
23. Wynne, I. D., Ryckoff, I. M., Day, J. and Hirsch, S. E. Pseudo-mutuality in the family relations of schizophrenics. Psychiatry, 21:205-220, 1958.

SOME VARIETIES OF PATHOGENIC
ORGANIZATION

Gregory Bateson and Don D. Jackson

It is necessary to delimit the subject of the present paper. First, the paper will not deal with that whole genus of interaction patterns which has been classified (1) as "symmetrical," i.e., the behavior in rivalries and other relationships, where A is stimulated to do something·because B has done this same thing; and where B does more of this because A did some of it; and A does more of it because B did some, and so on. This is the sort of symmetry characteristic of keeping up with the Joneses, some armaments races, and so forth.

This leaves the complementary side of interactive behavior, in which what A does fits, in some sense, with what B does but is essentially different from it. This category of complementary interaction includes, for example, dominance and submission, exhibitionism and spectatorship, succoring and dependence, and so forth --a series of patterns where there is a mutual fitting between A's behavior and that of B.

Within this category of complementary patterns of interaction, a number of subcategories may usefully be discriminated:

a) A very important subgroup is that which has been schematically organized by Erikson (2) in his analysis of behavioral modes and their relationship to the erogenous zones of the body. Characteristically, all the themes related to the erogenous zones--intrusion, invasion, exclusion, ejection, retention, and so forth-- are complementary.

Reprinted from DISORDERS OF COMMUNICATION, 42: Research Publications, A. R. N. M. D., pp. 270-283 (1964). Copyright, Association for Research in Nervous and Mental Disease; reproduced by permission.

b) To these we may add the themes related to locomotion and bodily mechanics--support, balance, rise and fall, control, reach, grasp, and the like.

c) A third category of complementary themes includes those related to sense organs and perception--understanding, ignoring, attending, and the like. Note in this connection that, probably for all animals, there is a strong tendency for organs of sense to become transmitting agents for outgoing messages. When the dog pricks up his ears, he is not simply improving his sensory reception, he is transmitting a statement about the direction of his attention, and in relationships between dogs to prick the ears becomes also a statement of self-confidence vis-a-vis the other individual.

d) Lastly, two important themes of complementary interaction are so closely interrelated that it is appropriate to mention them together. These are the themes of parent-child relationship and of territory. Neither can perhaps be separated clearly from a, b, and c above. The themes of parenthood are clearly closely related to the themes derived from the erogenous zones, and the themes of territory could perhaps be conveniently understood by regarding territory as an extension of body. It appears, however that, at least for mammals, the first learning associated with territory occurs in regard to territory defined by the mother (or possibly both parents) (3). The archetypal definition of territory might perhaps be "that area defined by mother's presence within which the infant has an autistic or absolute right to safety." Such a view of the relationship between parenthood and territory would explain not only such metaphors as motherland and patria but also the differential degree of confidence which an animal shows according to whether he is on or off his own territory.

In sum, restricting this paper to complementary patterns will focus attention close to the body and to parent-child relationship as the primary sources from which perhaps all behavior is derived. Further, any such classification as is attempted above makes certain assumptions about the role of learning in the development of behavior. The morphology of the erogenous zones and, in large measure, their erogenous character, are no doubt genotypically determined, but to assume transference of patterns derived from them to other spheres of life is to invoke learning. (If this sort of coherence should be demonstrated to occur in those invertebrates whose behavior is much more completely determined by the genotype and uninfluenced by relationship with a parent, this discovery would present serious problems for evolutionary theory.)

Second, another limitation is necessary. The paper will not deal with digital systems of message-making. Language, insofar as there is such a thing as pure language, is a digital business in the sense that the units of which it is made resemble numbers-- 1, 2, 3, 4, 5--from which of course the word "digital" comes. There is nothing particularly five-like in the number 5; there is nothing particularly table-like in the word "table." These words are arbitrary signs which can be manipulated according to various sorts of rules, called algorithms, and it is a characteristic peculiar to the human species that we have developed a very massive apparatus for communicating digitally. This linguistic system, as such, will fall outside the area of relevance of this paper, except insofar as the sequence of linguistic events may constitute analogue communication about complementary relationship, or insofar as the differences between analog and digital communication must be explored.

The other side of human and mammalian communication, namely that which one can refer to by the technical term, analog communication--this will be our subject matter. Here, the message material is much more directly recognizable for what it means. If you observe two natives of some unknown culture engaged in interaction, you will notice that you have no understanding of the words which they use but that you have at least a guesswork understanding of their gestures, postures, facial expressions, voices and silences. You may be seriously wrong in how you interpret these signals, but at least you are not faced with totally opaque material. When the natives raise their voices, you will guess (probably correctly) that the quantitative change, measurable in decibels, is simply analogous to some quantitative change in the intensity of relationship either between the persons or between them and the (unknown) subject of their discourse.

The primary definition of analog communication turns upon this notion of analogous magnitudes. The digital computing machine manipulates ciphers which have no magnitude, whereas the analog machine reproduces within the black box some physical process involving real magnitudes, which have direct relation to magnitudes existing within the subject matter about which the machine is being asked to compute. The digital machine is fed with bits of information and gives back its answer in a similar currency. The analog machine is fed with quantitative settings of dials and the like and gives back its answer in a similar quantitative form.

In addition, however, to this quantitative characteristic of analog communication, there is also the fact that in such systems patterns of relationship are likely to be formally analogous--a pattern
in the subject of discourse being represented in the discourse by
patterns or gestalten which are rather direct representations of
these. In many cases, it is actually impossible to separate the subject matter of complementary analog communication from the message material in which some proposition about the subject matter is
encoded. The actual events of the interchange may contain both:
a) an element of signalling, e.g., if A clenches his fist he is mentioning or proposing the possibility of violence and the gesture has
communicational function in that the clenched fist serves as a name
for a species of action and b) another, more direct element in that
the act of clenching the fist is a real change in A's readiness for
violent action. The statement of readiness is not separated from
the pragmatic reality of readiness by a step of coding. The
clenched fist is not just a name for a type of action, it is also a
part or sample of such action. It is therefore dangerous to use
in our thinking the very notion of coding which has been so fruitful in the analysis of digital communication. The relationship of
analog communication to the problems of logical typing is evidently
quite different from that which holds for digital systems.

One result of this direct relation between message and subject
matter will be that you, observing two individuals from some strange
culture, will be able to guess at complementary themes in their relationship. Watching their linguistic sequences but understanding
none of the words, you will still see who initiates segments of interchange and may well be able to detect patterns of respect, intimacy
or distance, if these are expressed in styles or overtones of language.

Moreover, as we proceed to the next higher level of abstraction,
it will probably be still easier for the observer to guess at what is
going on. He may have difficulty in evaluating the patterns of interchange so long as these are constant, but a change in expressions of
respect, intimacy or distance may be unambiguous.

Indeed, it would seem that precisely because the patterns of interchange are discussed by an exchange of samples of this interchange, the participants themselves are likely to be in some doubt
about what is going on. They too may have to rely more upon
changes in the pattern than upon ongoing constancy. The implications of a handshake or a kiss become blurred when these idioms of
interchange become constant. The relationship only becomes clear

as a result of changes in the kiss or the handshake. Lovers' quarrels are perhaps necessary for validation of the underlying patterns.

However, even if we disregard these higher levels of patterning, in discussing complementarity we are already concerned with an order of phenomena outside the field of behavioral psychology. There is, strictly speaking, no such thing as a complementary piece of "behavior." To drop a brick may be either complementary or symmetrical; and which it is depends upon how this piece of behavior is related to preceding and subsequent behaviors of the vis-a-vis.

It is, of course, as legitimate for the behaviorists to limit their discussion to those levels of abstraction in which they are interested as it is for us in this paper to limit discussion to the next higher level. What is important is to keep these levels clearly defined and to understand the difference between them.

The stimulus-response (S. R.) psychologist typically confines his attention to sequences of interchange so short that it is possible to label one item of input as "stimulus" and another item as "reinforcement" while labeling what the subject does between these two events as "response." Within the short sequence so excised, it is possible to talk about the "psychology" of the subject. In contrast, the sequences of interchange which we are here discussing are very much longer and therefore have the characteristic that every item in the sequence is simultaneously stimulus, response and reinforcement. A given item of x's behavior is a stimulus insofar as it is followed by an item contributed by y and that by another item contributed by x. But insofar as x's item is sandwiched between two items contributed by y, it is a response. Similarly x's item is a reinforcement insofar as it follows an item contributed by y. The ongoing interchanges, then, which we are here discussing, constitute a chain of overlapping triadic links, each of which is comparable to a stimulus-response-reinforcement sequence. We can take any triad of our interchange and see it as a single trial in an S. R. learning experiment.

If we look at the conventional learning experiments from this point of view, we observe at once that repeated trials amount to a differentiation of relationship between the two organisms concerned--the experimenter and his subject. The sequence of trials is so punctuated that it is always the experimenter who seems to provide the "stimuli" and the "reinforcements," while the subject provides the "responses." These words are here deliberately put in quotation marks because the role definitions are in fact only created by the willingness of the organisms to accept the system of punctuation.

The "reality" of the role definitions is only of the same order as the reality of a bat on a Rorschach card--a more or less over-determined creation of the perceptive process. The rat who said "I have got my experimenter trained. Each time I press the lever he gives me food" was declining to accept the punctuation of the sequence which the experimenter was seeking to impose.

It is still true, however, that in a long sequence of interchange, the organisms concerned--especially if these be people--will in fact punctuate the sequence so that it will appear that one or the other has initiative, dominance, dependency or the like. That is, they will set up between them patterns of interchange (about which they may or may not be in agreement) and these patterns will in fact be rules of contingency regarding the exchange of reinforcement. Although rats are too nice to relabel, some psychiatric patients are not and they provide psychological trauma for the therapist!

It is appropriate now to ask what is gained by the shift in our attention from asking about the response system of an individual to looking for contingency patterns within a relationship. The answer would seem to be that limitation to the S.R. level would limit us to the discussion of the non-verbal communication of inverte-brates with possibly some analysis of human _verbal_ behavior, and would exclude from our analysis almost the whole of mammalian non-verbal communication. When you open the refrigerator door and the cat comes and rubs against your legs making certain sounds, she is not touching off a reflex response in you--which might be the case if both you and she were members of some invertebrate species. Neither is she saying "Milk!" because she does not have denotative language. It would seem, rather, that the primary referent of her discourse is what we might call "dependency." She is asserting the contingency pattern of her relationship with you, or, in the language of the anthropologists, we might say that she is using something like a kinship term. In reply to this highly abstract message, you are expected to achieve a deductive step and guess that you should give her milk.

It is not possible to conduct any meaningful analysis of this order of communication in simple S.R. terms. It is absolutely necessary to conduct the analysis in terms of those units, which are the contingency patterns of the interchange.

If this argument be sound, it follows that mammals, including human beings, should be subject to pathologies of communication at this level, i.e., that errors regarding the contingency patterns

of relationship between individuals will be pathogenic. At the beginning of this paper, it was asserted that the complementary patterns of mammalian relationship have their roots in the body and
in primary interchanges between offspring and parent and in such
essential matters as physical balance and support. It is in these
areas that we must look for pathology when the premises of complementary relationship are disrupted.

In this connection, it seems that the experimental psychologists
have contributed crucial data. The classical experiments on breakdown of discrimination among dogs and other animals fall neatly into place as exemplifications of what happens when a mammal is
placed in a situation where he cannot be right about the contingency
patterns of his relationship to the outside world or to the experimenter. It is worthwhile to summarize the course of such an experiment. In the opening phase the animal subject is trained to
discriminate between two stimulus objects, e.g., ellipse and circle, one of which shall mean x, while the other is to mean y. When
this preliminary training is complete, the stimulus objects are
modified in the direction of greater resemblance. The ellipse is
fattened and the circle is flattened. In this stage the animal is
forced to make greater efforts at discriminating between them, and
if he is successful, he receives an even stronger impression that
the context in which he finds himself is one which demands discrimination. The same message also comes to be carried by the ancillary objects, the experimental harness, smell of the laboratory,
and so forth.

The experimenter, of course, will probably be guided by pencil
marks on the backs of the stimulus objects so that he may remember which is the "ellipse" and which the "circle"; and he will use a
tossed coin, or perhaps a table of random numbers, to decide which
object he should administer next. It would never do to have some
patterning of this order which the animal might detect.

Finally the stimulus objects become, from the animal's point of
view, indiscriminable, and at this point the animal is likely to show
non-adaptive or pathological behaviors. He may refuse food, go
comatose, bite his keeper or do something similar.

If we now ask about the contingency patterns of the contexts in
which the animal successively is placed, we observe that in the initial phase of the experiment the contingency patterns called for discrimination. In the middle phase of the experiment this demand was
underlined, but in the final phase of the experiment the most appro-

priate course for the animal would have been to stop trying to discriminate and to use a coin to decide which response he should give.
In this phase the context has become one for guessing or for gam-
bling, and indeed, the experimenter was guilty of some redundancy
if, in this final phase of the experiment, he continued to use two
stimulus objects instead of one; he might just as well have used one
stimulus object, consulting his random number table between each
presentation of the object to decide what it would mean. From where
the animal sits there is in this final phase only one stimulus object
seen in the trance of a strong expectation that the contingencies of
the context demand that he discriminate.

That some such reading of these experiments is correct is supported by other experimental data. Liddell has shown that without
the ancillary stimuli provided by the harness and the laboratory,
the pathological behavior does not develop, and it is also known that
the initial phase of the experiment in which the animal is trained to
discriminate is necessary. A naive animal faced with a stimulus
object which sometimes means x and sometimes y will in fact guess,
without any development of pathological symptoms.

It is not that the dog's discrimination broke down; it is that the
psychologist failed to discriminate between a context for guessing
and a context for discrimination while giving the animal the impression that there has been no change in context.

These classical experiments have been discussed here in order
to illustrate the difference between theory based upon S. R. be-
haviorism and theory which takes into account the contingency patterns of interpersonal relationship. If the reading here offered of
the cat's mew and of the classical discrimination experiments is
correct, it follows that mammals must be deeply and vitally concerned with correctness at this level.

The same considerations apply to human beings, who are similarly prone to exhibit psychotic symptomatology when placed in the
wrong regarding the contextual structure of their relationship. This
argument is, in fact, the core thesis of the so-called "double bind"
theory of schizophrenia (4-6), that schizophrenic behavior arises
in sequences of experience in which one or more individuals are
continually put in the wrong regarding the contingency patterns of
relationship.

A very little parlor experimentation along these lines will evoke
"schizoid behavior," i.e., the emitting of messages whose logical

type is obscured by their metaphoric form. One of us (G. B.), teaching a class of affiliate nurses at the hospital, talked to them about "Tiny, " the 5-foot sow at Cornell, who learned that she ought to recognize whether a given signal meant food or an electric shock in the food box. When the indiscriminable signal was given, Tiny would stand trembling for hours and finally make a great rush, smashing the food box and even forgetting to look for the food. The nurses wanted this translated into more human terms. The lecturer then picked one of the girls and started a conversation with her. Lecturer: "How are you enjoying your three months' psychiatric experience?" She: "Very much." Lecturer: "You had to say that, didn't you?" She: "But I really am." Lecturer: "Really? Really is one of those words we use when we want to overcompensate a little. Now honestly, how do you feel about your psychiatric experience?" She: "Oh, go play pig with somebody else!"

In this instance the hurt of both the nurse and the lecturer was relieved by the balm of laughter in which all joined, but this overt recognition of what has happened is not available in more malign settings.

A schizophrenic person is one who has learned to be abnormally cautious about committing himself to any particular view of the relationship between himself and important others. We may think of his messages as constructed according to the following recipe:

Imagine a Western Union telegram blank. It has on it a series of slots, one of which is for the text of the message. Others are marked "To whom"; "From whom"; "Time"; "Date"; "Code used"; "Priority"; and so on. All of these subsidiary slots are for messages about the message. In conversation we similarly accompany our messages with messages about the message, and it is these that the schizophrenic patient will selectively distort. These are the messages which would otherwise disclose his view of the contingencies of relationship between himself and the other. To use a first person pronoun is to refer to himself as in a relationship to you. To indicate that he cares about the content of his message is to imply that his relationship to you is such that an expression of caring would be appropriate. He will therefore distort the "priority" of his message. He may even change the address, making a message "from me to you" into a message "from Christ to the world. "

A schizophrenic patient was told by the therapist that the latter would be away for 2 weeks attending American Psychiatric Association meetings in Honolulu. The patient turned his back to the therapist and gazed out the window and said, "That plane is flying awfully slowly." The original form of this message before schizophrenic coding was perhaps "I shall miss you," but to have left the text in this form would have been to presume upon the relationship to the therapist. It was therefore safer to change the text to a more impersonal and metaphoric form.

It is, however, not sufficient to assert a) that mammals preponderantly communicate about the contingency patterns of the relationship and b) that traumatization at this level leads to schizoid manifestations. Over and above all this is the fact that while mammals, including man, primarily use analogic methods (intention movements and the like) in their discourse about the contingencies of relationship, man is unique in his attempt to combine digital language with this discourse.

Obviously an organism which uses two methods of discourse and which attempts to discuss the same subject matter with both of these methods will need to be able to translate from one method into the other. Any systematic errors in the machinery or rules of this translation will inevitably bring about pathologic behavior. It is therefore appropriate to consider the difficulties inherent in such translation and the probable forms of error.

We may note first that a combination of analogic with digital communication systems already has been achieved in mammals at the physiological level. Although the central nervous system at least in its microscopic functioning, is digital, depending upon the discontinuities provided by the "all or nothing" law (or some modification of this law), the hormonal system undoubtedly depends upon the use of real magnitudes and is to this extent strictly analogic.

It also appears that the whole evolutionary process turns upon a combination of digital with analogic communication. The corpus of genotypic messages is in the main digital, whereas the soma appears to be in every instance an analogic exemplification or trial model which tests the genotypic recipe. The analogic proof of the egg is the hen into which it develops.

These evolutionary problems have been discussed elsewhere (7) where it was argued that, while it is essential to embryology that there be a method for creating an analogic transform of the genotypic recipe, it is equally essential that the characteristics of the analogic model shall not be communicated back to the genotype but shall be tested and filtered through the processes of natural selection. Lamarckian inheritance would make evolution nonviable.

However, when we come to consider the weaving of analogic with digital process in the phenomena of interpersonal relations, i.e., in phenomena external to the body, it is clearly essential that the organism have means of maintaining some degree of consistency between its digital and analogic behavior.

What is needed is a digital transform of the analogic message material such that a) all important information be retained in the transform and b) that no new information of an unreliable or unsupported kind be added. We shall see that in fact there is a very strong tendency towards such inappropriate addition.

Three characteristics of the analogic material contribute to the difficulty of transformation into words; these characteristics must be considered together, because the difficulties of translation arise from a combination of the characteristics. First, the analogic material contains real (and therefore always <u>positive</u>) magnitudes; second, the analog material contains no simple negative, i.e., no word for "not"; and third, the analog material contains no morphemic signs. There is no analogue of "as if" or "perhaps," no differentiation between "and" and "or" and, in sum, no signs in analog communication which shall classify a message as to its logical type.

These characteristics of analog communication may be illustrated by considering the problem of translating the sentence, "The man did not plant the tree," into a purely pictographic script. We can readily imagine the series of pictures available: "man," "spade," "hole in ground," "tree," "tree in hole," and others, but what about the word "not"? We might perhaps be tempted to express this word by superimposing a deletion mark upon that word in the sentence to which the "not" most specifically applies. If it was not the <u>man</u> who planted the tree, we shall delete the picture of "man." Or if it was that he did not <u>plant</u> it, we shall delete "spade" or "tree in hole," and so on.

But now a serious difficulty arises. The receiver of the message will want to know whether we deleted one of these pictures because we made an error when we wrote the message. Or did we intend both the picture and its deletion to stand as part of the message? At this point the absence of logical typing signals has the effect that our negative cannot be understood by the receiver. What is precisely needed to discriminate between a correction and a negation is a logical type marker, and here no pictorial representation is available.

In fact, if the receiver of the message is sufficiently sophisticated to know that the sender could not, in the nature of the case, have inserted a negative if he wanted to, he will be able to deduce that the message can contain no simple indicative affirmative. Any sequence in the message which might appear to be an affirmative statement may owe this appearance only to the fact that the sender of the message had no meaningful negatives at his disposal. The analogic message can mention or propose; it cannot affirm or deny its own truth.

Similar difficulties will apply to a number of other elements in the sentence. We shall lack pictorial representation for the definite article and for the past tense, and more especially we shall lack that more fundamental logical type marker which would tell the receiver that we are not in this context talking about a man and a tree but only talking about a diagrammatic sentence created to illustrate a theoretical point.

In a word, the analogic communication about which we are talking suffers from the same limitations as those which characterize "primary process" and indeed, this finding is scarcely surprising inasmuch as these modes are evidently in an evolutionary sense much more archaic than the specifically human babel of language.

The limitations, however, can serve as a warning to the would-be translator who can be sure that if his verbal transform of the analog material contains simple negatives (or indeed, affirmative indicative statements) or logical type markers these must all have been added in the process of translation. The translation in fact will contain information which is unsupported by the analogic source and is therefore unreliable.

It is, of course, true that a major effort of psychoanalysis is to insert such markers and indicatives into dream material--a procedure which can hardly fail to induce change in the patient. The scientific problem remains: how much is the change caused by an accurate decoding of the patient's dream material, how much by the insertion of erroneous markers and how much by the fact that, right or wrong, acceptance has been extended to this material?

What has been said above has stressed the paucity of analogic communication, and it is necessary to insist that this paucity is systematic and arises out of the very nature of the analogic mode. In considering the case of an organism using both analog and digital modes for the same subject matter, there is, therefore, no question of this organism's achieving consistency by means of a translation process which would reduce digital material to the analog mode where the comparison might be achieved. Translation in this direction, from the digital to the analog, must always be accompanied by gross loss of information, unless the original digital material was so composed as to contain none of the elements which cannot be expressed in analog form. Presumably the genotypic corpus of instructions to the developing organism is limited in this way. [1]

However, when we consider the plight of man, we observe at once that he has great paucity on the digital side. There is probably no systematic reason why language should be so poor, but the fact remains that, for the discussion of contingencies of relationship, human language has yet evolved only a small vocabulary of words, which even the experts in human relations are unwilling to define in any critical manner. We refer here to such words as dependency, hostility, aggression, dominance, responsibility, spectatorship, prestige, respect, impertinence, rudeness, familiarity, intimacy, love, hate, and the like. For almost all these words it is unclear whether they are descriptive of an individual, of the actions of an individual or of a pattern of relationship; and almost every one of them contains that peculiar ambiguity (amphiboly) which is characteristic of the word "tender." We say that a bruise is "tender" but also that the nurse who handles the bruise is "tender." We may suspect that these words still carry with them some of the ambiguity with which we endow them in our attempts to translate from analogic representations of contingencies of relationship into digital language. There is, however, no evident limiting factor in the nature of language which would preclude the evolution of a more critical vocabulary.

Be all that as it may, the creature who must translate from analog to digital is continually liable to project upon his analog

---

[1] It is asserted by those expert in computing machines that any computation of an analog machine can be simulated on a digital machine, but that the converse does not hold. It is not possible to simulate all that digital machines can do on analogue machines.

sources the characteristics of the digital mode into which he is translating. The clenched fist of the vis-a-vis may be a signal that the latter is aggressive or that he is exerting self-restraint, or it may mean both of these, but the recipient is likely to translate it as a positive assertion of one or the other. The dream of a horrendous maternal figure may be a direct expression of the dreamer's fear, or it may be an ironic caricature either of mother or of the dreamer. The dreamer, with or without psychiatric aid, will tend to push this dream in one direction or another, adding logical type markers where there was none in the dream itself.

Finally, one other aspect of analogic communication about relationship must be mentioned, namely, that the message material is commonly empirical in nature rather than time-binding. The juxtaposition of these two terms, "empirical" and "time-binding" as contrasted opposites, may appear novel, but what we want to suggest is derivable from the traditional notion of empiricism. An "empiric" used to be a term of abuse for a medical practitioner who treated without theory, being guided only by trial and error. This is no longer considered to be discreditable, and indeed, the "empiric" has certain advantages of flexibility as compared with his colleague who is theory-bound. It is this order of contrast that we invoke in saying that analogic communication tends to be empirical while the digital tends to be time-binding. (A rather similar contrast between calibrational and feedback methods of adaptation has been discussed elsewhere (8)).

Precisely because no indicative, negative or affirmative statement can be issued in analog terms, this mode is appropriate for the trying out of styles of relationship, and in many fields of life, human beings have ritualized this fact. Courtship is noncommittal up to a certain point and consists very largely of analogic interchange. Finally the persons are ready for the contractual and digital statements of marriage and the shift from one stage to the other is marked in the analogic mode by ritual. The problem for the young people concerned may be stated in the language of the present paper: at what stage in the experimental and empirical interchange of analog signals does it become wise to translate these messages into affirmative digital statements with logical type markers?

A similar problem surrounds the matter of interpersonal anger. We live in a culture in which a very large number of people are afraid that to act in an angry manner will "tear" their relationships, and one of the recurrent problems of the psychiatrist is how to have the patient discover that it is all right to express his anger--by analogic modes. It has for some reason become difficult for us to believe that we can get, by the empirical use of anger, a new insight into important relationships--without destroying the relationship. Indeed, it is almost impossible for many of us to believe that sometimes only by this empirical use of anger can the relationship be saved. Our pathology derives from perceiving any expression of anger as an indicative negative and time-binding statement about the relationship.

And then there is the more complex problem of the relationship in which one spouse expresses anger freely and even compulsively, only to be met with a digital reply. "I was angry with my friend. I told my wrath, my wrath did end." But perhaps this relief could only be achieved if the friend was equally ready to express his wrath!

A converse--but much more complex--problem arises in regard to hysteria. No doubt this word covers a wide range of formal patterns, but it would appear that at least some cases involve errors of translation from the digital to the analogic. Stripping the digital material of its logical type markers leads to erroneous symptom formation. The verbal "headache" which was invented as a conventional excuse for not performing some task may become subjectively real and be endowed with real magnitudes in the pain dimension.

The essence of the matter is that an element of secrecy regarding the nature of the communication is conferred by the very fact of translation from the digital to the analogic.

In this connection it is interesting to consider the waxing and waning of conversion hysteria as a form of expression and interchange between humans, which has been the subject of numerous scientific papers. Viewed from the perspectives we are presenting, it could be predicted that advances in medicine and the current enormous consumption of placebos and analgesics (and the placebo effect of physiological analgesics) would go far to render hysteria untenable. In addition there is perhaps an increasing popular awareness of the functions of such symptoms in malingering and as protests in the field of relatedness. The hysteric thus finds himself in a dilemma--either his symptoms are spoiled by modern pharmacology which he must nominally accept, insofar as he claims that the symptoms have organic origin, or his secrecy is threatened by the suspicions of his friends.

In many cases, of course, the hysterically sick member of a family finds himself surrounded by other family members who are in a tacit coalition to regard the sickness as organic. This view frees them from responsibility and from the covert accusations which the symptom partly expresses and partly conceals. But it is becoming a little more difficult for such family systems to maintain their status quo. Medicine and health are becoming increasingly a duty, so that to maintain a sick member without recurrent appeal to the medical profession is becoming both difficult and guilt-provoking. On the other hand, the doctor, when they appeal to him, is more and more likely to expose the communicational aspects of the symptom.

REFERENCES

1. Bateson, G. Naven. Cambridge University Press, London, 1936.
2. Erikson, E. H. Childhood and Society. W. W. Norton & Co., Inc., New York, 1950.
3. Blauvelt, H. Neonate-mother relationship in goat and man. In Group Processes, (Transactions of Second Conference), pp. 94-140, Josiah Macy Jr. Fnd., 1956.
4. Bateson, G., Jackson, D. D., Haley, J. and Weakland, J. H. Toward a theory of schizophrenia. Behavioral Sci., 1:251-264, 1956. (See p. 31, this vol.)
5. Bateson, G. Minimal requirements for a theory of schizophrenia. A. M. A. Arch. Gen. Psychiat., 2:477-491, 1960.
6. Weakland, J. H. and Jackson, D. D. Patient and therapist observations on the circumstances of a schizophrenic episode. A. M. A. Arch. Neurol & Psychiat., 79:554-575, 1958. (See p. 87, this vol.)
7. Bateson, G. The role of somatic change in evolution. Evolution, in press.
8. Bateson, G. The biosocial integration of behavior in the schizophrenic family. In Exploring the Base for Family Therapy, Ackerman, Beatman and Sherman (Eds.), pp. 116-122. Family Service Association of America, New York, 1961.

SOME ASSUMPTIONS IN RECENT RESEARCH
ON SCHIZOPHRENIA

Robert E. Kantor and Don D. Jackson

INTRODUCTION

When Harry Stack Sullivan asserted psychiatry to be an interpersonal science, he adopted a set of tacit premises about the
social character of human conduct. To render these premises
explicit and to spell out their research consequences is the object of this paper. The profit from doing so lies in the fact that
Sullivan's assumptions have invisibly steered some of the present
courses in research on schizophrenia. Laying open these latent
influences may help to illuminate the paths of future leads.

At least three explicit propositions, each here illustrated by
an operational hypothesis on which significant research has been
performed, arise from Sullivan's fundamental position that man
is a social creature who depends for his sanity, and indeed for
his existence, upon the support and upon the continuous affirmation of his fellows:

1. The reciprocal adjustments of men to each other are primarily effected through channels of communication. Such learning starts early, and is transmitted to the child through a wide
range of verbal and non-verbal messages from his parents. Research applications have focused on schizophrenia as a result of
distortions in the vitally formative familial communications.

2. Human perception, another major modifier of behavior, is
essentially a selective process which begins when the child takes
the view of his "significant others" who teach him to pick out only

Reprinted from THE JOURNAL OF NERVOUS AND MENTAL
DISEASE, 135, No. 1:36-43 (July, 1962). Copyright © the Williams &
Wilkins Co., Baltimore; reproduced by permission.

certain events in his environment. Research here is based on the hypothesis that the level of the schizophrenic's perceptual organization can be a useful measure of the severity of his dysfunction, providing one knows something also of the context in which these perceptions occur.

3. Any human grouping consists of an enormous complex of expectations and comprehensions among its members which are continuously sustained and reinforced through acts of communication. The social world of the mental hospital, important for our purposes because schizophrenics are found here in large numbers, may be fruitfully studied as communication networks.

Corresponding to these three assumptions (and their research applications), the present paper, after setting the historical stage, will fall into three main sections, each indicating the kinds of studies now taking place, and something of their implications for an evolving definition of schizophrenia.

HISTORICAL BACKGROUND

A convenient date for the marriage between social theory and research on schizophrenia is 1929, when Professor W. I. Thomas pioneered the addition of a section of Sociology and Psychiatry to the program of the American Sociological Society. Presenting papers at that meeting (13) were Trigant Burrow, Benjamin Karpman, Adolph Meyer, George E. Partridge and Harry Stack Sullivan. The next two annual meetings also provided space for this area of "social psychiatry," focusing on society's sins in the production of emotional turmoil. Sullivan, for example, discussed the effects of urban density on the emotional conflicts of children.

In 1932, the sociologist Robert Faris argued that if there really are cultural factors in psychosis, it ought to be possible to demonstrate them empirically through differences in rates of admission to various mental hospitals, depending upon the areas of origin of those admitted. Faris found that a disproportionate number of schizophrenics came from "disorganized" ecological zones (15). He hypothesized that where social contacts are "adequate," and where social alienation is absent, schizophrenia is very infrequent (14). In his book with Dunham these theories were repeated (16), inspiring several validating studies which in the main supported Faris and Dunham's original findings. Among these are the works of Hadley (21), Mowrer (37), Queen (40) and Schroeder (43).

Fundamentally, the ecological position proposes that psychosis is a consequence of unfavorable social features. There are researches, for example, which inquire into the relationship between schizophrenia and neighborhood and occupational grouping (9, 48). Other work proposes that contemporary Western society, characterized as it is by high mobility both vertically and spatially, facilitates mental and emotional dysfunction of personality (11, 36, 47). Still other studies stress the role of the "sick society" (17). Halliday's work on the rising incidence of emotional illness in Scotland (23) was seen by him as the "medical approach to the study of the sick society." A frequent variation on this theme is the stress on intra-cultural contradictions as productive of mental breakdowns within individuals (27).

In its most recent version, the ecological frame of reference has led to investigations of the linkage between social class and mental disorder. Hollingshead and Redlich, utilizing as their sample approximately ninety-eight per cent of those under psychiatric care at a certain time in the city of New Haven, reported that a disproportionate number of the patients came from the less privileged classes, and when the members of the more privileged classes did get into mental hospitals they tended to receive more active courses of treatment (26). Regarding this latter phenomenon, a later empirical article (24) presents data indicating that "the lower the social class, the higher will be the percentage of male schizophrenics who are continuous long-term patients."

Intensively studying fifty patients and their families, Myers and Roberts concluded that the backgrounds of patients from different social levels differed markedly (38). The families, for instance, of those patients from less-privileged levels were more likely to abandon the hospitalized person. Significant differences in class orientations towards the institutionalized psychotic, were also discovered by another investigation (10).

Hollingshead has more recently proffered a rationale for this type of approach (called epidemiological by him, rather than ecological) (25). He suggests that the focus on the social context of schizophrenia is a "descriptive phase" which should form the necessary underpinnings for a "determinative phase" that comes later and that contains explanatory powers. The position taken here by Hollingshead puts epidemiological data in a useful perspective and meets in part the objections of Blumer (5) and by Zilboorg (52), who stressed the limitations of the ecological hypothesis; both noted that most individuals living in conflictful or

disorganized social groupings are not schizophrenic. What is
needed, both implied, is an explanation of how and in what manner the social pressures are rendered into meaningful individual
experience and conduct. In this same article, Blumer proposes
the beginnings of such an explanation by noting that the symposium of psychiatrists and sociologists about which his paper was
concerned presented a somewhat composite picture which conceptualized individual disorder as an end-product of unhappy experiences in childhood. What this really asserts, Blumer suggests, is the significance of the family group factor.

He thus clarified the fact that the psychiatrist's interest in environment is practically synonymous with the sociologist's interest in the totality of primary relationships in which the individual
participates. Pollack noted a similar fact when he declared that
what sociology can do for psychiatry "is to break down the concept of environment into its various components" (39). One sociologist (6) pointed out that a child's "family of orientation" may
include grandparents, or uncles and aunts, cousins or even
boarders, who may be in continuous proximity to the growing
child and thus may enter into significant inter-relationships with
him, and influence his growth processes nearly as much as do his
parents.

Viewpoints such as these make it easier to conceive that families exist whose constellations are unusually hospitable to the formation of schizophrenia among their members. The influence of
Sullivan also comes into play here, especially his recommenda-
tion to investigate the schizophrenic's whole pattern of interpersonal relations before his breakdown, as well as his idiosyncratic language (45).

In general, the writers are trying to show in broad outline that
these earlier approaches led up to contemporary studies (of family communications, of Rorschach assessments, of hospital networks) which endeavor to keep in mind and to get at the problems
posed by the original theoretical statements.

STUDIES ON FAMILY COMMUNICATIONS
One insight implied by a sociological orientation might usefully
be made plain: psychosis becomes understood as a situation within a primary group, rather than as the individual possession of one
of the group's members. Jackson utilized the idea, long circulated
among psychoanalytic writings, when he noted that the trauma dealt
to a schizophrenic is not necessarily a specific and transient hurt,

but is rather a "condition operating in the patient's environment
which has been non-discrete and continuing..." (28). As a logical
corollary, he introduced the concept of "family homeostasis" (29),
that schizophrenic conduct is a vital part of the precarious balance
of the whole family. Once the idea is grasped that all of the total
family personnel are interlocked in a pathological system of interaction, it becomes reasonable to study the communication channels
among them. Bateson et al. noticed that the schizophrenic makes
idiosyncratic and unshared interpretations of the information that
he receives, which led to their "double-bind" hypothesis that the
schizophrenic must have learned his communication procedures in
a family atmosphere where the verbal and non-verbal levels of
transmission clashed rather than meshed (1). This, in turn, resulted in the formation of a research project whose observations
are focused on the actual exchanges inside the family on at least a
triadic level (22, 30, 49).

EMPIRICAL STUDIES ON PERCEPTUAL ORGANIZATION

Obviously the kind of data needed to corroborate such a hypothesis about the family etiology of schizophrenia are best found in
longitudinal studies, but an implication, important for Rorschach
research, has arisen in the course of theorizing. Jackson high-
lighted the implication this way: "...the reporting of the patient
is more complicated than can be accounted for by repression or
denial... There is truly a perceptual difficulty involved, which is
partly a matter of what is paid attention to" (28). Essentially, this
is the more explicit version of Sullivan's general position that all
human perception is a highly selective process which enables
major modifications in conduct in accord with the shifting demands
of living. "Selective inattention" is determined by security operations and acts to limit what a person can communicate to himself.

Employing the idea that perceptual phenomena could throw light
on schizophrenia, Kantor, Wallner and Winder (31), using the vis-
ual productions (by Rorschach test) of 324 patients, demonstrated
that "schizophrenic cases can be reliably differentiated into process and reactive groups," and offered some evidence that the
former malignant type differed fundamentally from the latter benign type. Rabin and King (41), in an extensive examination of
the current contradictions in the literature on schizophrenia, noted that a great many of these contradictions disappear when the
syndrome is understood as a set of plural states rather than as a
unitary one, and declared that "the selection of a specific frame
of reference in the determination of samples, such as...reactive
vs. process...tends to be a most fruitful avenue of approach..."
(p. 278).

On the explicit assumption that the level of perceptual organization is somehow correlated with schizophrenia, Winder and Kantor (51) applied "personality-age-level" ratings as an operational
Rorschach device to differentiate successfully between the mothers of psychotic sons and the mothers of normal sons, using no
other external information than their Rorschach responses. The
device itself is of interest because it allowed further refinement
in the clarification of the plural states of schizophrenia. Basically, "personality-age-level" scores are obtained by defining the
protocol on a scale (five points in the cited study) whose points are
determined by published normative data on the level of expected
and average Rorschach performance at a given period of life,
ranging from very young childhood through adulthood. Process
schizophrenics tend to get the age-level ratings of early life,
whereas reactive schizophrenics score nearer the adult levels.
Used in this manner, the Rorschach test yields a reliable score
on the quantity of symptomatic severity, pointing to the possibility of being able to distinguish between groups of schizophrenic
persons.

Neither one of the last two studies attempted to apply a dimen-
sional approach to the problem, although an underlying dimension
was inherent in the idea of genetic maturation of perceptual organization. Nor was personality theory attempted. The developmental interpersonal theory of Harry Stack Sullivan (44) seemed to
offer an integrated set of concepts relevant to the next step in the
widening of a theory on the multiple states of schizophrenia.

Sullivan's theory of personality development referred to the
widely-utilized idea that there are sequential steps in experience
which all humans encounter in the course of maturation, and he
added that each step in the maturational sequence contains a central problem which must be at least partially "integrated" (Sullivan's term) before a new organization of experience can occur
successfully on the maturational continuum. At least five growth
steps are discernible. Ranging from infancy to childhood, they
are: the empathic, the prototaxic, the parataxic, the autistic and
the syntaxic.

This idea of growth stages was not extended by Sullivan to cover a theory about the schizophrenias. Kantor and Winder (32)
proposed that it might be operationally fruitful to describe the
schizophrenias as systematically distributed along the five-step
continuum of social maturity, using the etiological notion, early
proposed by Freud, that "incomplete integrations are antecedents

of regression, and that regressions and failures to progress developmentally are reflected in schizophrenia."

By using the Rorschach age-level score as an independent measure of regression or primitivization and then showing that it correlated significantly with case-history information as to the earliest developmental life-epoch in which the patient had encountered pathogenic situations, the authors, in an earlier paper (33), demonstrated that the schizophrenias may be quantitatively depicted, assigning reliable measurements to describe that level of life to which the schizophrenic has returned. Basically, this study mathematically described a widely-accepted concept: "The underlying psychological notion... proposes that the earlier in developmental history that severe stress prevails, the more damaging will be the consequences on the subsequent course of interpersonal relationships." The data of that study support the hypothesis that malignant schizophrenias result from early and extreme life deprivations, while the benign schizophrenias are associated with later and milder conflicts. Incidentally it seems probable that the semantically dysfunctional schizogenic families described by Jackson, Bateson, Haley, Weakland and other workers are producing schizophrenics of the more benign varieties, rather than the malignant types whose language and thinking functions are usually primitivized to the point of almost complete incomprehensibility.

Perhaps, as was mentioned earlier, the most promising aspect of this line of research which classifies schizophrenics on a malign-benign continuum, is that it offered a reasonable way of explaining why earlier research announced sharp differences between different samples of patients on such tested performances as perceptions, thinking, learning, intelligence and physiology (50). Benign schizophrenics do appear to be consistent on these measures among themselves, as do malignant types.

Interesting research benefits might be expected from the explanatory advantages of the reactive-process viewpoint. Becker's study, for example, used this concept of schizophrenia to reveal a worthwhile covariance between prognosis, case-history and test measurements (3). King added the variable of physiological reactivity to these three by demonstrating that "predominantly reactive schizophrenics display a higher level of autonomic responsiveness after the injection of mecholyl than predominantly process schizophrenics" (34). Brackbill and Fine found that signs of brain damage were statistically greater among the process schizophrenics than among the reactive ones (7).

Such findings are of especial interest because of the consistent failures of past studies to relate biological to psycho-social variables with schizophrenic samples which were either undifferentiated or classified on the orthodox nosology (35). Since the process-reactive idea implies a potential for change in the seriousness of the schizophrenic dysfunction from one pole towards the other, it also implies that time-change studies can utilize the quantitative measurements introduced by Becker (2), by Kantor and Winder (33) and by future efforts to study the effects of environmental and chemical agents on the retardation and advancement of schizophrenia by measuring changes in the distress of the illness. Changes in the communicative context of the schizophrenic's world, for instance, could be evaluated by their effectiveness in pushing him toward either polarity of severity.

EMPIRICAL STUDIES OF THE MENTAL HOSPITAL

Several striking studies described the mental hospital as a communicative system, basing their working assumption on the viewpoint that a social group is a communicative transaction which guides the orientations of the patients.

As well as reviewing previous research on this subject, Stanton and Schwartz (46) were able to show how psychotics' heightened unrest and loosening of reality ties related positively to staff indecision about handling of these patients' cases. When the same disagreements were worked through openly, the anxieties and dissociations of the patients tended to clear. Essentially, as Dunham and Weinberg emphasized, patients form social networks within the hospital which serve to convey information about ways to facilitate discharge (12). Caudill noted that greater status accrues to those patients nearer to discharge from the hospital (8), and that therefore the social groupings function primarily as communication centers which dispense information related to the problem of accommodating to the staff in the optimal way to insure the speediest release. Patients, for example, exert pressure on each other to acknowledge their mental illness openly and not to mislead themselves with other rationalizations which may impede medical assistance. Similarly, Goffman (20) observed that patients have to learn to picture themselves as mentally ill, and do so, in good part, because the other patients on the ward talk to them as if they were "sick."

Another form of communication in the mental institution is revealed in studies by Belkman (4), and by Scheff (42), whose interest focused on the "attendant system." Because the ward physician's duties are too numerous for effective ward supervision by him, the real control on the ward is exercised by the psychiatric attendant. What this means to the patient is that such essentials as access to the physician, ground privileges, eligibility for discharge, are all under the working sanctions of the attendant ideology; resentment on the part of the patient may be communicated to the hospital medical authorities as "disturbance" or "acute excitement," with the attendant thus achieving psychiatric authorization for the system.

It may be argued that both Belkman and Scheff were describing a state hospital model where the medical facilities tend to be minimal, and the tradition of psychotherapy relatively weak. However, their findings were confirmed by Goffman (18) who observed a large hospital with a comparatively vigorous medical culture. Focusing on the means by which the mental patient becomes incorporated into the social group of the hospital, Goffman comments that the "self is systematically, if often unintentionally, mortified," by an authority hierarchy which, in effect, creates a staff elite which may punish any member of the inmate class for offenses which are not classified as illegitimate outside the hospital walls. An oligarchy is thereby created, at least from the patient's viewpoint, which may decisively intervene in the vital matters of therapy and discharge.

Perhaps it is relevant to comment here that Goffman is particularly shrewd at discerning what is really operating for both patients and personnel in the mental hospital situation. He notes, for instance, that given the type of privilege system (18), the patient's most imperative need is not to cope with the internal pressures of mental dysfunction, but to survive emotionally under the unfamiliar vagaries of the hospital world. At another place (19), he offers the idea of the "ratifier's" role as important not only as society's agent in the incarceration of the psychotic patient, but also for lifting the onus of betrayal from the shoulders of the family of the patient in that he, the "ratifier," rather than the relatives, is the one who "enforces an estrangement which the next-of-relationships can enjoy yet feel no guilt of having created." Again, noting that society's actions implicitly define normality or abnormality, Goffman says (20), "the psychiatric view of a person becomes significant only in so far as this view itself alters his social fate--an alteration which seems to become fundamental...when...the person is put through the process of hospitalization."

CONCLUSIONS

Schizophrenia is undergoing a gradual redefining process as the research focus shifts toward the facts-of-life as they appear variously to sociologists, the anthropologists and the social psychologists. In this regard, it is of considerable importance that some studies on schizophrenia (here regarded as of significance) have tacitly adopted a social-science viewpoint by defining communications and perceptions, no longer merely as vehicles for the transferral of information, but as forms of conduct conducive to adjustment or maladjustment among interacting humans.

The present paper has proposed that flourishing lines of inquiry into the nature of schizophrenia (citing family, Rorschach and mental hospital studies) have been nourished by the particular position of the social scientist--a position that adds new dimensions to the traditional psychiatric inquiries. The adoption of this particular position bypasses the study of the biology of schizophrenia but, of course, does not exclude or supersede it; in our present state of darkness, illumination from any direction seems equally beneficial.

REFERENCES

1. Bateson, G., Jackson, D.D., Haley, J. and Weakland, J. Toward a theory of schizophrenia. Behav. Sci., 1:251-264, 1956. (See p. 31, this vol.)
2. Becker, W.C. A genetic approach to the interpretation and evaluation of the process-reactive distinction in schizophrenia. J. Abnorm. Soc. Psychol., 53:229-236, 1956.
3. Becker, W.C. The process-reactive distinction: A key to the problem of schizophrenia? J. Nerv. Ment. Dis., 129: 442-449, 1959.
4. Belkman, L. Human Problems of a State Mental Hospital. McGraw-Hill, New York, 1956.
5. Blumer, H. Social disorganization and individual disorganization. Amer. J. Soc., 42:871-877, 1937.
6. Bossard, J.H.S. The Sociology of Child Development. Harper, New York, 1948.
7. Brackbill, G.A. and Fine, H.J. Schizophrenia and central nervous system pathology. J. Abnorm. Soc. Psychol., 52:310-313, 1956.

8. Caudill, W., Redlich, F.C., Gilmore, H. R. and Brody, E.B. Social structure and interaction processes on a psychiatric ward. Amer. J. Orthopsychiat., 22:314-334, 1952.

9. Clark, R.E. The relation of schizophrenia to occupational income and occupational prestige. Amer. Sociol. Rev., 13:325-330, 1948.

10. Cumming, E. and Cumming, J. Closed Ranks: An Experiment in Mental Health Education. Harvard Univ. Press, Cambridge, Massachusetts, 1957.

11. Davis, K. Mental hygiene and the class structure. Psychiatry, 1:55-56, 1938.

12. Dunham, H. W. and Weinberg, S. K. The Culture of the State Mental Hospital. Wayne State Univ. Press, Detroit, 1960.

13. Eliot, T. D. Interactions of psychiatric and social theory prior to 1940. In Rose, A. M., (Ed.) Mental Health and Mental Disorder, pp. 18-41. Norton, New York, 1955.

14. Faris, R. E. L. Cultural isolation and the schizophrenic personality. Amer. J. Sociol., 40:155-165, 1934.

15. Faris, R. E. L. Insanity distribution by local areas. Proc. Amer. Statist. Ass., 27:53-57, 1932.

16. Faris, R. E. L. and Dunham, H. W. Mental Disorder in Urban Areas. Univ. of Chicago Press, Chicago, 1939.

17. Frank, L. K. Society as the patient. Amer. J. Sociol., 42:335-344, 1936.

18. Goffman, E. The characteristics of total institutions. In Symposium on Preventive and Social Psychiatry, pp. 43-84. U. S. Gov. Print. Office, Washington, D. C., 1957.

19. Goffman, E. On some convergences of sociology and psychiatry. Psychiatry, 20:199-203, 1957.

20. Goffman, E. The moral career of the mental patient. Psychiatry, 22:123-142, 1959.

21. Hadley, E. E. et al. Military psychiatry: An ecological note. Psychiatry, 7:379-407, 1944.

22. Haley, J. The family of the schizophrenic: A model system. J. Nerv. Ment. Dis., 129:357-374, 1959. (See p. 171, this vol.)

23. Halliday, J. L. Psychosocial Medicine. Norton, New York, 1948.

24. Hardt, R. H. and Feinhandler, S. J. Social class and mental hospitalization prognosis. Amer. Sociol. Rev., 24:815-821, 1959.

25. Hollingshead, A. B. The epidemiology of schizophrenia. Amer. Sociol. Rev., 26:5-14, 1961.

228

26. Hollingshead, A. D. and Redlich, R. C. Social Class and Mental Illness. Wiley, New York, 1958.
27. Horney, K. The Neurotic Personality of Our Time. Norton, New York, 1937.
28. Jackson, D. D. A note on the importance of trauma in the genesis of schizophrenia. Psychiatry, 20:181-184, 1957. (See p. 23, this vol.)
29. Jackson, D. D. The question of family homeostasis. Psychiat. Quart., 31:79-90, 1957. (See p. 1, this vol.)
30. Jackson, D. D. and Weakland, J. Conjoint family therapy. Psychiatry, 24: Suppl. to No. 2 (Chestnut Lodge 50th Anniversary Symposium) 30-45, 1961.
31. Kantor, R. E., Wallner, J. M. and Winder, C. L. Process and reactive schizophrenia. J. Consult. Psychol., 17: 157-162, 1953.
32. Kantor, R. E. and Winder, C. L. The process-reactive continuum: A theoretical proposal. J. Nerv. Ment. Dis., 129:429-434, 1959.
33. Kantor, R. E. and Winder, C. L. Schizophrenia: Correlates of life history. J. Nerv. Ment. Dis., 132:221-226, 1961.
34. King, G. F. Differential autonomic responsiveness in the process-reactive classification of schizophrenia. J. Abnorm. Soc. Psychol., 56:160-164, 1958.
35. King, G. F. Research with neuropsychiatric samples. J. Psychol., 38:383-387, 1954.
36. Merton, R. K. Social structure and anomie. In Wilson, L. and Kolb, W. L., (Eds.) Sociological Analysis, pp. 771-780. Harcourt, Brace, New York, 1949.
37. Mowrer, E. A study of personality disorganization. Amer. Sociol. Rev., 4:475-487, 1939.
38. Myers, J. K. and Roberts, B. H. Family and Class Dynamics in Mental Illness. Wiley, New York, 1959.
39. Pollack, O. et al. Social Science and Psychotherapy for Children. Russell Sage Foundation, New York, 1952.
40. Queen, S. A. The ecological studies of mental disorder. Amer. Sociol. Rev., 5:201-209, 1940.
41. Rabin, A. I. and King, G. F. Psychological studies. In Bellak, L., (Ed.) Schizophrenia: A review of the Syndrome, pp. 216-278. Logos Press, New York, 1958.
42. Scheff, T. J. Control over policy by attendants in a state hospital. J. Health Hum. Behav., 2:93-105, 1961.
43. Schroeder, C. W. Mental disorders in cities. Amer. J. Sociol., 47:40-47, 1942.
44. Sullivan, H. S. Conceptions of Modern Psychiatry. William Alanson White Psychiatric Foundation, Washington, D. C., 1947.

45. Sullivan, H. S. The study of psychiatry. Psychiatry, 10:355-
    371, 1947.
46. Stanton, A. H. and Schwartz, M. S. The Mental Hospital.
    Basic Books, New York, 1954.
47. Tietze, C., Lemkau, P. and Cooper, M. Personality disorder
    and spatial mobility. Amer. J. Sociol., 48:29-39, 1942.
48. Tietze, C., Lemkau, P. and Cooper, M. Schizophrenia,
    manic-depressive psychosis and social-economic status.
    Amer. J. Sociol., 47:167-175, 1941.
49. Weakland, J. The "double bind" hypothesis of schizophrenia
    and three-party interaction. In Jackson, D. D., (Ed.)
    The Etiology of Schizophrenia, pp. 373-388. Basic Books,
    New York, 1960.
50. Winder, C. L. Some psychological studies of schizophrenics.
    In Jackson, D. D., (Ed.) The Etiology of Schizophrenia,
    pp. 191-247. Basic Books, New York, 1960.
51. Winder, C. L. and Kantor, R. E. Rorschach maturity scores
    of the mothers of schizophrenics. J. Consult. Psychol.,
    22:438-440, 1958.
52. Zilboorg, G. Sociology and the psychoanalytic method. Amer.
    J. Sociol., 45:341-355, 1939.

A METHOD OF ANALYSIS
OF A FAMILY INTERVIEW

Don D. Jackson, Jules Riskin
and Virginia M. Satir

I. INTRODUCTION

During recent years evidence has been accumulating which suggests that a significant relationship exists between family interaction and mental illness. However, hypotheses concerning this relationship have been derived primarily from experience in conjoint family therapy and attempts to validate them have been essentially retrospective. We are in the process of setting up a longitudinal predictive study of families, in order to test predictively some of these clinical impressions. Currently, we are focusing on the development of methods which will enable us to identify more precisely different patterns of family interaction, and relate these patterns to various forms of mental illness. Specifically, this paper presents a brief theoretical framework followed by a detailed illustration of one such approach. [1] Also, we believe that this report offers (postdictive) evidence in support of hypotheses relating family interaction to mental illness, or in more general terms, to personality development.

The article presents the analysis of the first 5 min. of a "blind" tape. The tape was kindly supplied us by Dr. Lyman Wynne of the National Institute of Mental Health. [2] The only identifying data accompanying the tape was the notation that this was the 80th session of the family in which mother, father, and son (identified patient)

---

[1] See References for discussion of theoretical base.

[2] Dr. Wynne's detailed comments on this analysis are included at the end of this paper. We wish to express our appreciation to him for his cooperation on this project.

Reprinted from the A.M.A. ARCHIVES OF GENERAL PSYCHIATRY, 5:321-339 (October 1961).

were present. We were told that there was a younger son who was not present at the interview and that the identified patient did not participate until late in this particular session. [3] We therefore deliberately focused on the intial stages of the interview in order not to be influenced by the way the patient sounded.

Our immediate impression, after hearing only 2 or 3 min. of the tape, was that this was not the family of a chronic schizophrenic with either insidious or acute onset. We also felt that it was not likely to be a family in which any of the children had had an acute schizophrenic episode. However, as it will be detailed below, we were much less sure of the second assumption than the first. The mother and father interact rather overtly with each other and there is open argument. Although each qualifies his statements (especially father) in a manner we have not yet encountered in an apparently healthy family, there is more open challenging criticism than we had experienced in families containing a chronic schizophrenic member. The parents of an acute schizophrenic with a good prognosis are somewhat less direct than this couple, although superficially, the argumentation may sound rather similar. [4] In the present excerpt, the criticism is explicitly directed and explicitly responded to. In the family of the acute schizophrenic, it is our impression that critical statements are more covert and/or the response is rendered tangential by laughing, changing the subject, etc.

The material presented below attempts to demonstrate 2 kinds of analyses of the data: A. The patterns of communication between the parents are examined from the standpoint of communication theory as containing a primary message and the manner in which it is qualified. B. In addition, inferences are made as to the kind of individual who would produce such a message in such a manner. Thus one method is to describe formal communication patterns between the parents; and the other makes inferences about their motivations and the kind of life experiences that might have led to such

---

[3] This was an error on our part. Actually, as Dr. Wynne pointed out in a later note, there were three sons, not two. Dr. Wynne also stated that although he appreciated that this first attempt at analysis be as "blind" as possible, in the future it would be important to know a) more of the context of the session being analyzed, and b) essential identifying data about the family.

[4] These comments apply primarily to middle-class families. Our experience with upper and lower class families is very limited.

behavior. It is obvious that these approaches are complementary rather than mutually exclusive.

A. Introduction to Communication Analysis. -- The system of annotations on communication patterns has been described at length elsewhere (1, 2, 4-6); we summarize it here. Statements may be judged as "symmetrical" or "complementary." A symmetrical statement is a comment on the equality of some aspect of a relationship. The most commonplace example would be in the conversation of adolescent peers engaged in a competitive relationship. For example, A says "I can hit a ball better than you" and B replies "I can hit farther than you." Equality may be expressed by the general notion, "I have the right to say this to you at this time," or it may be expressed in obvious form through content. A complementary statement is one that "asks" or "offers." Arbitrarily, we call "asking" the complementary one-down position and "offering" the complementary one-up position. Complementarity may have to be judged in terms of content and in terms of following statements. If one is presented merely with the statement, "I feel lousy," it may not be possible to judge whether this is merely a statement which refers to parasites, whether it is an asking for help or sympathy, or whether it means, "You are difficult to be around," unless the response and the response to the response are included. If the context is known, for example, if such a statement is uttered in a doctor's office and the vocalization is characteristic of a particular mood expressed in a particular tone in our culture, then one may feel reasonably sure as to whether it is a complementary one-down or one-up statement.

The justification for the use of "complementary" and "symmetrical" is described by Jackson (5). Briefly, the use of these terms is based on the assumption that the individual is constantly attempting to define and influence the nature of his relationships. It is conceivable, after making due allowance for context, that the patterning of complementary and symmetrical responses will give a rough and simple index to varying types of communications in families, and that these patterns in turn will be correlated with specific manifestations of mental illness.

Communications may also be analyzed from a somewhat different, yet related, point of view. Since all communications contain more than one message, one may qualify another in a contradictory fashion or the messages may be consistent. If there is a contradictory message, we label that message a "disqualification." If the disqualification occurs within a single communication, it may be either a "sequential" disqualification (verbal contradiction), or an "incongruent" disqualification. The latter may be either an affect-verbal discrepancy or a statement-context discrepancy. Thus, "go away closer" is a sequential disqualification, since one phrase "go away" is opposite to the following word, "closer." "Go away" uttered in a warm, loving tone is an incongruent message of the verbal-affect type, since there are opposite meanings conveyed in the verbal and tonal aspects of the statement. A wealthy man telling his wife he can't afford a new dress for her is an example of the statement-context type of incongruency.

One reason for making this distinction between sequential disqualification and incongruency between messages is that, in our experience, the more disturbed families utter a greater number of incongruent messages as compared to sequential disqualifications than do healthy families. A commonplace kind of sequential disqualification, for example, "yes" and then "no" is evidence of unsureness, doubt, and so on and may occur in any family particularly under stress. If it occurs frequently in a family without an appropriate context (for example, as being on the witness stand), it may be a sign of fairly severe family pathology. Incongruent messages may be labeled by the family as jokes, sarcasm, or special types of personal family humor, but if they occur in response to a message from another family member that requires an answer, and then the incongruency is not commented upon, it is usually a sign of pathology. "Pathology," in this sense, may refer to as simple a measure as the fact that incongruencies bring ordinary family business to a halt. The wife doesn't know what her husband "really" would like for supper, etc.

If disqualifications of any sort are frequent in a family's exchanges, the observer will be struck by the number of unresolved or "incomplete transactions." A will respond to one of B's messages, and B will respond to A with evidence that he, B, was not understood. The amount of unfinished business (incomplete transactions) with consequent dissatisfaction becomes very striking. To put it another way, the transaction is incomplete because B does not insist that A make himself clear and this lack will lead to further noncompletions, since B will respond with only partial information about A's meaning and so on. For example, a wife says to her husband: "I think you ought to go on that fishing trip, since you will make it unpleasant for the family if you don't." If, in addition, this statement is uttered in a biting, cold tone, then there are several messages at different levels to which the husband might respond. Our analysis of his relationship to his wife would be based

on which aspect of her statement he responds to and how he qualifies his own communications. There is quite a difference between
his stating, "You just put me in a bind. If I go, you will be angry;
and if I don't go, you'll be angry because you'll be expecting me to
make trouble"; and his stating in an explosive manner, "Dammit
why can't I ever do what I want to. Okay, I'll stay home, but I don't
think you're being very fair."[5]

The type of family just described, we have labeled elsewhere
(2) as "unstable, unsatisfactory," for issues are always being
raised but never concluded. In this type of family, an event which
calls into question "who has what rights in the relationship" will
provoke discord without solution. The cardinal principle in this
kind of family (unstable, unsatisfactory) is that neither husband nor
wife will be able to deal with the issue of who has the right to determine the nature of their relationship and under what kinds of circumstances. Hence, children, sex, relatives, recreation, and
other areas that call for collaboration or at least cooperation immediately bring up the question of "who will decide what," which
leads almost invariably to discord.

Another kind of response to the wife's statement given above
would be casual and quiet, and on the surface it would appear that
the husband and wife got along very well. An example of such a response would be the husband's stating, "Oh dear, I can't go this
week end anyway. My boss will be coming to town." This change
of context avoids the issue of "do you have the right" and "under
what conditions to tell me what to do." The cardinal principle in
this kind of family (stable, unsatisfactory) is that the question "who
will decide what" is never raised. It might be followed by the wife's
asking about the boss's plans and concluding with the statement, "I
wish you had let me know sooner. I want to get the house cleaned
up." The husband could then respond, "Now, now, dear, you're a
good housekeeper--it's just that you have so much to do." This kind
of exchange, apparently friendly and superficially agreeable, is
characteristic of some of the sicker, middle-class families we have
seen. Since the complexities of modern living demand that each
spouse have certain areas in which he or she must make decisions

---

[5]This latter response is characteristic of the husband in the
family being presented in this paper. The husband gets angry,
creates tension in the family, but obeys his wife's command, thus
making his show of strength a sham and forcing on her a responsibility she hasn't asked for.

that affect their relationship, avoiding this issue or failing to resolve it makes for an increasing complexity. As a consequence, behavior by the family members becomes apparently inappropriate and
unpredictable. Symptoms are the outcome. They are related to
shifts in the levels of communication which, in turn, are the results
of attempting to respond with multileveled statements to disqualifications in messages among the members.

B. Introduction to Interactional Dynamics. -- In this section we
describe how each individual's expectations are revealed through
family interaction in the interview situation. We focus on the individual's perception of the self (how I see me), the perception of the
other (how I see you), and the perception of the other in relation to
the self (how I see you seeing me).

Given these perceptions, we are then able to make further inferences in relation to motives. In particular, we are interested in
those attitudes such as: "am I lovable?", "am I acceptable?", "do
I have self-worth?" We are also concerned with how an individual
responds in the interview situation when his expectations and needs
are frustrated. In other words, we are looking for what a person
is implicitly trying to say in terms of his relationship with other
family members. This can obviously be considered from many
points of view, but we are focusing on how one individual tries to
influence the other to respond to him in terms of his perceptions
and expectations.

Another dimension of the analysis of interactional dynamics involves making reconstructions (postdictions) of the early life experiences based on our observation of the current interaction. This is
based on the assumption that earlier experiences with parental figures affect the ways that one later perceives one's self and others,
and that early patterns become "ruts," so that every problem tends
to become a replica of the original problem.

Further, given an assessment of the interacting parental dynamics, we want to indicate how the children are integrated into the parental relationship. For example, such questions as: Do the children
fill an emotional void in one or both parents resulting from a lack of
gratification in the marital relationship; are the children essentially
outside the relationship; are the children seen as narcissistic extensions of one of the marital partners; are the children seen as essential communication links between the parents since direct channels
are blocked; does the child who becomes a "cross-monitor" help
block more direct communication (4).

Transcript	Interactional Dynamics Analysis	Communication Analysis
1. Husband Well, last time we were together Mrs. Bryant gave a very . . . well a rather (Pause) dissertation, and one of the things I got out of it was she said that uh if I seem to make up my mind sometime and go ahead and do something I want to do and have the courage to do it, or something of that sort (evidently turns to wife) you remember that? (hedging —slightly whining)	1. Husband reminds therapist that last week wife said "I should do what I wanted to do." (Husband is saying "last week wife gave me permission to please myself and indicated by so doing I would please her.")† (Does this complaining tone mean wife doesn't keep promises?) (*I am a little boy who must ask permission from mother.*)	1. (CD)* The message "I should be more assertive" is framed by: (a) My wife told me to, and (b) you therapists are responsible —isn't that right? Thus, the interview begins with the husband's difficulty in making a symmetrical statement because it would raise the question with his wife, "Who has what rights in our relationship." Anything that is further stated must be viewed in the framework of "she told me to" and "you said it was all right."
2. Therapist Uh-huh.	2. Therapist makes affirming response indicating husband should continue.	2. Therapist makes a neutral comment which in this context means go ahead.
3. Husband Well so when I tried a little sample of that Saturday, she just *raised* hell. (mimics, with raising voice) (he laughs) (evidently turns to wife) Your reaction was interesting. I just said that I was going to play . . . this was Friday, wasn't it? (tries to sound factual)	3. Husband tells therapist he tried to please himself but wife objected. ("Wife doesn't mean what she says. She gives permission but takes it away, and this is what I expected. As usual, I can't please her.") (Husband's comments are indirect criticism of wife and at the same time a plea for understanding from her.) (*You must never make women angry. Women don't like grown-up men. I resent this.*)	3. (Sym ‡ to CD) Husband starts again with a symmetrical statement "My wife is like this." He almost immediately disqualifies himself by "little sample" and by using an exaggerated tone, for example on the word "raised," thus criticizing her without risking being overt about it. He does not state "I am critical of my wife." Instead, by mimicking her, he implies "this is what she sounds like."
4. Therapist You were what?	4. Therapist asks for more information.	4. Therapist asks for more information.
5. Husband This was Friday (sounds factual) I'd been away on this trip. Didn't have any vacation Friday. Thought I was going to play golf, (pause) and so made this statement, I was going to play golf, and she started in (apparently mimics her complaining tone) well, Dick wanted some kids to go swimming and one thing and another. And she had to do some shopping because Pete was coming over, bringing his friends over. And immediately got *angry* about this. (someone coughs) At one point, it involved things about (mimicking) I was selfish and I wasn't thinking about anybody else and all this sort of thing. (back to reportorial tone) Meanwhile I had arrived at the suggestion that part of this was because Pete had to have the car over him. That, I imagine Pete had nothing to do Friday morning and he could solve this whole thing extremely simply by just coming home and taking his mother shopping. (sounds heroic) And I would call him up and ask him to do this. At which point (mimics) *don't you dare*—all that sort of thing. (suffering, complaining) I mean everything here was pinning this whole business on what Dick wanted to do with his little children, what Pete might be just inconvenienced one way, slightly one way or another. And you were just going to see by God if you could not keep me from, if you could keep me *from* playing golf, I *do* believe. (pause) But I did. . . .	5. Husband says "after working hard, I wanted to enjoy myself." ("I had justification for enjoying myself but my wife says children's needs come first. Wife criticizes me for not dropping my needs and meeting children's needs, but I saw a reasonable way that both my needs and theirs could be met.") ("Wife refused to accept this way, but continued to favor the kids. My wife is unreasonable. You, wife, lie when you say you want me to do what I want to do.") ("If I want to do what I have to defy you, wife. Doing what I want to do can only be an act of rebellion.") (*You always have to defy mothers to get what you want. If you rebel you make them angry, but if you don't rebel they think you are weak and you remain a little boy.*)	5. (Sym to CD) Again he starts out with a symmetrical statement but again disqualifies himself in 2 ways: (a) He gives up his reportorial tone and factual reporting and then mimics his wife again, implying that she is unreasonable and she will not let him determine what goes on in the house: (b) he then adopts a suffering, complaining tone during which he apparently turns to his wife and addresses her directly in a challenging way. In addition, he seems to be indicating to the therapist what he has to put up with.
6. Wife (Overlaps husband's statement) The way you take it. (quietly determined)	6. Wife denies husband's accusation. ("I am not bad, you are. You are misunderstanding me.") (Wife feels that men are really just little boys, they are to be humored, not to be taken seriously.) (*Father was ineffectual and treated by mother as a little boy.*)	6. (Sym) The wife's statement, "The way you take it" is said in a quietly determined voice, indicating all too clearly "you are unreasonable and I have to put up with you." The measured tone is an appropriate qualification of the content.
7. Husband And I called up your son and he was glad to come over and help you and all this and that. So this was your reaction to me deciding I wanted to do something and meaning it. (more tentatively) Wasn't it?	7. Husband says ("I proved to you that I had a reasonable idea but you won't accept proof. You just want to deprive me. You are unreasonable.") (*Mothers lie when they say they want to be accepting. They are always depriving. Men have no way of influencing women.*) ("You want children on your side and are against me. You make me feel that my children and I are rivals: When I try to be the father, I am left out. You don't really want a man.") ("Isn't it true that you are unreasonable? If you can admit to being unreasonable, then we both can feel equal. How I feel depends on how you feel.")	7. (Sym to CD) Husband ignores the challenge, apparently, and resorts again to an attempt at a symmetrical statement. Again he backs down by ending on a question "Wasn't it?" This is an invitation to being cut down. (Note that so far there have been no completed transactions.)
8. Wife (With a sigh—icy) That's the way you like to take it. You must remember when you left (deadly, bitter) you said (mimics) that you *may* not be here. . . .	8. Wife says "I am justified in criticizing you because you are so unreasonable." (*You can't count on men.*)	8. (Sym to CD) Wife repeats her statement with greater emphasis, for example the sigh implying his unreasonableness. Although the statement is uttered generally in a deadly bitter, icy tone and she continues in that symmetrical position, she disqualifies it slightly by mimicking him in the words, "May not be here." She ends in a one-down position as she appeals to the therapist, "Listen how unreasonable he sounds."

† Statements range from those being of low inference (having no parentheses), through those of medium inference (having parentheses), to those being highly inferential (having parentheses and italicized).

* CD—Complementary one down comment.
‡ Sym—Symmetrical comment.

9. *Husband*
(Filling in her last statement) Thursday. And you know my custom is I would let you know. (injured innocence) (Wife murmurs) So what's the difference? (loudly)

10. *Wife*
What's the difference? (exaggeratedly factual) Because Pete had called me very nicely and asked if you were back yet or if I knew and I said—No, I didn't. So he said he'd like, he'd bring the car back but I couldn't as I explained to you, (slightly faltering) get the car and drive Pete back to the hospital because he had booked up the evening, because that was the night that Dick had a baseball game which you simply accepted. And I, I uh, (exaggeratedly factual) we had made our plans because we hadn't heard you'd come back or not. Dick invited some boys over there and when you came back and you were sore at me. It wasn't that . . . (mimics) you just came out and said (mimicking—slightly faltering) by God, I'm home, by golly I'm going to have the car by golly, I'm going . . . the hell with—(Wife gets increasingly louder) (factual tone—mimicking attitude)

11. *Husband*
(Interrupting) (sounds very defensive) I wasn't saying anything like that. (loud) I just said I was going to play golf.

12. *Wife*
(Mock horror) Oh-h-h you just when I said—

13. *Husband*
(Sharply interrupting) It was not until you started (she interrupts, some overlapping) (fast, sharp interaction, each being exaggeratedly factual), not until you started.
13a. *Wife*
I said . . .
13b. *Husband*
. . . yelping about it. This seems almost petty of me to bring a thing like this in here but it goes back to this point that you were saying (mimicking) by golly you would like to see me make up my mind some time or other what I wanted to do and do it.

14. *Wife*
What did you learn that week end, John? (quietly determined, matronizing)

15. *Husband*
Hm?

16. *Wife*
What did you learn (pause) after all that snorting around? (more critical and with slight edge)

17. *Husband*
I learned that you just do a lot of yelping

9. (Husband says "You are unreasonable for labeling me as unreasonable.") (*Men can't please women.*)

10. (Wife says "How can I help but criticize you when you are so unreasonable; you are just a blustery little boy.") (*Men cannot be counted upon. Men are unreasonable. Father was an unreliable, unpredictable, unreasonable man who couldn't be counted on either.*) (Wife has a need for a husband who will confirm her expectation that men are unreliable, but on the other hand desperately hopes they won't turn out that way.)

11. Husband rejects wife's accusation. By defending himself husband automatically denies wife's plea for a strong man who will understand her. (He comments instead—"I didn't mean to hurt you, I just wanted to do something for myself.")

12. (Wife attacks him for being a little boy.)

13. (Husband says "I am not a bad little boy, you are the unreasonable one.") (If this interaction continued, their mutual hurt would show. In order to avoid this, husband joins in setting the automatic governor in motion and returns to opening gambit saying—"I don't want to hurt you, I am only trying to do what you want me to do. Damn you. Please let me!")

14. Wife changes subject ostensibly. (Wife implies she is speaking to a little boy who is bad—she therefore acts ostensibly like a solicitous mother. Wife is wanting to give by being mothering to husband even though critical. The tone is softer—making a bid for closeness—conciliation to husband.) (Wife, if denied gratification of her needs is to be given to further denies them by defensively taking the role of mother.)

15. (Since this mothering is seen by husband as defensive, as a disguise to the lack of gratification of her needs, it is not possible for him to fully respond to it. Husband seems taken aback and behaves as though he doesn't hear.) (Mothering probably feels phony to him.)

16. Wife initially repeats mothering tone, but changes to critical one in tone and word after being denied any response for her offering. (*Wife feels confirmation of her expectation that men will not accept any giving from women, therefore women are useless in the eyes of men.*) (Wife denies being put in this position by accusing husband of being incapable of giving or receiving.)

17. Husband denies wife's accusation ("I am not ungiving; your demands are insatiable.")

9. (Sym to CD) Husband again resorts to making a symmetrical maneuver by simply reporting the facts, but ends again on a question "What is the difference?" which obviously calls for a response from her, thus putting him in a complementary one down position.

10. (CU § to CD) Wife responds to his one-down position by taking the complementary one-up position, stating by her tone and her factual content "I am reasonable; you are unreasonable." She then weakens her position when she uses his technique of mimicking again, again asking for his support.

11. (Sym to CD) Husband responds to first part of wife's message by attacking. He becomes literal "I just said I was going to play golf" rather than dealing explicitly with her message that he is unreasonable. He thus invites a reiteration from her. His defensive tone (hurt?) is perhaps a comment on her using the one-up position to criticize him.

12. (Not determined) Her exaggerated mock horror is a comment on his being a child, but she is utilizing a child-like technique and it is thus not a strong ploy. She does not continue to usurp the one-up position, perhaps because she recognizes that she has gone too far in criticizing him. This pattern would suggest that apparently they have an inflexible set of rules as to how far they can go in devastating each other. Wife attacks husband for being a little boy, which makes her seem like an evil mother because husband cannot better tolerate her criticism. She is hurt by his being hurt. And this circularity seems to serve as a governor on the extent of their relatedness.

13. (Sym to CD) The governor now in effect, husband returns to the starting statement. Even the content of his statement says clearly "You went too far and now let's start over." He is back to his original position.

14. (CU to Sym) In the absence of an intervention by the therapist, wife responds to husband by asking a therapist-like question, thus switching the context from their private circular interaction. Wife's attempt to get out of the rut misfires because she frames it with a superior tone, thus baiting him; so he must reattack instead of responding helpfully.

15. Husband is unclear which message to respond to, therefore he stalls.

16. (CU to Sym) Wife interprets husband's stalling as a lack of response to the helpful aspect of her statement and reinforces the superior aspect in order to punish him. This is not being a "good therapist" and invites attack from husband by her failure.

17. (Sym to CU) Husband responds with the expected attack, using "yelping" instead of

---

§ CU—Complementary one-up comment.

no matter what. (sharply critical) Another thing is yesterday was another example. (Wife—"um hum") Uh, *you* wanted to go swimming. (gentle, definitive, teaching quality) And because Dick—

18. *Wife*
(Interrupts) I *didn't* say I *wanted* to go swimming. I said I *may* go swimming. But I didn't want to rush. (edgy, exasperated) (tersely) And we were going out at 4 o'clock. (Defensively starts to get legalistic)

19. Husband
(Interrupting) But you hinged all this around Dick not liking to do something or other. (Patient, patronizing—trying to be factual)

20. Wife
Well, I didn't want to go swimming by myself. (defensive) (faster) You were (quite fast, almost stumbling) I was half planning on doing something like that and I (defensively)

21. Husband
(Interrupting) Then you couldn't. (indignantly) You had to rush back to cook him his supper and the other night you cooked him his supper and he didn't even eat it. (pause) I mean all this stuff starts hinging around what do these little *rascals* want to *do* (mimicking) all the time (pause) and are they absolutely first?

22. Wife
Well I always (quieter—regaining her composure)

23. Husband
(Interrupting)—interfere with you and interfere with me and interfere with everything else. (Indignant and angry)

24. Wife
I always knew you were jealous of your children. (contemptuous, cold, critical, definite, sounds almost triumphant)

(*Your needs, like those of all women are so great that they are incapable of satiation.*) (Wife says apprehensively—"Go ahead, I know you are going to blame me but you are not going to get away with it.") (Husband continues . . . "You say you want to do something for yourself, but you let the kids interfere just as they interfere with my pleasures. You blame me for not pleasing you when you really won't let yourself be pleased.")

18. (Wife denies she desires pleasures. "My concern is for you and the children. My pleasures are only secondary to yours and the children's.") (*Women dare not expect pleasure or gratification. Wife's mother was a martyr, thus she expects it is woman's role to suffer.*)

19. (Husband says, "You, wife, can't openly ask to have pleasure though you really want to. You can only attain it under the guise of doing it for the children.") (*Husband's mother would have used him against his father as wife uses Dick against him.*) (Husband feels competitive with son and at the same time critical of wife for using Dick.) (It could additionally be that husband suspects women can ask for what they want, but they consciously deny this. Husband is attempting to get wife to acknowledge this.)

20. (Wife denies that she can't ask for pleasures. "It appears that I can't because you desert me and I have to turn to Dick. It really is your fault since you don't give to me. I'd really want to receive.")

21. (Husband says "I don't believe you want to give me anything. The children get more than I do and they are not as appreciative as I would be." (*Husband feels unloved and that his mother was depriving in a manner that prevented overt labeling by him. Thus it is important that he get his wife to openly acknowledge her deprivation of him.*)

22. Wife is taken aback by the extent of husband's accusation that children come first, especially since wife views him as one of the children. She views his accusation of partiality as a comment on her being a bad mother. (Her need to maintain a good-mother image might also relate to her not perceiving illness in Pete until external factors force it to her attention.)

23. In order to avoid a direct frontal attack on wife for not caring about him, husband points to the children as the reason for his being left out, inferring that wife would care for him very much if she were able to, that is, the children prevent her from doing this. It would be dangerous openly to accuse wife of not caring lest he receive concrete evidence of her not caring, that is, his own unworthiness. (*His mother's preferential treatment of him, much like his wife's treatment of Pete, resulted in feelings of privilege, and, at the same time an inadequacy to live up to them.* He repeats this pattern with his wife.) (*Husband's preferential position with his mother makes him a hopeless competitor with his father and denies him an identification which would enable him to carry out his fathering role. Thus fathers can't help their sons because they are rivals. They can only look out for themselves.*)

24. (Wife says "I knew you always felt like a rival with your children. Which means that you make me a mother instead of a wife. Thus I am deprived of a husband.") (Her cutting tone indicates the attitude, "You aren't a man.") (*Since wife married such a "man," she has no expectations of being treated as a wife.*) (Her mother did not openly label her

---

"snorting." As soon as he is critical, he attempts conciliation by being solicitous in the manner of a therapist. However this effort on husband's part to become a therapist, although conciliatory, labels her a patient and will bring forth a rebuttal, which will lead to a symmetrical relationship such as these two have.

18. (Sym to CD) The expected rebuttal occurs but with a revealing edge to it. By denying husband's implication that she is entitled to want for herself, she indicates that their relationship is one in which wanting is bad. However, her defensive tone disqualifies this definition and invites the husband to pursue his attack. They have now reversed roles. He is telling her she should be more assertive, and she is denying it as he was doing earlier. It is as if each had told the other: "If you would get more for yourself, I could too." Although husband has her on the defensive, it is the same old issue; there has been no progress toward clarification.

19. (Sym) This again is a symmetrical statement in which he accuses her of taking second place to the children. At the same time in this context he removes himself from the charge of being a spoiled child since he, too, is put in second position.

20. (Attempts CU but settles for CD) She again switches context by ignoring the "Dick" charge. This may have been partly caused by his ignoring her statement "and we were going to go out at 4 o'clock." Her content is disqualified, however, by her fast, defensive vocalization. She again uses a similar type of message to his—an apparently factual statement disqualified by hurt defensiveness and inviting further movement from the spouse. Wife has ignored husband's implication that when she puts children first, she suffers.

21. (Sym to CD) Here he nearly reaches his finest hour. "You sacrifice me for the kids and it doesn't pay off." But on the threshold of becoming one-up, he backs down and asks: "Is it necessary?" which is an invitation for wife to take a CU.

22. (Sym) She doesn't immediately respond to his invitation to take the one-up position, perhaps because she is still caught by the first part of his message.

23. (CU to Sym) Her refusal to accept his message that "we are both losing out to the kids" leads to further attack, in which he overgeneralizes and thus leaves himself open.

24. (Strong Sym) Again as in sequence 14, she nails him with a "therapeutic" interpretation, which fails for the same reason. (Cf. 14).

25. *Husband*
I (only mildly defensive) am not jealous of
them.
25a. *Wife*
Yes you are (as he says)
25b. *Husband*
I just expect equal *rights.* (long pause) You
do all this self-sacrificing all the time and
what does it get you? (righteously indignant)
26. *Wife*
I am not self-sacrificing, John. (pause)
(soft) You think so . . . (mimicking through
phony toughness) you·want me, it's like the
last time, you want me to treat your children.
the way your mother treated you. (bitter contempt) She ran her little roost over there
and this thing was done this way. You liked.
it. (biting)

father as *"no good" but implied men are
ungiving and women must be the responsive
ones. Wife's father cooperated in this attitude
by being dead tired, too busy. Thus she was
denied an opportunity of being a Daddy's girl
and thus was not prepared to be given to by
a husband.*)
25. Husband denies rivalry with children. ("It's
your fault that I am not a man. It is not
the children but your preferential treatment
of the children that makes me feel deprived.
Why do you treat yourself this way? I could
help you if you would let me.") (This man
needs the evidence of external validation from
wife to give him feelings of self-esteem.)

26. (Wife says "I almost believe you would like
to be a man, which means I could be a wife,
but I know really you want me to be a mother
to you. I can't even be a mother to you because
your picture of a mother is unacceptable to me
and I can see what your mother did to you.
I deny that she and I have anything in common. Your attitude prevents me from having
anything to offer.") (Thus wife expects
external validation is necessary for her own
feeling of worth as a wife or mother.)

25. (Sym to CD) He attempts to escape a
damning charge by restating his message,
"Don't put them in front of us." As usual,
however, his bid is double-edged and difficult
to respond to. His major message is, "Why
can't we get together?" but it is disqualified
by his angry tone and the label, "You are
bad" attached to being self-sacrificing.

26. (Starts Sym and ends CU) She responds
to his implicit charge rather than to his
attempts to get together. Again she out-
maneuvers him by switching the context to
"You loved your mother and she was wrong
so I won't be like her." This is a double-
leveled message that is difficult to respond to.
If he accepts the "You liked it," he accepts
a damning charge as well. If he agrees mother
was wrong, he is ignoring the charge "you
loved her" and may step into further difficulties, namely "You don't love me any more
than you loved your mother." If he could
rise to a new level, namely, "I care for you as
much as I did my mother," he could handle
her message.

II. TRANSCRIPT WITH INTERACTIONAL DYNAMICS AND COMMUNICATION ANALYSIS

There are several generalizations that might orient the reader toward following the parental interaction in the transcript to be presented:

1. The parents make no attempt to include the identified patient (their son) and they speak of him and his brother (who is not present) in much the same manner.

2. The parents are defensive and righteous and each is insecure in regard to his role. Thus, they cannot aid one another and must resort to blaming each other.

3. The mother appears to achieve an edge in the power struggle between them but as mentioned below, this position is not maintained. She is able to use the children against the father and he is unable to avoid falling into this trap because he is defensive about his attitude toward his sons. Apparently he competes with his sons for his wife in a fashion which makes him feel like one of the children, thus lowering his own self-esteem and elevating the relative position of his wife. This makes the husband defensive and he attacks wife for being a bad mother. The wife then becomes anxious and feels deserted over the husband's abdication of his role, which is seen by her as neglect. She then reinstitutes the struggle by attacking him for his neglect of her. This pattern between the parents produces an oscillatory interaction which is apparent even in this brief excerpt.

4. Although we state that the fighting between the parents is more overt and explicit than the family of the acute or chronic schizophrenic, it should be pointed out that this couple is unable to resolve anything by their struggle and this is an indication of significant pathology. They play what Berne has labeled "The Game of Uproar (3)."

5. Because the therapist makes no attempt to break up the parental struggles, we can assume that he has been through this before. Since there is more impotence than destructiveness in the argumentation, the therapist is not alarmed by any untoward effects. This hypothesis is supported by the cyclical nature of the parents' encounters. One or the other backs off before things get out of hand and reenters the area and a new fight starts. Without the therapist's intervention, the couple behaves as if a psychological governor were limiting the range of their oscillation. One

can, therefore, imagine this couple going through life not agreeing but not disagreeing to the extent of separation.

III. CONCLUSIONS
On the basis of the analysis of the above portion of the tape, we make the following conclusions about this family:

A. We view these parents as upwardly mobile, middle-class individuals.

1. Wife expects men to be unpredictable, weak, withholding, and unnurturing, as seen in her expectations of her husband. Because of men's weakness, wife feels that women must, of necessity, step in and be the strong ones as her mother probably did. Women cannot hope to be protected, cared for, and understood by men because men prevent it by being weak. This is a comment on her feminine identification. These expectations blind her to any evidence to the contrary.

Her hopes on the other hand are that men be predictable, strong, giving, and nurturing; thus her frequent verbalizations "Be a man, don't be a man." "Be aggressive. Don't be aggressive." The former aspect represents her hopes and the latter, her expectations, which she succeeds in evoking. Because wife expects that men are responsible for how women are, women are weak and helpless. This would seem to be a clue to wife's relationship to her mother, who was likely withholding. In relation to women, wife probably sees herself as undesirable, inadequate, and basically a child.

2. Husband expects women to be overwhelming, the mainstay of the family, partial, depreciating, unpleasable, infantilizing, as seen by his expectations of his wife. "Women do not like grown-up men. They only say they do." Husband hopes that women will permit him to have a position of equality with them, will relate to him as though he were strong, important, and grown-up. On the other hand, he expects this not to happen. We see that he ignores efforts on the part of his wife to treat him this way. He behaves according to his expectations of women's expectations and depreciates his own hopes. Therefore by necessity, he must communicate in multilevel messages. In relation to men, husband probably feels unable to compete and be esteemed.

3. All of this results in a lack of mutually satisfying communication between husband and wife--"no closeness," about which the couple openly complain. They feel inadequate, undesirable, un-

loved, incapable of loving or being loved. This is spelled out in terms of criticism of each other. The communication is carried on at the level of their defenses against their mutually felt but unverbalized low feelings of self-esteem. Each is trying to force the other to increase his feelings of self-worth, which, however, because of the other's low expectations and his own low feelings cannot be supplied. On the other hand, despite the long history of deprivation, each still is actively trying to increase his feelings of self-esteem and be giving to the other, unsuccessful as these efforts turn out. This pattern is in contrast to families which seem sicker to us, where there seems to be only futility and despair.

B. From our knowledge of the present interaction between the husband and wife, we may make further inferences in relation to their own respective families of origin. It would seem that the expectations of each spouse, as revealed, for example, by their criticisms or demands on each other, would enable us to speculate as to what kinds of relationships their own parents might have had in order to provide the matrix for the development of these expectations. We therefore make the following reconstructions on the families of origin:

1. Husband had a father whom we would consider withholding, restrictive, punitive, an average provider but basically ineffective. Husband's mother was probably a "giving," strong, (iron-hand-silk-glove) orderly, demanding woman. We would see her as depressed and unhappy, with husband feeling ineffective in being able to please her. Husband's mother was the openly accepted, undisputed authority with father being covertly rebellious, particularly with money, but openly accepting her authority. Husband's mother was a precise, aggressive woman, socially adept. His father was also a socially correct, but passive businessman who was probably closely tied to his business.

2. Wife had a fairly materially successful father. Mother of wife was an overly demanding woman who expressed this covertly. We would expect that wife saw her father as literally absent or remote, ineffectual and unable to provide emotionally. Wife's mother was the boss in the family, but this could not be explicitly spelled out. Wife's father covertly acted out against mother's covert authority in some self-punishing way so that it turned out that mother was a martyr and father was an unfortunate man. Wife could not comment on the relationship between her parents.

The chances are, in our experience, that in a family which is characterized by a symmetrical relationship such as in this one, the first child brings up the question of "Who is in charge of what?" In such a family, the first child also may be made a bearer of the parental ambitions, as well as a repository for their uneasiness and self-doubt. In this family, then, we would expect that the first child, Pete, would be used by the parents to facilitate communication between them. (We would predict that if something were to occur to prevent their using Pete, they would use the second child in the same way.) The second son, Dick, might have an easier time of it. In view of this mother's overprotectiveness and the father's helpless competitiveness, Dick is apt to be the spoiled child with some ability to manipulate other people and some acting out behavior.

C. The identified patient, Pete, might manifest some of the following symptoms because of his focal position in the parental struggle.

1. He must be responsible and succeed, yet success would increase father's competitiveness and reveal the shallowness of mother's attachment to Pete. Therefore, Pete must also fail. These mechanisms occur against the backdrop of the parents' mutually depriving interaction. The parental interaction heightens Pete's success-failure conflict, and in turn this conflict highlights the parents frustrating struggles with each other.

2. Pete must fail in such a way that neither parent can view the failure as a comment on their relationship with their son. His failure is apt to provoke comments from each in blaming the other. At the same time, since he perceives himself as outside their relationship and feels hopeless about breaking into it, he would be fearful that both might turn on him. His failure, therefore, would be of the "quiet type" such as increasingly poor grades, decreasing socialization, etc. Failure of this sort would lead to evanescent concern and interest as well as criticism on the part of his parents, but there would be no follow-through until he becomes so overtly symptomatic that they seek medical help. It is postulated that there has been a long delay in seeing difficulties as "symptoms," since each parent would label some aspect of Pete's behavior as an extension of faults in the other person, therefore "bad" rather than "sick." They would each procrastinate, blaming the other for the "bad" behavior in Pete, for which they hold the other responsible.

3. Withdrawal would keynote Pete's defensive operations because it allows him to feel he leaves the relationship rather than

being left out of the parents' interaction. In addition, withdrawal
will dull the hurt of experiencing their bitter clashes. This family is intact enough so that Pete could not withdraw in an obvious
fashion such as becoming a vagabond or hiding in his room, but he
might withdraw by preoccupation, especially if his parents' striv-
ings link this to intellectualism, "the absent minded professor,"
and if his fantasies take the form of noncomments on his relationship to his parents, e.g., concern with ideas, with self-improve-
ment, etc., rather than with what he would like to do either with
or to his parents. Pete's comment is "I am not separated from
you; I am just involved with myself." As long as the parents accept this thesis, Pete is forced to acknowledge that he is alone,
and this will lead to depression which will be noticed by them.
The parents are then forced to view him as sick. If they delay in
this recognition, the next step might be suicidal comments and
possibly a suicidal attempt. Although we have no direct data on
this, we would not be surprised if he had actually threatened to
make a suicide attempt.

4. Pete's model from both parents is a longing hunger that one
must not reveal lest he become vulnerable. Therefore, blame and
alibi play an important part in accounting for why things are not as
they should be. While there is no evidence from the tape directly,
one might infer that Pete used physical illness, procrastination,
and "I don't feel like it" as part of his avoidance mechanisms.

5. There is a family fiction that Pete and Dick both must go
along with. This includes:

(a) Father is stereotyped as trying hard, but he shouldn't put
the family last as he does. He is also depicted as a dictator who
invokes fear.

(b) Mother is more loving and reliable and puts the children
first. Actually, it seems to us that father identifies with his sons
and is more forgiving than mother represents him as being, even
though he is competitive and temperamental. He is not much of
a dictator and his wife indicates he is more of a windbag than a
strong force. He supports her view by being unable to make symmetrical comments without framing them as "This is the way you
told me I should be." Such a comment frames the whole session.
Mother is such a deprived person that much of her apparent giving
to the children is actually using them against father to point up his
deprivation of her and to replace him via the sons. This retalia-
tory gesture states "Since you won't give to me, I have to use my

sons." Pete's understandable failure to fill father's shoes, would decrease his self-esteem, and produce sexual problems. While there is no direct data, the problem would take the form of concern over masturbation, (5) and doubts about his masculinity. Such problems would increase the parents' anxiety and render them incapable of aiding Pete.

Rather than being discrepant as being presented in the family fiction, both parents are evenly matched. They are in a constant struggle for love from each other and only tangentially relate to their children. They are mirror images and use much more similar communication devices than any set of parents we have so far analyzed. The extent of their involvement with each other leaves little involvement with the children except as the child: 1) reminds each parent of some aspect of himself; 2) can be used to replace deficiencies in the relationship of the one spouse with the other; 3) can be used as a weapon by one spouse against the other. Pete, then, serves as a repository for the faults they see in the other, and simultaneously disguises these faults in them, thus resulting in labeling Pete the sick one. Dick, on the other hand, might be the child who represents the more carefree wish of each, and any problem he might show would be interpreted as "cute" or childlike.

IV. SUMMARY

In this paper we have presented an analysis of the first 5 minutes of a family therapy interview. The analysis has been from two viewpoints: 1) in terms of communication theory, which is concerned with the formal aspects of the interaction; 2) in terms of the interacting dynamics of the spouses, with emphasis on how each one's needs and defenses are affected by and affect the other spouse. We have tried to reconstruct (postdict) the possible bases for their interaction in terms of their early life experiences. From their patterns of interaction we have attempted to predict the psychiatric symptoms of their oldest son, and also some character traits of his younger brother. Our immediate purpose in this analysis has been to illustrate a method of analyzing family interaction, with the ultimate intention of applying this method to a longitudinal predictive study which would test hypotheses relating family interaction to mental illness.

REFERENCES

1. Bateson, G. Minimal requirement for a theory of schizophrenia. A. M. A. Arch. Gen. Psychiat., 1:477-491, 1960.

246

2. Bateson, G. Jackson, D. D., Haley, J., and Weakland, J. Toward a theory of schizophrenia. Behav. Sci., 1:251-264, 1956. (See p. 31, this vol.)

3. Berne, E. Unpublished manuscript.

4. Haley, J. The family of a schizophrenic: a model system. J. Nerv. Ment. Dis., 129:357-374, 1959. (See p. 171, this vol.)

5. Jackson, D. D. Guilt and the control of pleasure in schizoid personalities. Brit. J. Med. Psychol., 31:124-130, 1958. (See p. 12, this vol.)

6. Jackson, D. D. Family interaction, family homeostasis and some implications for conjoint family psychotherapy. In Individual and Family Dynamics, Jules H. Masserman (Ed.), Grune & Stratton, New York, 1958.

7. Jackson, D. D. The Analysis of Schizophrenic Families. Read before the Group for the Advancement of Psychiatry, November, 1959.

* * * * *

COMMENTS ON THE PRECEDING ANALYSIS

Lyman C. Wynne, M. D.

These comments are based upon clinical work with this family over the past 2-1/2 years. The therapy has included conjoint family sessions twice weekly, individual psychoanalytic therapy with the son Pete for 2 years, and individual psychotherapy with the mother for 3 months. The family therapists involved were Drs. Lyman C. Wynne and Juliana Day, and the individual therapists were Drs. Leslie Schaffer and Irving Ryckoff.

The authors are correct in concluding that this family is psychiatrically disturbed but does not contain a schizophrenic offspring. The presenting patient in this family is a young adult man who has been diagnosed clinically as primarily an obsessional character, with obsessional symptoms appearing sporadically. He also has a definite tendency to depressive illness. Although at times he has seemed somewhat schizoid, he has not had acute or chronic schizophrenic psychotic episodes of a clearly definable sort. Rated on a continuum of "degree of schizophrenicness," this young man is actually not very far removed from being schizophrenic. Some clinicians would regard him as "borderline." Therefore, the conclusion made on the basis of the parental interaction, without this son verbally participating, involves a high degree of accurate discrimination.

Like Jackson and his colleagues, I too have repeatedly found such impressionistic judgments about families in conjoint sessions can be made very quickly and, thus far in my experience, always accurately.* If it can be shown that such judgments by persons experienced in conjoint family therapy can, in fact, be made consistently, this finding deserves intensive study. After family-therapy experience it seems possible to make such diagnostic evaluations accurately without being able to specify fully the cues which have helped form the impression.

In the report on this excerpt, it was noted that the parents argued more openly than seems characteristic in schizophrenic families and "the criticism is explicitly directed and explicitly responded to." This statement about the openness and directness in this family is a kind of communication analysis, on the level of clinical impression, and is spelled out in more detail in the speech-by-speech "communication analysis" of the excerpt. I do not have any special comment to make about the notation method of the communication analysis in this report, compared to other descriptive techniques. I feel that its ultimate merit hinges upon its demonstrated usefulness in discriminating various kinds of families and in evaluating various hypotheses about family patterns.

Whereas the communication analysis seemed to be most useful in deciding whether or not this was the family of a schizophrenic, the interactional dynamics analysis seemed to contribute more to the description of the personal characteristics of the family members. This difference between the uses of the 2 approaches seems natural if we regard dynamics as more closely related to personality characteristics and communication patterns as more closely related to the nature of a social system which might produce an offspring of a particular variety.

On the whole, the detail and accuracy of the conclusions about the characteristics of the parents is indeed remarkable. It had been only too true that the first child, Pete, had been an intermediary between the parents, both facilitating communication between

---

*Relevant here is a comment which Dr. Stephen Fleck, of New Haven, made in reviewing this paper: "Before turning to Dr. Wynne's notes, I made the following notations: There is nothing pathognomic of a schizophrenic process in the parents' exchange as far as I could tell. The quarreling is hot but relatively direct and on a defensive level indicative of lack of psychological sophistication rather than masking or obscuring" (D.J., J.R., V.S.).

them and being used as a weapon by one spouse against the other. This pattern, which actually had started to change at the time of this session, stemmed from the history of deprivation and low self-esteem of each parent. The narcissistic needs of both were so great that they could not risk asking directly for affection or comfort from one another. Instead, each demanded that the other stop feeling anxious and be satisfied and appreciative of what had been done and given. However, each felt undeserving and fearful of the passive vulnerability associated with being given appreciation or anything else positive from the other. Thus, feeling deprived and vindictive, each "gave" to the other with sufficiently negative overtones so that the painful expectation that no solace was forthcoming from the other was in fact regularly confirmed.

The consequent shared communication pattern constitutes an example of what I have called pseudohostility, hostility in which the fangs are always pulled at the last minute because of the disguised underlying dependent attachment. If Pete or the therapists served as intermediaries between the parents, or as an agent for either of them, the direct impact of the hostility between the parents would be toned down, blurred, and partially evaded. Such participation by either Pete or the therapist in this struggle would thus support the marital pseudohostile defenses and would delay feared clarification and change in the marital relation. In earlier sessions in which Pete was more vocal, his ambivalence about being in the middle of the parental struggle was spelled out in some detail. Pete's failure to establish a life of his own maintains a place for him in the lives of his parents, a place which they all had come to experience as somehow necessary, although in some respects very distressing.

Thus the main features of these intrafamilial relations as described in the excerpt analysis are substantially supported by clinical study of the family. Some relatively minor points, mainly about the background of the mother, are not borne out by the clinical material, but these are not crucial. For example, the prediction that the wife's father was fairly successful materially was incorrect; the wife's mother expressed her demands both overtly and covertly, not just covertly as predicted. On the other hand, essentially everything about the father's family background was predicted accurately. The description of Pete was also correct on the whole. Although there had been a period, contrary to prediction, when he had retired to his room and looked like a hobo, this behavior was cut short when his parents insisted that he get back to school, get into the army, or get out. The parents of a schizophrenic would, it is my impression, be unable to set and stick to such limit-setting.

There was one misinterpretation of this excerpt which might have been corrected by direct observation or filming of the session. It was incorrectly assumed in the first speech by the husband that the husband had turned to the wife. Actually, he turned to the therapist and both spouses continued to orient themselves visually toward the therapist throughout the session. Judging from their nonverbal behavior, they were not so much talking to each other as they were talking about each other toward the 2 silent participants, the therapist and Pete.

Although each complained that the other was insatiable, it is noteworthy that the complaint was saved to be presented in this session, with the implicit plea from each parent that the therapist or Pete do something to pound sense into the other's head. The therapist's silence was a frustration for them both, which he intended would, as it later did, bring out more into the open their implicit wishes to have the therapist appease or deal with the spouse.

In the earlier sessions, Pete had regularly stepped into the middle of parental quarrels of this kind and had quieted each parent alternately. This pattern had been repeatedly interpreted by the therapists. Pete had been recently expressing a wish to stay out of such entanglements, but this was one of the first occasions in which he had actually stayed out. At the time of this excerpt, the parents were transferring to the therapist certain expectations which they previously had held toward Pete. Much later, after a little over 2 years of family therapy, Pete had become sufficiently disentangled emotionally so that he left the family therapy with general agreement. He went on with individual therapy, while the parents continued in conjoint marital therapy. The prediction of a favorable prognostic outlook with family therapy seems to have been confirmed.

There was one other feature about this particular session which was not apparent from the tape-recording and may have affected its form. This session occurred after a 10-day vacation and was also unusual in that only a single therapist was present. (The female cotherapist had become ill just before the session and there was no opportunity to alter the schedule.) While chairs were being moved around at the start of the session, the therapist told the family that the other therapist was not going to be present, but this does not come through on the tape-recording. The family did not comment on either this absence or the vacation, but judging from other times when such interruptions to the therapy routine were discussed, they very likely felt angry and deprived. Thus, the unusual aggressiveness of the parents toward each other was probably in part a displacement and an acting-out of the reaction to the separation from the therapist. In addition, there was a clear tendency for the sexes to align in this family therapy group; since the wife did not have her female "ally" during this session, this probably gave courage to the husband. It may also have contributed to the wife's using the tactic of defensive "superiority," without attacking in forays of her own as much as usual.

These final comments suggest the minor modification in future "blind" studies of single tape-recorded excerpts that the tape-analysts be given a description of the principal nonverbal features of the session and of major events in the context of the particular session. Alternatively, multiple excerpts from different phases of therapy would facilitate understanding of other facets of the family patterns which are not apparent in a single excerpt and also might give added clues to changes associated with the therapeutic process.

METHODOLOGY FOR STUDYING
FAMILY INTERACTION

Jules Riskin

Much of clinical psychiatric research and therapy has been
traditionally oriented towards the individual patient, in particular
toward the "intrapsychic meaning" of his behavior. In recent
years, however, there has been increasing attention devoted to
the interpersonal aspects of an individual's behavior, especially
his interaction with other members of his family. This shift in
emphasis has paralleled the development of the therapeutic technique of conjoint family therapy, in which the identified patient
and his family meet together with a therapist. (2)

Along with the therapeutic implications of this change in focus,
much more explicit attention has been given to the complex relationships between the specific patterns of family interaction and
the developing personalities of the children. In only a few years
much clinical material has been gathered, suggesting the specific
kinds of family environments in which a child learns those patterns of behavior which contribute profoundly to his character.
However, the hypotheses derived from clinical experience so far
suffer from serious methodological flaws. The subjective biases
of the therapists or observers are a continuously operating yet
inadequately evaluated factor. Further, there is the retrospective
fallacy, namely, the possibility that patterns observable in a family may, on the one hand, themselves be a result of emotional illness, or on the other hand, that they may have been present before the overt illness but etiologically irrelevant.

Our research group is convinced that clinically derived hypotheses causally relating family interaction to psychopathology in
the children, or more generally to the personalities of the children, must ultimately be tested by long-term (longitudinal) pre-

Reprinted from the ARCHIVES OF GENERAL PSYCHIATRY,
8:343-348 (April 1963). Copyright, American Medical Association,
Chicago; reproduced by permission.

dictive studies. To take a highly oversimplified example: if interaction X in a family is thought to be necessary for the development of schizophrenia 10 to 15 years hence in a child, then
we should be able to predict that if factor X is present (along
with other specified conditions), a child will become schizophrenic in 10 or 15 years; if factor X is not present, none of the
children in the family will later become schizophrenic. Clearly,
however, before such a predictive study could be attempted, certain prerequisites must be met. A reliable and empirically valid
method is needed to describe family interaction. In addition, both
the theoretical structure and the operations by which variables
will be identified must be more clearly established.

The purpose of this paper is to outline the project at the Mental
Research Institute of the Palo Alto Medical Research Foundation
to develop concepts and techniques with which to analyze family
interaction, techniques which would provide the theoretical and
empirical basis for carrying out a longitudinal predictive study.

The following aspects of the Methodology project will be considered: 1) theoretical framework; 2) procedural matters;
3) data collection, analysis, and progress; 4) clinical examples.

THEORETICAL
By now in various research centers many hypotheses have been
derived from experiences with families in conjoint therapy. Historically, with our own group at least, the earlier work was done
primarily with families of schizophrenics. More recently, clinical experience has broadened to include work with families containing delinquents, neurotics, asthmatics, and school under-
achievers. Our hope is to have a sufficiently broad clinical pool
of families from which to establish a general framework relating
family interaction to the children's personalities, which would be
applicable regardless of the presence, or absence, the kind or
the degree of psychopathology. Although hypotheses (ranging from
quite specific to highly abstract) have been formulated, we still
lack a consistent, integrated theory, including both general concepts and detailed operations by which these concepts can be identified. However, a beginning has been made towards constructing
a theoretical structure, which I should now like to outline.

The family is viewed as an ongoing system. (1) It tends to
maintain itself around some point of equilibrium which has been
established as the family evolves. The system is a dynamic, not
a static, one. There is a continuous process of input into the

system, and thus a continuous tendency for the system to be pushed away from the equilibrium point. The input may be in the form of an external stress such as a job change, war, or depression; or it may be an internal stress such as the birth of a new child, a death, or a biological spurt such as the onset of puberty. Over a period of time, the family develops certain repetitive, enduring techniques or patterns of interaction for maintaining its equilibrium when confronted by stress; this development tends to hold whether the stress be internal or external, acute or chronic, trivial or gross. These techniques, which are assumed to be characteristic for a given family, are regarded as homeostatic mechanisms. In the above description, the family is described somewhat analogously to an individual with his drives, defenses, character traits, and ego functions. However, these concepts differ from classical psychoanalytic ones in that they refer primarily to interpersonal organizations of behavior rather than to internal mechanisms.

Given this abstract framework, we then turn to what goes on among the family members, that is, their patterns of communication. Their manner of communicating, we believe, will elucidate the underlying interactional patterns of behavior. From the communication point of view, we focus on the messages which members send to each other. Messages, even the seemingly simplest ones, are regarded as having multiple aspects, or levels. These various levels may be consistent or inconsistent with each other; if inconsistent, they may be inconsistent in certain highly specific ways. Also, the various levels may be overtly or covertly labeled. Further, the person to whom the message is directed has the option of responding to different aspects of the message, and the particular level he does characteristically respond to may be significant. For example, father may come home and announce that he had a difficult day at work. Depending on his tone of voice, his accompanying physical gestures, and the context in which he speaks, he may also be sending out messages that he needs an opportunity to let off steam, or that the day actually was quite pleasant, or that he doesn't want to talk about the day's work, or that he does, or that tonight no one has the right to disturb him in the slightest way, etc. Mother might respond by saying she had a worse day, or that he shouldn't be so complaining or how about a drink before dinner to help relax him, etc. In addition, from a somewhat different perspective, the verbal message may carry an implicit accompanying comment on how the speaker regards the other person, as well as the literal meaning of the words. For example, in the above illustration mother may interpret father's comment to mean that his day was ruined because she burned his toast that morning, that if she really loved him she would have prepared the toast properly, and that therefore he must certainly be convinced that she doesn't love him. Our impression is that generally the more covert messages there are present, the more pathology will be present in the family, and also that the specific kinds of covert messages will influence the kind of pathology.

Analysis of family communication also leads to insights concerning family "laws" and "rules." The laws are more or less consciously held values which are related to the values of the family's cultural environment. Rules are hypothetical constructs formulated by the observer to account for observable behavior in the family. The family may be totally unaware of them. For example, we might observe that every time daughter makes a direct assertive statement to her parents, they criticize her in some way. We would then hypothesize that the family had a rule which leads them to behave as if they cannot tolerate her making such assertive statements. Further, when she does, homeostatic mechanisms, e.g., the parental criticism, are invoked which have the effect of preserving the rule.

Although we are primarily interested in cross-sectional behavioral patterns, we are not neglecting the insights which have come from ego psychology. From this point of view, we would consider the interacting psycho-dynamics of the spouses, and of the parents and children. For example, what psychological needs does each spouse satisfy in the other, or what unacceptable impulses of his own has a parent projected onto a child. Clues for this kind of analysis come from such projective-type questions as asking how they first happened to get together, and focusing particularly on any indications of discrepancies between one spouse's own self-perceptions and the other's perceptions of him.

Proceeding from the general concept that the family is a dynamic system, it follows that the children have an important function in maintaining an effective balance in the system. The children learn to "fit in" to the system; these learned patterns will be highly influential in determining their future patterns of interacting with other people, i.e., in forming their character structure. (There are, of course, "accidental" factors that a child brings with him into the family, e.g., his sex, ordinal position among the siblings, constitutional sensitivity, and the status of the family at the time of his birth. It seems likely, however, that even these kinds of characteristics will affect, and to some extent be affected by, the family pattern.) I will list some of the functions which we have observed children to fill in the family.

1. If the parents are not able to talk directly with each other, they may tend to talk "through" a child. For example, a husband may express irritation with his wife by criticizing a child, or express affection similarly.

2. Children may be indirectly rewarded by acting out some unconscious wish of one or both parents.

3. A child may be placed in the role of achieving high social performance, in order to validate the feeling of self-worth of a parent who has strong feelings of inadequacy, and who does not obtain sufficient emotional support from his spouse.

4. Parents may, without being aware of it, use a child as a scapegoat in order to express mutual disappointments in each other.

There is evidence that these kinds of behavior patterns tend to be associated with pathology in the children. On the other hand, to the extent that a child is not seen as an extension of one or both parents or as some sort of communication link, but is accepted as an individual in his own right, he will tend to acquire high feelings of self-esteem, and an identity of his own.

PROCEDURAL

We have worked out many of the mechanical aspects of the methodology study. The project is being limited to the intensive investigation of approximately ten families so as to avoid our becoming swamped by excessive amounts of raw data. In order to reduce the number of variables, we are working with families who meet the following criteria: white, middle-class, at least second generation American, of Western European background, the biological family intact and living together; at least three children, no younger than six nor older than 21. These families are obtained randomly through the local school system. [1] The presence or absence of psychopathology in the family does not enter into selection criteria, since we are interested in comparing and contrasting pathological and nonpathological patterns of family inter-

---

[1] The Palo Alto School authorities have been exceedingly helpful in making families available to us.

actions. Earlier we had been concerned whether families would be willing to participate in a program which might demand up to ten or more hours of each member's time. So far, however, we have been gratified that five out of five families contacted have agreed to participate. [2] The initial interview is made at home; further interviews are done at the Mental Research Institute. We are making every effort to avoid the development of a treatment-oriented relationship but rather keep the family's contacts with us as much as possible in the context of "pure research." In addition to families obtained through schools, we are utilizing as another group a few families with labeled psychopathology who are in treatment with various members of the project.

DATA COLLECTION, ANALYSIS, AND PROGRESS

So far, the theoretical point of view and procedural matters have been discussed. I will now turn to a description of the observational data with which we have been working. We have been developing a series of standardized structured interviews which are taped, transcribed, and observed behind a one-way screen. (For certain theoretical and technical reasons we are not filming interviews and are therefore excluding the systematic analysis of body movement.) The interviews include a meeting between the spouses and the investigator, one with the whole family, and a series with the individual family members. So far, most of the analysis had been done on the conjoint family interview. The parents are asked how they happened to meet each other, what their hopes and expectations of the marriage were, how they have handled certain inevitable contingencies such as relationships with in-laws, and birth of children. The whole family is then asked to participate in discussing the following kinds of problems: Plan something together you would all like to do as a family. Who is in charge of the family? Here is a picture of a family--tell a story about what you see. Here is an unfinished story--complete it. [3]

A major task has been to identify reliable, specific variables which can be derived from the theory, and are at least to some extent quantifiable. Many kinds of observations such as how long does each person talk, or who talks the most, can be made and quite precisely quantified, but their value for our purposes seems

---

[2] One of these families which was willing to participate was rejected because they were first-generation American citizens.

[3] For example: "Mother and father go to a movie, leaving their three children at home alone. The parents return home at midnight and are shocked to find..."

negligible. Using a detailed, "microscopic" approach to the
analysis of each interchange (including verbal and tonal aspects),
we are constructing a series of scales to measure the family interaction. Raters are asked to score several factors along a
scale ranging from: factor is present to factor is absent. These
variables are somewhat, but not completely, independent of each
other. So far, the scales include:

1. Clarity. Is what the speaker says clear to the observer?
(Here we are concerned with the most immediate meaning, not
with assumed motives.)

2. Content. Does the speaker stay on the same verbal content as the person to whom he is talking?

2A. When the speaker changes content is this change appropriate or inappropriate?

3. Agreement. Does the speaker agree or disagree with the
other person's verbal message?

4. Commitment. Does the speaker meet the issue, that is,
take a stand on the main point of what the other person said, when
a stand would have been appropriate?

5. Congruency. Are the verbal and tonal aspects of the
speaker's message consistent with each other?

6. Intensity. How emphatic or forceful is the speaker?

7. Relationship. Does the message contain an element of
attack or acceptance of the other person?

In addition to these scales, the observer must also judge what
role the speaker is taking in relation to the other person, namely,
a dominant accepting, dominant rejecting, submissive accepting
or submissive rejecting. (4) We are now in the process of comparing the responses of various kinds of families to a standard
stimulus along these variables, and it is our initial impression
that these scales do indeed differentiate among families. We
have also done some preliminary runs of having nonprofessional
technicians score the interactions, and so far our results tend
to be reproducible.

Complementary to this approach is a more "macroscopic" one, using the concepts of rules, laws, and homeostatic mechanisms previously mentioned. These terms apply more to an impressionistic or global response to the whole interview rather than primarily to an analysis of each interchange, although the two approaches are closely related. A clinical example might illustrate how these latter concepts are used. In one family (one in which we see no evidence of significant pathology) the parents interact as if they had a rule that they must remain equal at all times in all ways. They are not consciously aware of such a "rule." Nor is this striving to maintain equality accomplished by any grossly competitive means. Thus we find, for example, that if husband indicates achievement or accomplishment, then almost immediately, as if a homeostatic mechanism had been automatically triggered, he will either give his wife an opportunity to express her accomplishments or she will gently make some assertive statement.

There is so far some suggestive evidence that this kind of analysis and conceptualization has predictive power and thus has empirical validity. For example, recently Jackson, Riskin, and Satir, using a slightly modified form of communicational and interactional dynamics analysis, were able to reconstruct the family background of a family and some of the identified patient's symptoms, by examining intensively five minutes of interaction between father and mother. (3) We are planning to make various kinds of short-term predictions to test these variables further, e.g., on the basis of the analysis of a family's response to "plan something together," predict how they will respond to "who is in charge."

CLINICAL ILLUSTRATIONS AND IMPRESSIONS

1. It appears that in families with schizophrenic children, there is a rule, with quite specific exceptions, that there must be no coalitions of any two members to the exclusion of a third.[4] For example, if mother and father seem to be reaching agreement on some issue, the psychotic daughter will intervene precisely at this point with some apparently grossly bizarre comment. Oftentimes these schizophrenic families will appear at first glance to be talking on the same content. However, closer examination will show that they are rarely committing themselves on the other

---

[4] The exceptions include, e.g., agreement by mother and father that the psychotic child is ill.

person's position, or that they are carrying on independent mon-
ologues which do have some words in common, but actually have
a "pseudocommunicational" quality about them.

2. In some families without pathology (and it is our impression at this time that these families will not produce children who
later will have serious psychopathology), other patterns emerge.
The family mentioned above which has the rule about equality, reported the following incident which occurred early in their marriage. In discussing their first few months together, they mention a bicycle trip on which they had a quarrel. As a result they
each turned and drove off in opposite directions from each other.
After spending the night alone, each, quite independently, decided he couldn't continue alone. Each one turned back, and they
met exactly in the middle of the highway that had separated them
the previous night. This family seems free to speak directly,
freely, and to the point with each other, without any feeling of
personal attack, within rather clear limits which they have e-
volved in order to maintain their equilibrium as a system. One
has the impression of a harmonious team. [5] In terms of the
effect of this kind of family climate on the children, one would
not expect, for example, that the son will become a "rugged
individualist." Another family acts as if they must present to
the world a picture of father as the leader, although a more detailed analysis would indicate that mother often appears to be
the final arbiter. Evidence that father is not the boss is based
on such observations as father's asserting his role in an exaggerated, almost caricaturing manner, or his assertions being
responded to by giggles from the children. One would expect
that the boys in this family would likely marry women who would
tend quietly to "take charge" of the family. However, much of
the communication in this family does remain quite open, and
there is no evidence of gross pathology.

SUMMARY

To summarize, this paper has attempted to point out on the
one hand a considerable amount of clinical experience with families, and on the other hand, to show that we do not have yet
available adequate tools for evaluating the assumed relationship

---

[5] We are not, of course, concerned here with questions of
value, i.e., whether this particular brand of "harmony" and
reasonableness leads to a desirable way of life; or even if there
is one kind only of psychological health.

between family interaction and personality formation. A pilot study whose aim is to develop a conceptual framework and methods for investigation of this relationship has been described, using both detailed and more global approaches to analysis of family interaction. It is planned eventually to test hypotheses relating family patterns to future behavior of the children by doing a long-term predictive study. Ultimately it is hoped that the knowledge thus gained will be applied toward more effective treatment and eventually the prophylaxis of mental illness.

REFERENCES

1. Jackson, D. D. The question of family homeostasis. Psychiat. Quart. (Suppl.) 31:79-90 (Pt. 1) 1957. (See p. 1, this vol.)
2. Jackson, D. D. and Satir, V. Family diagnosis and family therapy. In Exploring the Base for Family Therapy, N. Ackerman, F. Beatman, and S. Sherman (Eds.), Family Service Association of America, New York, 1961.
3. Jackson, D. D., Riskin, J. and Satir, V. A method of analysis of a family interview. Arch. Gen. Psychiat., 5:321-339, 1961. (See p. 230, this vol.)
4. Leary, T. Interpersonal Diagnosis of Personality. Ronald Press, New York, 1956.

FAMILY EXPERIMENTS: A NEW TYPE
OF EXPERIMENTATION

Jay Haley

In the search for more satisfying ways of explaining differences
between individuals, the emphasis in psychiatry and psychology
has been shifting from the study of the processes within an individual to the study of the processes which occur naturally between
people. There are increasing attempts to classify and describe
the functioning of married couples and families as well as ongoing
groups in industry, military organizations, different psychotherapy situations, and other "groups with a history." The study of
established relationships offers an opportunity for a new type of
experimentation on human behavior; new because the variables to
be measured are those which other psychological experiments are
designed to eliminate. This paper will present some of the problems in design, sampling, and measurement as well as the results
of a pilot experimental program on families containing a diagnosed
schizophrenic.

THE PURPOSE OF FAMILY EXPERIMENTS

If there were a satisfactory descriptive system for families,
questions like the following might ultimately be answered: Does
the delinquent come from a particular kind of family? Is there a
similarity between the family of one schizophrenic and the family
of another which could be related to the peculiar disorders of the
patients? Is the family containing a schizophrenic different in any
important way from the family which contains a psychopath or al-
coholic? Is there a "normal" family system which could be differentiated from one where psychiatric symptoms exist or are
likely to occur? These rather practical questions could be extended to include inquiries about the family as a system of influence,
questions of cultural differences between families, the persistence
of family patterns over generations, and so on.

Reprinted from FAMILY PROCESS, 1, No. 2:265-293 (September
1962). Copyright, The Mental Research Institute of the Palo Alto
Medical Foundation and the Family Institute; reproduced by permission.

Answers to such questions will come only with the development
of a descriptive system which will rigorously classify families and
differentiate one type from another. The basis for classifying
families into groups is only now beginning to be explored. Such a
classification cannot be a characterization of individual family
members, e.g., what sort of personalities the mothers and fathers
have. Similarly, impressionistic descriptions, such as statements
that a family exhibits covert resentment or has shared delusions
will not lead to rigorous classification. The crucial differences
between families would seem to reside in the sorts of transactions
which take place between family members; the study of differences
becomes a classification of communication patterns in the family.

There are several basic assumptions to family study: (a) family members deal differently with each other than they do with other
people, (b) the millions of responses which family members meet
over time within a family fall into patterns, (c) these patterns persist within a family for many years and will influence a child's expectations of, and behavior with, other people when he leaves the
family, and (d) the child is not a passive recipient of what his
parents do with him but an active co-creator of family patterns.

Various research groups, including those of Bateson (1),
Bowen (3), Lidz (5), and Wynne (6), have observed families of
schizophrenics and are in general agreement that there are similarities among these families other than the schizophrenic behavior of one of the members. The ways the parents deal with
each other, as well as the ways they behave with the psychotic
child, seem to follow consistent patterns from family to family.
All of the researchers seek some way of describing the unique
kind of interactive process observed when these family members
are brought together. Further, the goal is to phrase such a description in a way which would ultimately permit quantitative validation of descriptive statements.

Clinicians usually are uneasy about quantification, feeling that
those variables least relevant to the real problems are always
chosen to be counted. Yet it would seem inevitable that study of
the family must lead to quantification of some sort. If one suggests that schizophrenia (or any characteristics of an individual)
is related to the family, he is implicitly suggesting that there are
two types of family system, the schizophrenic and the non-schizophrenic. He is immediately involved in a sampling problem and a
problem of measurement. If he suggests that one type of family
produces a schizophrenic and another does not, the investigator

must support such a hypothesis by observation and description of the two types of family. If his emphasis is upon the family rather than upon the individuals within it, he must bring family members together in some situation where he can observe and record their activity together. Such research inevitably tends toward the arrangement of structured settings in which samples of families can be placed to observe their similarities and differences.

It is becoming more common for families to be brought together and tape recorded or filmed while having a conversation. The investigators attempt to classify the transactions which take place between family members and note which families use which range of transactions. Yet the process of communication between people is extraordinarily complex; they communicate verbally, with vocal inflections, with body movement, and with reference to unique past, familiar incidents. Any classification of this complex of communication will depend upon the skill of the observer--and the skill in observation of those he reports his findings to. Should an investigator note, for example, that a mother has a certain response whenever her child joins with father in some agreement, he would need a way of identifying that "certain response" whether it was a verbal statement, an inflection of voice, or a slight body movement. Other observers might overlook her response or interpret it differently. The ultimate verification of typical family patterns would seem to be possible only if the family is placed in some experimental situation where the responses can be recorded by some other means than the quick eye of an investigator, as necessary as his observations might be before such experimental situations could be devised.

The Bateson project developed a theory and a descriptive system for families, with data drawn from therapy sessions with families of schizophrenics. They placed schizophrenic as well as non-schizophrenic families in a standard interview situation, which included leaving the family alone to talk together, in order to note similarities and differences in the responses to the situation. Finally, the project began to devise explicit experimental settings for measurement of family behavior. When actual experiments were attempted on families, it was found that there was little general theory available to isolate the important variables to be measured, and that the type of experiment and the sampling problems were without precedent.

UNIQUE PROBLEMS IN EXPERIMENTATION
There is a history of psychological experimentation with animals, with individuals, and with small groups, but experimenta-

tion with family systems is a discontinuous change from that history. There is no adequate precedent for this type of experiment; the methodology which has been developed to experiment with individuals and with artificial groups does not apply to the measurement of typical patterns of an ongoing system.

The Family Versus the Individual

When one experiments with individuals, it is conventional to eliminate the influence of interpersonal factors. Quite the reverse is the goal of experimenting with an ongoing relationship; the interpersonal factor is to be measured.

Experimentation and testing of individuals classifies different types of individuals or measures some factor which is thought to be generally characteristic of people. These investigations usually emphasize some internal process within the person: his learning ability, his perception, the way he makes decisions, amount of anxiety, and so on. Typically a standard situation is created in which the experimenter exposes a series of individuals to some sort of stimuli and measurement is taken of their responses. It is hoped that the standardization of the situation will mean that the relationship with the experimenter is the same for all subjects so that the only variables will be differences between subjects. When a shift is made from experimenting upon individuals to experimenting upon a relationship, a quite different procedure is necessary. One must create some standard context and place two or more people within it and measure their responses to each other. Then one must place two or more other people, presumably involved in a different type of relatedness, in the same situation and measure their responses. Whereas in individual experiments it is necessary to eliminate as much as possible the subject's response to another person, in experimenting with ongoing systems the typical response of one person to another must be measured.

In general, most psychological experiments could be called Inferential Experiments. Certain inferences are made about an individual, and experiments are designed to test those inferences. For example, an inference is made that individuals will learn more rapidly with reward rather than punishment. An experiment is designed, and the results indicate whether the inference could be said to be accurate or not. What is measured is not the process of learning, but certain behavior which is inferred to have occurred because the process of learning took place. Family experiments could be called Descriptive Experiments. After observation of certain behavioral patterns in a type of family, an experiment is designed to test the behavioral description which has been made. These shifts of emphasis leave the family experimenter unable to use as precedent most of the previous experimentation done in psychology.

The Family Versus the Small Group

Although it might be thought that family experiments would be comparable to small group experiments because the family is a small group, there are marked differences. In the usual small group experiment a situation is arranged and several unrelated people are placed within it. Measurement is then taken of the effect of that context on their behavior. The people are carefully chosen so they are not acquainted, far less related, to eliminate any variable other than the effect of that particular setting on their performance. In the family experiment precisely the opposite is the goal: The problem is to measure how members of a "group with a history" typically respond to each other, while attempting to eliminate as much as possible the effect of that particular setting on their performance.

An illustration will clarify the difference. A small group experiment might be designed in which three people, A and B and C, are placed within a communication network where A can communicate with B and B can communicate with C, but A and C cannot communicate with each other. Another network can be set up in which all three people can communicate freely with each other. The two groups are then given a task to perform. Measurement is taken to discover whether the group which can communicate freely has less or more difficulty with the task than the group where individual A and individual C can only communicate with each other through B.

In contrast, suppose an experiment is attempted with the Jones family after preliminary observation indicates that father and mother rarely speak to each other, if at all, but talk to each other "through" their daughter who can communicate with both of them. Instead of merely pointing out this "obvious" communication pattern in this family, we wish to devise an experiment which will show by quantified results that the family follows a typical pattern of speaking through the child.

Although the limited communication network set up for the small group experiment and the limited communication network which this family has developed for itself are similar, the problem of measurement is obviously not the same. Our problem in experimenting with the family is not to show whether with their particular network they have more or less difficulty with a task, but to show what their particular network is. We might, for example, place the family in a situation where they could communicate freely or follow their typical restricted communication. Measurement could be taken of how often they chose either method of communication.

The difficulties involved in this type of experimentation are quite different from those in small group experiments. The Jones family in its natural state might consistently follow one pattern, but placed in an experimental setting where they are being observed they might follow another pattern. In this case, for example, father and mother might wish to conceal the fact that they don't usually speak to each other and so during the period of the experiment they might converse.

Although some adaptation of small group experiments might be possible for family experimentation, it would seem that measurement of typical patterns in a particular family, even quite rigid and crude patterns, will differ markedly from measurement of the effect of different contexts on unrelated people who have been placed in them.

THE SAMPLING PROBLEM

A major purpose of any family experimental program would be to provide some statistical evidence to support points of a hypothesis derived from natural history observations of families. This evidence would presumably be in the form of counting events which did or did not occur or counting units of time in the accomplishment of some task. As a reluctant choice, there might be some use of verbal materials rated by judges along some pre-set scale.

Presuming an experiment were devised where totals could be counted, it would be necessary to run sufficient schizophrenic and non-schizophrenic families to have two sample groups. The average performance of these groups, when contrasted, makes it possible to compare the two types of family. A basis of comparability would be an acceptance or rejection of one or both of two possible hypotheses: (a) we can attempt to accept or reject the hypothesis that there is no difference between the family of the schizophrenic and the non-schizophrenic on the factors being measured, (b) we can set out to accept or reject the hypothesis that there is no more similarity between one schizophrenic family and another on the factors being measured than there is between any schizophrenic family and any non-schizophrenic family.

Whether "statistically significant" differences between types of families imply real differences in the populations sampled must depend upon the sampling procedure. A level of significance which might be adequate with samples selected randomly from well-defined populations could be quite inadequate with the sort of sampling problems involved in family work.

Most sampling designs in psychology are based upon the characteristics of individuals, i.e., the populations to be sampled are defined in terms of the characteristics of individuals. Any individual can be classified according to a pre-existing set of characteristics which can be listed and are considered important, such as sex, age, marital status, religion, education, and so on. If one wishes to take a sample of families, it becomes immediately apparent that the relevant characteristics of families have never been listed.

The rather vague classifications of families which exist are actually based upon the characteristics of individuals in families. For example, the economic level classification of a family is essentially a statement of father's income, the classification "Catholic family" or "Protestant family" is a statement of the religious affiliation of individual family members. A classification of families as families, would require some statement of the characteristic patterns of responsive behavior in that family. The ways family members deal with each other, if these could be listed, would provide a classification of types of family systems. Any classification of this nature would require statements which describe the interaction of two or more family members. For example, there might be a class of families whose characteristic is an inability to maintain any coalitions between family members, or there might be a class in which the parents maintain coalitions against the children but no child can maintain a coalition with one parent against another, and so on. Such a classification of types of relationship in the family does not exist, and in fact there is not as yet a language to build such a classification. Yet a proper sampling of families should be of types in this sense since the sample should be based upon the characteristics of the system being studied rather than upon the characteristics of an element in that system.

At this time schizophrenic families are identified by the presence of a member diagnosed schizophrenic. To substantiate the hypothesis that schizophrenia is somehow related to the family, one must deal with the definition of a schizophrenic and the defini-

tion of a family. The diagnosis of schizophrenia is based in part
upon an archaic set of premises dealing largely with unobservable
processes occurring within the patient. It is not even generally
agreed that there is a schizophrenia, but some insist there are
multiple types of schizophrenia. It is also not entirely clear that
three psychiatrists would make the same diagnosis of schizophrenia in any particular patient except in those cases where the
patient has long been hospitalized and is chronic. Recently the
question has been raised whether the chronic schizophrenic is actually much more than a person responding to long-term hospitalization in a total institution, and so even that diagnosis might not
be useful for doing a family study. Further, there is the question
of including under schizophrenia not only different types, such as
paranoid, hebephrenic, or catatonic, but borderline diagnoses such
as schizo-affective states, schizoid, autistic, and so on. The time
interval of a diagnosis also becomes a problem: Is a patient always schizophrenic once that diagnosis has been made, or does he
remit and so can no longer be classified as schizophrenic? Is a
schizophrenic who has had apparently successful therapy a candi-
date for experimentation, or is he no longer a schizophrenic?
What of spontaneous remission--is a patient who went through a
schizophrenic episode but now appears in good shape still to be
classed as a schizophrenic? Further, can a patient currently in
a psychotic episode be classed with a patient who is no longer manifesting overt symptoms but is still hospitalized?

If we assume that family systems will differ from each other if
any one member is systematically behaving differently within the
family and further assume that the pre-schizophrenic, the overt
schizophrenic, the remitted schizophrenic and the schizoid are
systematically behaving differently from each other, then it would
follow that within the category "schizophrenic family" there would
be at least four different types of family system. These types
would be in addition to the possibilities of sub-species of families
based on the presence of different types of overt schizophrenia.

A further difficulty in definition resides in the question of what
is a family. Is it essential to include the extended family, including grandparents and other relatives? Is the family containing a
stepfather comparable to a family containing natural parents? Is
a patient with a father and older sister but no mother comparable
to a patient with a mother and father? If the patient has had little
or no contact with his family for some years, can he be classed
with the patient living at home? Could a chronic patient's ward

doctor and nurse be comparable to a family? Is a family with six children comparable to one where the patient is an only child?

Rigor in Sampling

To clarify the sampling difficulties, let us suppose an ideal situation. Let us suppose that there exists a population of clearly diagnosed schizophrenics whose parents are alive, available, and involved with the patient. We shall refer to this population as the group of schizophrenic families. Let us further suppose that there exists another population of parents whose children are not schizophrenic. We shall designate this population as the group of nonschizophrenic families.

Since we cannot experiment with all the families in these two groups, we will take a sample of each group. Our samples must be chosen in such a way as to justify some inference about each of the total groups. We must, therefore, take a random sample of each group in such a way that any family has an equal chance of appearing in our sample. Once we have our two sample groups, we place the families in the same experimental situations and quantify the results. We may be then able to make statements about real differences between the two types of families which are inferred at some designated level of significance.

There are two crucial points in such an ideal situation: (a) to determine whether a difference is real or not, our samples must be selected randomly, and (b) the families must be placed in the same experimental context. When we leave the ideal situation and approach the actual situation both criteria are difficult to meet.

The Selection of a Sample of Families

In reality a sample of schizophrenic families is not only doubtfully diagnosed and often shattered with divorces and separations, but also many patients have left home and are more involved with spouses than with their family of origin. However, including only those patients "involved" with their parents, they are identifiable only through an institution or through a psychiatrist in private practice and must "volunteer" to come in and be experimented upon.

In a preliminary attempt to build a sample of families with schizophrenics, it became apparent that a suitable random sample would be difficult to obtain. The reactions of the families indicated that a considerable bias might be apparent in those families who do cooperate. Since the parents assume they are being ob-

served to see what they have to do with the child's illness, they
have nothing to gain except embarrassment by coming in, except
in those cases where the parents see in such a venture some hope
for some help for themselves. The parents' stout defense that
they do not have anything to do with the child's illness, which is
typical of these families, tends to be a highly selective factor unless the families are required to come in as part of the child's
treatment.

The selective problem also is present with a "non-schizophrenic"
group. "Non-schizophrenic" families who agree to come in might
differ markedly from those who refused. A family having difficulty between members would doubtfully come in to put their difficulties on public display--except in those cases where the difficulty
was so extreme they were seeking help. Interviews with "non-
schizophrenic" families tend to indicate they are either reasonably
amiable with each other or rather desperate, but at any rate they
are doubtfully a random sample.

Yet another problem with such a "non-schizophrenic" sample
is the fact that the families may not have had contact with a psychiatrist, but a good percentage might well contain a pre-schizophrenic or an undiagnosed schizophrenic. The child brought in for
the experiment might be in one of those categories, or the child
might be the sibling of a hidden schizophrenic at home. Therefore, our "non-schizophrenic" sample could predictably be expected to include a percentage of families similar to our schizophrenic sample.

Further, it would seem illogical that a "non-schizophrenic"
sample would be homogeneous and therefore easily sampled in
regard to any aspect of families that we might choose for our purposes. That is, it would be naive to think that there are "schizophrenic" families and "non-schizophrenic" families. Actually,
there will be in any normal sample a variety of types of families
rather than a single "non-schizophrenic" type, just as there will
be a variety of kinds of symptoms in the children in any random
sample of the normal population.

The Same Experimental Context
The second criterion of any experimentation, that the two groups
be placed in the same experimental situation, is also difficult to
achieve. It would be naive to assume that if two families are given
the same verbal instructions for an experiment, they will be in
the same experimental context. If a schizophrenic family is

brought in feeling accused because something has gone wrong with their child and defensive about what will be shown wrong in their family, they are hardly in the same experimental context as a family coming in with no accusation of anything wrong in the family but merely to be cooperative with some research. Inevitably in a schizophrenic family any request that the parents be brought together with the patient is a suggestion that they have something to do with the patient's illness. A contrast family without a patient cannot approach the experimentation with the same frame of reference. Even if the "non-schizophrenic" family is told that the research centers on family organization and mental health, this is doubtfully accusation enough for the family to be as defensive in proving their mental health as is the schizophrenic family where the patient has been diagnosed and hospitalized. (This problem is quite separate from the question of whether a major characteristic of the schizophrenic family is some form of defensiveness, and therefore something to be measured with experimentation.) It is not possible to separate the performance in any experiment from the context in which the experimentation takes place, nor is it a simple problem to find a way to provide a "schizophrenic" and a "non-schizophrenic" family with the same context. If the context is not the same, performance differences are doubtfully valid.

THEORY AND METHOD

To choose one family and pluck it from the network of families whose totality make up the culture is to do some violence to the wider influence on the family. Having chosen a family, to select a few family members from it and discard the others means ignoring the complex influence of grandparents, aunts and uncles, and all those related people whose ideas affect the ways individual family members deal with each other. Further, to take a few members of a family and examine only certain species of their interaction together requires an extraordinary simplification of the complicated gestalt of their life together. Yet to build a theoretical conception it would seem necessary to begin with the less complex whenever a relevant formal pattern appears to be present and to proceed from there to additional complexities. An arbitrary decision was made in this research to begin with the central nucleus of the family--mother, father, and one child--and to develop the most elementary types of experiment for this three-person system.

The investigation was preliminary and exploratory; the sampling problem was examined rather than solved, with the empha-

sis on experimenting with experiments rather than producing con-
clusive findings about families. The theoretical problems, and
an example of a type of experiment which was run on a small sample of families, will be reported here.

The Search for Testable Hypotheses

To classify into groups a number of three-person families, one
must be able to label typical patterns of the ways the three people
deal with each other. These patterns must be described rigorously enough so that it is conceivable to devise an experimental situation which would prove or disprove a statement about a family.
The ingenuity required to devise an experiment which will emphasize rather than obscure a family pattern is one problem; to make
a descriptive statement which can be potentially tested is the problem of the moment.

The clue to an approach to this sort of investigation lies in the
basic premise on which such a study is based: any one family is
a stable system. It is stable in the sense that statements about
the family have ongoing truth over time. Such a premise follows
from the fact that a family is an organization and so follows a
limited range of behavior. This premise is also supported by observations of family members talking together week after week
and month after month. Certain sequences occur again and again.
Approaching a three-person family as a system which is stable
over time, one is led naturally to the kind of theory concerned
with the maintenance of stability in any system. If a system is
stable, there is a governing process at work which maintains the
limits of variability of the system. A family system may break
down, and the result is separation and divorce, but if people continue to live together there is a self-corrective process at work
which makes their continued association possible, even though this
self correction may make continued conflict. If one person goes
too far in any direction and exceeds the limits of tolerance of other
family members, they will respond in such a way that the extreme
behavior is corrected. The system must correct itself or dissolve
into separate entities. From this point of view the family is a governed system with each family member one of the governors of
that system. [1] The self-governing process within the family ap-

---

[1] It is possible that organized relationships follow abstract laws
which would not be apparent as long as the focus of interest was
upon the individual or the artificial group. If one draws upon cybernetic theory and describes a family, or any ongoing relationship,
as a self-corrective system with individual functioning as governors

pears particularly important in the family of the schizophrenic. The influence of an external governor is minimized by the ways these family members isolate themselves from other people.

The function of a governor in the usual self-corrective system is supervisory; it takes action when some variable in the system is exceeding a certain range. For example, the household thermostat will turn on a furnace when the room temperature drops below a certain point and turn off the furnace when the temperature exceeds a certain point. The system will regulate itself, fluctuating within a limited range. However, this range is pre-set for the thermostat, usually by a human being who sets the range of temperature he prefers. The thermostat may govern the system, but since the human being sets the thermostat he is the governor of the governor.

If we use the analogy of a self-corrective system for describing a family, we must include as the function of each family member two sorts of supervisory capacity: each person not only responds in an "error activated" way if another family member exceeds a certain range of behavior, but each person also attempts to preset the range of behavior for the other people. A mother and child may be in conflict over whether mother takes care of the child properly, but they also may be in conflict over whether a "taking care of" relationship is the type they should have together. What sort of relationship people have together is a matter of presetting limits on behavior; whether one or the other is responding appro-

in their relationships with one another, and if one accepts the idea that it is the function of a governor to diminish change, then one can derive a law of human relations. This First Law of Relationships could be stated in this way: <u>When an organism indicates a change in relation to another, the other will act upon the first so as to diminish and modify that change.</u>

Assuming that people follow this law in their relationships, families would be stable systems because each attempt by a family member to initiate a change in relation to another would provoke a response to diminish that change. It would also follow that people in the business of changing people, such as psychotherapists and discontented family members, would find it necessary to avoid straightforward requests for change and would attempt to bring about change in more devious ways, e.g., with a denial that a change is being attempted. This might be why psychotherapists do not say to patients, "I'm going to change you," but rather emphasize self-understanding and self-help.

priately within that sort of relationship is another level of governing process (2, 4). These two levels may be separable for purposes of analysis, but often they occur simultaneously. The message which indicates that certain behavior is inappropriate in that relationship also is questioning, reinforcing, or re-defining, what sort of relationship it is. If mother says to father, "You treat me like a child," she is indicating that some statement he made is inappropriate to a relationship between two equals and thereby defining their relationship as one between two equals. However, she may also be provoking her husband to treat her like a child and then protesting when he does and so be maintaining a continual confusion as to their type of relationship.

If we examine parents and child as a stable system with each person governing the behavior of the other two, it is possible to describe patterns in the ways they influence each other. These patterns will be abstract in the sense that they are formal rather than concerned with content. One way to conceptualize the governing processes in a family is to approach families as a system of rules established by the ways family members deal with each other. The members of a particular family will not use the full range of behavior possible to them; the potential behavior of any one member will be limited by the responses of the other members. These limitations are rules for what sort of behavior is to take place in the family. If father tells daughter to help mother with the dishes, he is establishing, or reinforcing, a variety of rules. A few can be suggested: he is indicating that in this family daughter helps mother, he is indicating that in this family father decides who shall help whom; he is indicating the rule that he is allowed to comment on what sort of relationship mother and daughter are to have, and so on. He may also be cooperating in a situation where he is dragged into a conflict between mother and daughter and so be following a rule that mother require him to join her. Whether the rules are accepted or not depends not only on father's directions but daughter's response to those directions as they work out an agreed upon set of rules. In some other family the mother might ask father to tell daughter to help her with the dishes and he might say that it is not his business to do so. By responding in this way, he would be establishing, or reinforcing, a different set of rules.

Classifying the rules which any one family develops, and the processes whereby they work out these rules, could conceivably lead to a way of classifying families into groups. However, these rules are not necessarily explicitly stated by family members or even known to them. They are a format of regularity imposed upon a complicated process by the investigator. If the investigator is accurate in his observation that a particular family follows such and such a rule, then it should be possible to place the family in an experimental context where they would follow such a rule. The difficulty in such an endeavor rests on the fact that these rules are not simple but always function at several levels: there are not only rules, but rules about making rules and rules about how not to follow rules. For example, one might observe a family and note that whenever the family is asked to decide something, father announces the decision. One might say that father is the prime indicator of what is to happen in the family. Yet mother and child might typically not do what he decides. Or mother might consistently say, "You decide, dear," so that the decision may be in his hands, but who is to make the decision is in his wife's realm according to the rules. Any statement about a simple rule a family appears to follow may become more complex the more the context of the rule is explored.

The Family of the Schizophrenic

From this general point of view, suppose one imagined a family which was manifesting the following rule: no family member will permit another family member to set rules for his behavior. If a family behaved in this way, there would be a central paradox. The family might be a stable system with each family member governed by the response of other family members, but each would be indicating that the others were not to govern his behavior. If one directed another to do anything, the other would have to indicate that he was not to be governed by that person. This refusal to be directed might be expressed directly, it might be expressed by the person doing what he is told reluctantly, or it might be expressed by the person "taking over" the direction with an indication that he is doing it but for some reason other than the person's direction.

The idea of one person directing another to do something can be enlarged beyond mere requests for specific activity. Actually any message from one person to another must include a "command" or "directive" aspect. The existence of the message, as well as the way the message is given, may compel a certain sort of response from the other person. If one person says to another, "It's a nice day today," he is not explicitly directing the other person how to behave, but he is indicating what sort of behavior the other person should deliver. If a person is "programmed" to refuse to follow any direction from anyone, he must respond in a complicated way even to the most simple sort of message.

The family of the schizophrenic--mother, father, and schizophrenic child--would seem to be following the rule that none of them will permit the other to govern his behavior and so elicit a particular response. The result is a peculiar kind of communication in this sort of family. Whatever one says, the other indicates that he shouldn't have said it or it wasn't said properly or not at the proper time and place. If one says, "Let's do such and such," the others must follow the rule that their behavior is not to be governed by that person, and so they cannot merely reply, "Yes, let's do," and then do it. They may say, "Yes," and then not do it. They may say, "Yes," but qualify it with an indication they really would rather not. They may agree and do it and then later say they hadn't really wanted to. They may say they had that idea earlier themselves and are willing to do it not because they were asked but because they really initiated it.

All of these examples of types of response to direction are formally the same: each example represents an incongruence between what a person says or does and the way he qualifies what he says or does. Just as one can have two levels of governing process when one governor governs another, so one can have two, or many, levels of message when one message qualifies another. When parents and child in this type of family are brought together, they consistently manifest an incongruence between these levels. As a result you rarely hear one affirm what another says, unless at some other time this affirmation is negated. It would naturally follow that if there were a rule in the family that no one was to concede that he was governed or directed by the others, and if every message they exchanged directed a certain sort of response, then they would need to "disqualify" each other's messages consistently.

Since the incongruence between levels of message which these family members consistently show is often subtle as well as crude, such an observation can only be verified if the observer is skillful and then two observers might disagree. At this point experimentation becomes relevant. It is not a simple matter to construct an experimental situation where the family members can communicate with each other at two levels and which involves each directing the others how to respond. Yet from the point of view of this research, it is this sort of patterning of communication which is most relevant to the development of psychopathology in a family and to the classification of families into groups.

A way to create a hypothesis which might be validated by experimentation is to examine one of the results of this peculiar type of communication pattern in the family. It should follow that if the members must "disqualify" what each other says, they would have difficulty forming and maintaining coalitions in the family. Observations of the family of the schizophrenic indicates that this is so. When any one member tries to get together with another, the other responds in a way that disqualifies that invitation. For example, should father and mother join together in an attempt to discipline their child, they typically end in a row with each other with one or the other saying the other is too mild or too severe.

The hypothesis that this type of family has more difficulty forming and maintaining coalitions between two members should be verifiable with an experiment, and a report of such an experiment will be given here. Several versions of an experiment designed to test this hypothesis were attempted. The final version offered family members both the opportunity to form alliances and the opportunity to communicate at two levels. Before describing this particular experiment, a few generalizations can be made about the criteria for this kind of experimentation:

1. The experiments must deal with the responses of family members to each other rather than their individual responses to stimuli from the experimenter. The measure is of the system rather than the individuals within it, and so the experiment must require family members to interact with each other.

2. At least some of the experiments must be of such a nature that any one family will behave in a consistent way in that experiment over a period of trials. If one family behaves differently each time on the experiment, it is difficult to argue that two families who behave differently are really different.

3. The experiments must be of such a nature that it cannot be argued that intelligence, education, or manual dexterity of the family members was a major determinant of the results, unless one assumes the psychopathology being measured is based upon intelligence, education, or manual dexterity.

4. The experiments must be such that it cannot be argued that because one member is a schizophrenic the results of the experiment inevitably follow. For example, it should not be a task which the schizophrenic could not, or would not, participate in so that it could be said, "No one could do that task with him involved."

5. It must be a type of experiment which a family will participate in, willingly or not. That is, the task must be something
everyone in the family can do.

6. The experiment must be of such a nature that it does not
impose patterns on the family by forcing them to change under
duress their typical patterns, unless measurement is being made
of the ability of a family system to change under stress.

7. The experimentation must involve multiple experiments to
measure multiple factors in families. There are possibly no single differences between any one type of family and any other type.

8. The experiments must show extreme differences between
types of families, granted the sampling problems in this sort of
study.

In summary, family experiments must meet some rather complicated criteria, besides providing the usual problems of theoretical conception and problems of measurement, and there is little
precedent for the required experimental designs.

A COALITION EXPERIMENT

Father, mother, and child are placed at a round table with high
partitions so they cannot see each other. In front of each person
there is a small box with a window in it. This is a counter, like
an automobile speedometer, which runs up a score visible only to
the person in that area. Also in front of each person there are
two buttons which are labeled for the persons on the left and right.
That is, in mother's position she has a button labeled "husband"
and a button labeled "son" (or "daughter" as the case may be).
Besides these two buttons, which we shall call the coalition buttons,
there are two more buttons, one on each side. These are signal
buttons. When pushed, the signal button lights up a small light in
the area of the person on the other side of the partition. By pushing either of these two buttons, for example, mother can signal
father or child. All of these buttons are connected with pens on
an event recorder in the control room so that all button activity is
recorded during the experiment.

The table is wired so that the counters begin to add up a score
whenever two people choose each other by pressing each other's
coalition button. When mother presses the button labeled "hus-

band," nothing happens until father presses his button labeled for her. When both buttons are pressed at once, then both counters add up a score at the same speed and continue to do so (making an audible sound) as long as both buttons are pressed. Therefore each person can gain a score only if he joins another person, and then he and that person gain exactly the same amount of score. Each person can signal another with the signal button to invite a coalition. The family is asked not to talk together during the experiment so they can only communicate by button pushing.

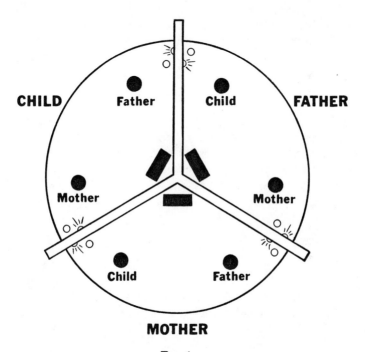

FIG. 1

Father, mother, and child are placed at this table and told this is a game they are to play together. They are instructed that they should each try to win by getting the highest score. They may push buttons one at a time or two at a time or not at all. The only rule is the prohibition against talking during the game.

The "game" consists of three rounds of two minutes each which are begun by the experimenter and ended by him. At the end of each round the family members are asked to read off their scores, and then the next round is begun without setting the counters back to zero so the score is cumulative.

In this situation each person must form a coalition with another to make a score, and yet he can only make the same score as the person he joins. To win, each must shift coalitions and gain score from both of the other two players. That is, if mother only joins father, she will have a high score at the end of the two minute round but father will have the same score if he has only joined her, and neither can win.

The family members are free to signal each other to indicate they want to form a coalition; they are free to signal without following the signal with a push of the coalition button; they can signal one person while forming a coalition with the other; they can form coalitions by getting together without any signalling; and they can form one or two coalitions simultaneously. Therefore the table permits a range of family behavior and all this behavior is recorded.

In addition to the three round game, the family is asked to have a fourth round. Before they begin the fourth round, they are asked to talk together and decide who is to win that round and who is to lose. Then they are to have another two minute round and see if they can make the scores come out the way they planned. This conversation is recorded.

THE SAMPLE
A total of sixty families was run in this experiment. Thirty normal families were selected on the basis of a random choice of students from a high school directory. The parents of the students were telephoned and the sample consists of those families whose members had never had psychotherapy and who were willing to come in for the experiment. The children ranged in age from 14 through 17, and there were 13 girls and 17 boys in the sample. The educational background of the families can be described in terms of the highest educated member of the family; there were 5 high school graduates, 9 who were high school graduates with some additional training, and 16 college graduates or above.

The group of thirty families containing a schizophrenic child were chosen on the basis of availability. Some families were obtained through a family therapy program, others from the records of state hospitals, and others included children actually hospitalized at the time. The children ranged in age from 11 through 20. The sample included one family with a stepfather who was in the home three years prior to the child's breakdown.

In the sample there were 3 girls and 27 boys--a more equal distribution could not be obtained. In education, taking the highest educated member of the family, there were 4 who had completed less than four years of high school, 7 high school graduates, 7 who were high school graduates and had additional training, and there were 12 college graduates or above.

Of the sixty families, twenty normal families and twenty families containing a schizophrenic child were run with the instruction that they could push buttons in any way they pleased and therefore they could form coalitions with one or two people simultaneously. This procedure is called Experiment One. Another 10 normal and 10 schizophrenic families were run with the instruction that they could form only one coalition at a time and so could not score with two people at once. This is called Experiment Two. On certain measurements the combined totals of the two experiments are reported.

PREDICTIONS AND RESULTS

Certain predictions were made about the differences between these two groups in the experiment. These predictions will be summarized here along with a brief summary of the actual results.

1. It was predicted that the family of the schizophrenic would have more difficulty forming and maintaining coalitions. Therefore the schizophrenic group would have a higher percent of time when no member of the family was in coalition with any other member.

The twenty normal and twenty schizophrenic families which were run in Experiment One where the family members could push buttons in any way they pleased differed significantly in the percent of time no member was in coalition with any other member. (The differences was significant at the .05 level[2].)

The ten normal and ten schizophrenic families which were run in Experiment Two where the family members could only score

---

[2] The statistical test used was the Median Test. In certain cases the t-test was used with the assumption that differences in population variants affected the t-score only very slightly. All P values could legitimately be reduced by half when the results were predicted, but this reduction has not been made on these figures.

with one person at a time also differed significantly in the percent of time no member was in coalition with any other member. (The difference was significant at the .05 level.)

The combined results of Experiments One and Two, totalling 30 normal and 30 schizophrenic families, differed significantly on this measurement with a level of significance of .01.

2. It was predicted that the family of the schizophrenic would have longer continuous periods of time when no two family members were in coalition.

The longest periods of continuous time when there was no coalition in three rounds of the game was significantly greater in the schizophrenic than in the normal group. In Experiment One, with twenty families in each group, the difference was significant at the .005 level. In Experiment Two, with 10 families in each group, the difference was significant at the .01 level. The results of the two experiments combined showed a significant difference at the .001 level.

3. It was predicted that the average lengths of time in coalition would be shorter in the schizophrenic group.

The two groups did not differ significantly on this measurement.

4. The members of the schizophrenic family would be less consistent with each other than the normals. There would be less consistency in following a signal with a press of the coalition button, and less frequent response by the person signalled.

The two groups only differed significantly in the consistency of family members in the case of the child. The schizophrenic child followed a signal with a coalition press less often than did the normal child (significant at the .05 level). There was no significant difference between the parents of the normal child and the parents of the schizophrenic child on this measurement.

The child in the schizophrenic family was also less responsive to both parents than the normal child when his parents signalled him and then pressed his coalition button (significant at the .01 level). There was no significant difference between the parents in the two groups on this measurement.

5. It was predicted that the members of the schizophrenic family would be less "successful" than the normal group, measured by the amount of time pushing the coalition button in proportion to the amount of time they spend scoring with someone.

The two groups differed significantly in the parent's "success" with the child but not in their "success" with each other. That is, if the amount of time mother and father are actually in coalition with the child is divided by the amount of time they are pressing his coalition button, the resulting percent differs significantly from the results of the parents in the normal group (the difference is significant at the .05 level on the t-test and the median test).

Actually the parents of the schizophrenic child tended to be more "successful" with each other on this measurement than the parents of the normal child, although the difference was not significant.

6. In the planned round, it was predicted that the schizophrenic families would have more difficulty reaching agreement on who was to win and who to lose, and it was predicted that they would have more difficulty making the round come out with the winner and loser they had agreed upon.

The problems of classifying verbal material were such that it proved too difficult to measure whether the schizophrenic families had more difficulty reaching agreement on who was to win and who to lose than the normal families.

However, there was a striking difference between the two groups in their success at making the winner and loser come out as they agreed.

	Chosen to win			Succeed	
	Normals	Schizo-phrenic		Normals	Schizo-phrenic
Child	20	20	Yes	28	15
Father	6	5			
Mother	4	5	No	2	15
	30	30		30	30

Most of the normal group could make the round come out as they planned, as far as getting the winner right, whereas half the schizophrenic group could not. (The difference was significant at the .001 level on the chi square test.)

	Chosen to lose			Succeed	
	Normals	Schizo-phrenic		Normals	Schizo-phrenic
Child	7	4	Yes	29	19
Father	16	10			
Mother	7	16	No	1	11
	30	30		30	30

Most of the normal group could make the loser come out as they planned, and they differed from the schizophrenic group at the .01 level on the chi square test.

In summary, out of 30 families in the normal group, 27 succeeded completely in doing what they planned and 3 failed. Out of 30 families in the schizophrenic group, 11 succeeded completely in doing what they planned and 19 failed.

Unpredicted Results

An unexpected result was based upon the simple measurement of who won the first three rounds of the game. The normal family members shared about equally in winning while in the schizophrenic group the father won the majority of games and the child hardly won at all. The difference was significant at the .01 level on the Chi Square test.

	Won				Lost	
	Normals	Schizo-phrenic			Normals	Schizo-phrenic
Child	11	3	Child		9	21
Father	9	21	Father		7	5
Mother	10	6	Mother		14	4
	30	30			30	30

This result is similar to the measurement of how the family members divided up the total time in coalition. In the normal group the family members shared about equally in the time they were in coalition. In the schizophrenic group the mother-child coalition was significantly less than the normal (a difference at the .05 level) and the mother-father coalition was significantly greater than the normal (a significant difference at the .01 level).

If one measures the amount of time that family members were not pressing a button at all, the schizophrenic child spends significantly less time pressing buttons than the normal child (significant at the .01 level). The parents of the schizophrenic child also spend significantly less time pressing buttons than the parents of the normal child (a significant difference at the .05 level).

In signalling, the fathers in the schizophrenic group signal the children more frequently than the fathers in the normal group. The mothers signal the fathers more units of time in the normal group than the schizophrenic group. The normal child presses his parents' coalition button more than the schizophrenic child.

SUMMARY

Although it was expected that the schizophrenic group would be more homogeneous than the normal group, the reverse proved to be the case. On almost all measurements the normal families tended to be more like one another while the schizophrenic families showed a considerable range of variability.

The family members in the schizophrenic group press their buttons less than the members of the normal group, and they spend less time scoring with each other and have longer periods of time when no one is scoring. Of the amount of time they spend in coalition together, the normal family members share coalitions about equally, while the parents of the schizophrenic get together with each other more than the normal parents do and they get together with their child less than the normal parents do. The schizophrenic child tends to get together with his father more than he does with his mother. The family members of the two groups signal each other about equally, although the fathers in the schizophrenic group signal the children more, and the mothers in the normal group spend more time signalling their husbands than the schizophrenic mothers do. The child in the schizophrenic group presses his buttons less, is more inconsistent, and is more unresponsive than the normal child.

When asked to plan the winner and loser of a round of the game, the family members in the schizophrenic group tend to predict how the round will come out rather than plan it. That is, the normal family members will say, "Let's have mother win," whereas often the members of the schizophrenic family will say, "Well, father won before so I guess he will win again." They then must be re-instructed that they are to decide who is to win and lose and try to make it come out as they planned. Almost all of the normal families could make the winner of the round come out as they planned, while half the schizophrenic group could not. Since it might be argued that this inability to do what they plan in the schizophrenic group is related to intelligence rather than ability to cooperate, it should be pointed out that the two groups do not particularly differ in education. There are a few with less than high school education in the schizophrenic group, and a few more in the normal group with a college education or above. There seems to be little correlation between education and inability to make the round come out as planned. (Since the question of ability to understand the procedure is at least partially relevant to this result, a group of six families with a mentally retarded child--IQs from 60 to 90-- were run in this experiment. All six chose the child to be the winner of the planned round, and all six succeeded in having the child win.)

THE NEED FOR BASIC RESEARCH

The results of the experiment in this pilot study indicate that on certain measurements there are differences between the group of families which contain a schizophrenic member and the group that does not. Can we then say that families containing a schizophrenic member are actually different from families who do not have such a member? Such a question raises more problems than it answers. It is doubtful whether this experiment differentiates families on the basis of schizophrenia; more than likely it differentiates a "disturbed" family from a non-disturbed family, whatever psychopathology might be present in the family. However, more important questions are raised than the sample, the methodology of this particular experiment, or the question whether the differences in the child's behavior alone accounts for the differences in result. There are more basic questions about the validity of this type of experimentation. We cannot say whether the behavior of a family in an experimental context accurately represents the typical pattern of that family until further research is done upon the possibilities and limitations of family experiments. An immediate task is the exploration of a single family, or a small group of families, with a variety of experiments to test the process of experimentation itself rather than testing a difference between groups. Actually the study which has been done is premature. Before one can experiment with differences between groups of families, basic research on the methodology should be done. There are various questions which need to be answered about the approach itself. Will a family show consistent patterns on the same experiment over a number of runs? In other words, can it be demonstrated that a family is an organized system? Will there be correlations between different experiments which presumably measure the same pattern? How can the factor of the family disguising its typical patterns when on display be minimized? Do the necessary limitations which must be put upon family communication for measurement purposes distort the typical patterns of the family more than they reveal them? Are the statistical methods which have been developed for measurement of individuals and unrelated people appropriate for the study of ongoing systems? What differences are there between single exceptions in the classification of families and the classification of individuals--is the mean or median a significant measurement when dealing with groups of organized systems?

The work done so far in this pilot study has centered largely upon differentiating one type of family from others. The theoretical approach has centered largely upon one dimension--given three people in a room, there is a potential range of communicative behavior possible and any one type of family will habitually confine itself within limits of that range. In that one dimension, the focus ultimately centered upon a single aspect--the measurement of coalition patterns. In the area of coalition patterns, the work was further narrowed down to the patterns involved among only three people in a small sample of families.

The final narrow focus of this study was partly a product of elimination and partly the result of problems in time, personnel, engineering, and availability of families. The process of working out the problem, and the results achieved, indicate to us that the approach is well worth further exploration. This exploration should be of two sorts: (a) the exploration of the process of family experimentation itself, with the emphasis upon experimenting with experiments rather than attempting to test out particular differences between particular types of families, and (b) the development of other dimensions on which to classify families with appropriate experiments.

To select families on the basis of a characteristic of a member would not seem to be the most sensible approach to the problem of family classification. Should one, for example, wish to compare the families of schizophrenics and the families of delinquents, he is immediately involved in the unfortunate problem of defining schizophrenics and delinquents for sampling purposes. Any approach based upon the individual will immerse the research in age old problems of individual psychology.

A proper classification system for families should be based upon types of interaction in families rather than characteristics of individual members. Such a classification problem is formidable, but it would seem the next logical development in the social sciences. Just as the first half of this century has been largely devoted to classifying and describing individuals, it seems probable the second half of the century will be devoted to classifying ongoing systems of two or more people. The dimensions upon which such a classification system will be based have yet to be devised. An exploration of this field must include developing a theory of family organization which can be experimented upon, classifying families on several dimensions, designing and conducting appropriate experiments, and pursuing and entrapping the appropriate families for adequate samples. The theoretical problems are formidable; the problems of experimental design and sampling are exasperating. Yet it would seem that family experimentation is the most appropriate procedure for putting a wedge into the large and important problem of devising a classification system for the human family and other ongoing organizations. These types of experiments would seem to require exquisitely precise theoretical formulations and ingenuity in devising experimental situations; sufficient challenge for any experimentalist.

REFERENCES

1. Bateson, G., Jackson, D. D., Haley, J., and Weakland, J. Toward a theory of schizophrenia. Behavioral Sc., 1:4, 251-264, 1956. (See p. 31, this vol.)
2. Bateson, G. The biosocial integration of behavior in the schizophrenic family. In Exploring the Base for Family Therapy, papers from the M. Robert Gomberg Memorial Conference. Nathan W Ackerman, Frances L. Bateman, and Sanford H. Sherman (Eds.), Family Service Association of America, New York, 116-122, 1961.
3. Bowen, M. Family psychotherapy. Am. J. Ortho., 31: 1, 40-60, 1961.
4. Haley, J. The family of the schizophrenic: a model system. J. Nerv. & Ment. Dis., 129:4, 357-374, 1959. (See p. 171, this vol.)

289

5. Fleck, Stephen. Family dynamics and origin of schizophrenia. Psychosom. Med., 22: 333-344, 1960.
6. Wynne, L.C., Ryckoff, I.M., Day, J., and Hirsch, S.I. Pseudomutuality in the family relations of schizophrenics. Psychiatry, 21:205-220, 1958.